ORGANIZATIONS THROUGH THE EYES OF A PROJECT MANAGER

Harvey F. Hoffman, Ed. D.

Technical Career Institutes, College for Technology
Fairfield University

Prentice
Hall

Upper Saddle River, New Jersey
Columbus, Ohio

Library of Congress Cataloging in Publication Data

Hoffman, Harvey F.
    Organizations through the eyes of a project manager / Harvey F. Hoffman.
      p. cm.
    Includes bibliographical references and index.
    ISBN 0-13-033971-7
    1. Project management. 2. Employees—Training of. 3. Organizational effectiveness. I.
Title.

HD69.P75 H64 2003
658.4'04—dc21
                                         2002025132

Editor in Chief: *Stephen Helba*
Executive Editor: *Debbie Yarnell*
Editorial Assistant: *Sam Goffinet*
Production Editor: *Tricia L. Rawnsley*
Design Coordinator: *Diane Ernsberger*
Cover Designer: *Linda Sorrells-Smith*
Cover Art: *Linda Sorrells-Smith*
Production Manager: *Brian Fox*
Electronic Text Management: *Karen L. Bretz*
Marketing Manager: *Jimmy Stephens*

This book was set in Trump Mediäval by Preparé, Inc. It was printed and bound by R. R. Donnelley & Sons Company. The cover was printed by Phoenix Color Corp.

Pearson Education Ltd.
Pearson Education Australia Pty. Limited
Pearson Education Singapore, Pte. Ltd.
Pearson Education North Asia Ltd.
Pearson Education Canada, Ltd.
Pearson Educación de Mexico, S.A. de C.V.
Pearson Education—Japan
Pearson Education Malaysia, Pte. Ltd.
Pearson Education, *Upper Saddle River, New Jersey*

Prentice
Hall

10 9 8 7 6 5 4 3 2 1
ISBN 0-13-033971-7

CONTENTS

PREFACE   ix

CHAPTER 1   ORGANIZATIONAL EXPECTATIONS
AND PROFESSIONALISM   1
Introduction   2
Employer Expectations: Technical Competence,
Attitude, Communication, and Teamwork (TACT)   2
Employee Expectations   5
Professionalism   7
Trades and Crafts   12
Review Questions   12
Chapter Test   17

CHAPTER 2   THE ORGANIZATION   19
Introduction   20
Core Identity   20
Goals and Objectives   23
Sidebar: A Personal SWOT Analysis   25
Activities   26
Standards   27
Policy, Process, Procedure, Rule   29
Sidebar: Public versus Private Companies   29
Review Questions   32
Chapter Test   32

CHAPTER 3

PROJECT MANAGEMENT: ORGANIZATIONAL OVERVIEW **35**

Introduction 36
Why Project Management? 39
Project Manager's Responsibilities 41
Organization Charts 42
Line Organization 46
Review Questions 48
Chapter Test 48

CHAPTER 4

MANAGEMENT CONCEPTS **51**

Introduction 52
Management 52
Managers and Supervisors 54
Historical Overview 55
Classical Management 56
Human Behavioral Management 60
Human Resources School 62
Management Styles 70
Power 71
Teams 73
Leadership 76
Leadership versus Management 78
Competitive Advantage 81
Review Questions 81
Chapter Test 82

CHAPTER 5

PROJECT PLANNING **85**

Introduction 86
Request for (a) Proposal and Request for (a) Quote 86
Project Charter 88
The Project Plan 90
Plan Benefits 93
Review Questions 114

CHAPTER 6 **PROJECT TIME MANAGEMENT** **117**

Introduction 118

Rudiments of Developing a Schedule 119

Creating a Schedule 123

Sidebar: The Eight-Hour Day 135

Summary 136

Review Questions 137

CHAPTER 7 **PROJECT ESTIMATION AND COST** **143**

Introduction 144

Direct and Indirect Costs 144

Indirect Costs 146

Bottom-Up Estimating 147

Example: Villa-Tech Bid 151

Project Spending Profile 158

Bottom-Up Estimate 161

Top-Down Estimate 161

Rule-of-Thumb Cost-Estimating Approach 161

Parametric Modeling 162

Estimating by Analogy 163

Learning Curve 164

Project Estimating Summary 168

Cost Management 169

Review Questions 173

CHAPTER 8 **PROJECT COMMUNICATION** **179**

Introduction 180

Communication Management 180

Communication Process 183

Conducting Effective Meetings 184

Memos 186

Listening 187

Verbal Communication 188

Review Questions 189

CHAPTER 9   **QUALITY**   **191**
Introduction   192
The Quality "Gurus"   193
Quality and the Project Manager   197
Quality Policy   198
Quality Planning, Assurance, and Control   199
Responsibility for Quality   217
Review Questions   217
Chapter Test   219

CHAPTER 10   **PROJECT RISK**   **221**
Introduction   222
Risk Identification at the Proposal Stage   222
Mitigating Risk   233
Review Questions   234

CHAPTER 11   **PROJECT TRACKING, REPORTING, AND PROCUREMENT**   **237**
Introduction   238
Project Tracking Example   239
Summary of Monitoring and Tracking Activities   258
Subcontracting   258
Project Completion   262
Review Questions   263

CHAPTER 12   **EPILOGUE**   **271**
Introduction   272
Project Management Career   273

APPENDIX **TYPICAL EMPLOYEE PERFORMANCE APPRAISAL FORMS** **277**

APPENDIX **ETHICAL CODES OF SELECTED PROFESSIONAL**
 ORGANIZATIONS **285**
American Chemical Society 285
American Society of Mechanical Engineers (ASME) 286
The Institute of Electrical and Electronics Engineers (IEEE) 287
Project Management Institute (PMI) 288

APPENDIX **WILDERNESS SURVIVAL ANSWER AND RATIONALE**
 SHEET **301**

APPENDIX **ISO 9000 QUALITY MANAGEMENT PRINCIPLES** **305**

REFERENCES **311**

INDEX **315**

PREFACE

I know I could never forgive myself if I elected to live without humane purpose,
without trying to help the poor and unfortunate, without recognizing
that perhaps the purest joy in life comes with trying to help others.
—Arthur Ashe

ABOUT THE AUTHOR

During the first year of my tenure as the dean of technology at Technical Career Institutes (TCI), I spoke with human resource personnel from more than 20 companies that hired the college's graduates. Each company representative praised the technical abilities of the TCI students, but indicated that the students needed to improve their social skills and their understanding of an organization's operation. The department chairs and I discussed the type of course that would help our students, and the outline for this book evolved. The book reflects my experiences as an engineer, department manager, and project manager in my 30-year career in industry.

INTRODUCTION TO THE TEXT

Today, medium-sized to large organizations routinely use project managers. Technology students will likely encounter a project manager in their first job. The students may be part of a project team, or if the organization does not use the project manager methodology, they will meet that person as a supplier or customer. Most undergraduates have little understanding of how an organization operates or what an organization's expectations are. Who makes which decisions and why? Who manages the group? How does one get things done? What does an organization's culture permit? Seasoned employees realize that success in one's employment depends not only on technical abilities, but also on the ability to interact well with colleagues and to quickly learn the organization's standard operating procedures.

This book serves five purposes. First, it introduces students to project-based information technology, manufacturing, and research-and-development business environments. Second, it encourages students to learn business and industry's vocabulary, processes, and procedures. Third, it enables students to ask intelligent questions about an organization during a job interview. Fourth, it enhances students' ability to evaluate different organizational management styles, in order to decide what is best for them. Fifth, and most important, it prepares students to step into a new job and have some understanding of an organization's expectations.

To accomplish the first objective, the book examines the project manager's role. A large number of organizations use the project manager model to cut across the entire set of departments in an effort to get a job done on time, within budget, and without compromising quality. Understanding the project manager's function will enable the new employee to quickly adjust and contribute to the work environment.

In the discussions that ensue, ethical questions may arise. The book will familiarize students with ethical issues that arise in the business and industry context. Questions throughout each chapter will promote class discussions and serve to sensitize students to the moral dimensions of an organization's issues.

Organizations Through the Eyes of a Project Manager will assist students in their preparation for the Project + certification examination, offered by CompTIA, and the certified associate in project management (CAPM) degree offered by the Project Management Institute. These certification programs prepare new practitioners for introductory project management positions with titles such as coordinator, expeditor, planner, project administrator, and project management assistant.

The book includes information from the Project Management Institute's Project Management Body of Knowledge (PMBOK) and covers many of the topics required for CompTIA Project + certification.

TCI instructors have successfully used *Organizations* for a one-term, 45-hour introductory project management course. Instructors select from the following topics:

- Chapter 1: *Organizational Expectations and Professionalism*
- Chapter 2: *The Organization*
- Chapter 3: *Project Management: Organizational Overview*
- Chapter 4: *Management Concepts*
- Chapter 5: *Project Planning*
- Chapter 6: *Project Time Management*
- Chapter 7: *Project Estimation and Cost*
- Chapter 8: *Project Communication*
- Chapter 9: *Quality*
- Chapter 10: *Project Risk*
- Chapter 11: *Project Tracking, Reporting, and Procurement*
- Chapter 12: *Epilogue*

I recommend allocating six hours to the Microsoft Project software application. During the first three hours, introduce students to preparing a schedule using this software. Work in a computer laboratory during this session, if possible, and have each student use his or her own computer. In the second three hours, assign an in-class student project. I find that organizing students into groups of two or three works best for learning. Each group uses one computer during this session.

Organizations contains a large amount of information on the topic of quality. It is ideal for students to prepare reports and make class presentations. Consequently, allot up to six class hours to discuss quality. I suggest lecturing for $1\frac{1}{2}$ hours and allocating the remainder of the time to team presentations.

Many of the quotes at the beginning of each chapter have influenced my thinking over the years. Others I discovered while doing this research. I hope that they will influence the reader positively.

ADDITIONAL RESOURCES

The website, which can be found at *www.prenhall.com/hoffman*, contains several files useful both for students and for instructors.

Chapter 1, question 14, contains a Wilderness Survival Worksheet. The purpose of the exercise is to increase the student's confidence in team decisions. The teacher may use the file to create a worksheet for distribution to the class. Questions 5 and 6 in chapter 6 requires the student to modify and manipulate task lists in both Microsoft Word and Microsoft Project. The files on the website enable the student to focus on the learning aspect of the assignment and not be concerned with the task of entering data into the computer.

ACKNOWLEDGMENTS

I would like to thank the reviewers of the initial text drafts for their valuable and insightful comments. TCI teachers Roy Lau, Pedro Lopez, Gilbert Chan, Steve Maybar, and Dr. Bert Pariser tested versions of the manuscript in their classes and provided constructive criticism of the work. I am also indebted to the TCI students who suffered through the MOT-200 notes phase and the CD-ROM PDF file. I am grateful for their suggestions, which helped me a great deal.

Many thanks go to Harley Cudney of Virginia Tech, Kenneth Merkel of the University of Nebraska, and Marv Crowe of Spartanburg Technical College for reviewing the final manuscript and offering suggestions for improvement.

Finally, I want to express my appreciation and thanks to Cristina Hernandez of the art history department at Mt. San Antonio College and to Tony Mattrazzo, a public relations specialist at the New York State Archives Cultural Education Center, for the images that they furnished for this project.

DEDICATION

I have worked with nontraditional college students for many years. I dedicate this book to the hard work and perseverance of this group of people:

- To the nontraditional college-aged men and women who commute to college after (or sometimes before) a day's work.

- To the student parents who have concerns about the whereabouts of their children while they attend school.
- To the student caregivers who worry about the health and welfare of their children, parents, friends, or relatives.
- To the significant others, spouses, and children who give up time during the evenings and weekends so that nontraditional students can complete homework or prepare for a test.

Keep plugging. It may take a while, but graduation will come—and success will feel so good!

Harvey Hoffman

CHAPTER 1

ORGANIZATIONAL EXPECTATIONS AND PROFESSIONALISM

*Whether you think you can
or whether you think you can't,
you are right.*
Henry Ford

OBJECTIVES

After studying this chapter, you should be able to

- Understand an organization's expectations
- Understand the components of an employee assessment
- Understand the elements of professionalism

INTRODUCTION

Among the characteristics of the business environment during the 1990s were rampant technical innovation, a global economic perspective, a free market, and a requirement for continuous employee learning. The 21st century began with the lowest unemployment rate in 30 years (4.1%). African-American and Hispanic workers had the lowest rates (8% and 6.4%, respectively) since the Labor Department began breaking out statistics.[1] Even during those good times, layoffs, downsizing, restructuring, and de-layering occurred due to numerous corporate mergers and reorganization. To ensure quarterly sales growth and regular profit increases, organizations focused on productivity. The economy then cooled down in 2001, when telecommunications, Internet, data-processing, dot-com and other companies slashed their workforces. A good example of this can be seen on the Washtech.com Technology Layoffs Watch Website at *http://www.washtech.com/specialreports/layoffs_bydate.html*. Unemployment has since risen. Knowledge-workers who maintained necessary skills kept their jobs. Others survived on a mixture of part-time and contract work. Those who didn't update their knowledge base had difficulty obtaining employment. The lesson is clear: People *must* take responsibility for *continuously* managing their careers.

Business and industry provides a service or a product to both internal and external customers and exists not only to make money, but also to make a profit. Today's corporations require employees who are responsive to a customer's needs and who will *delight* the customer while maintaining sensitivity to the bottom line. Table 1–1 compares the forces and factors confronting modern corporations and employees with those of several years ago.

Corporations now move quickly through uncharted waters, proceeding toward a defined corporate mission, but frequently making seemingly chaotic excursions from their goals. Employees must empower themselves and embark on lifelong journeys to update skills and pursue opportunities that will help then meet professional objectives. Maintaining accountability to oneself increases one's value to a corporation. Demanding new work experiences, requesting challenges, and developing new skills makes for a more valuable employee. Paradoxically, the selfish attitude of looking out for "number one" makes the employee a valuable resource for the company.

EMPLOYER EXPECTATIONS: TECHNICAL COMPETENCE, ATTITUDE, COMMUNICATION, AND TEAMWORK (TACT)

Consider the position of a corporation's chief executive officer (CEO). Suppose a company has merged with another, resulting in the duplication of some jobs and services. Keeping every person employed in the newly formed company

---

[1] Stevenson, R. W., "Growth in jobs at end of year beats estimates," *The New York Times* (January 8, 2000): A1.

TABLE 1–1

Forces and Factors Confronting Corporations and Employees

	Traditional	Modern
Corporations	Long-term profits	Immediate profits! Quarter-to-quarter earnings growth
	Insulated	Competitive
	Hierarchical	Flat: fewer managers
	Parent	Employer
	Rich	Lean: fewer employees, but employees who do more, increased employee responsibility
	Thorough	Fast and good
	Stable	Changing, hectic, chaotic, turbulent
Employees	Specialized talents	Broad capabilities
	Dependent	Empowered
	Comfortable	Stressed
	Loyal to company	Loyal to self
	Entitled	Accountable
	Learn and then earn	Learn to earn: lifelong learning

Adapted from Goldman (*http://www.asee.org/assessments/html/goldman.htm*)

represents an unacceptable expenditure of funds. Stockholders demand profits and expect increased employee productivity because of the merger, so the company decides to reduce its workforce by five percent. What guidelines should be proposed to managers in order to help them decide whom to lay off?

Technical competence, attitude, communication, and teamwork (TACT) together define four categories of employer expectations. (See Figure 1–1 for a complete description.) Technical competence would probably be most people's first choice on the list of important employee capabilities. Every employee must have the unique training, knowledge, and skills required to perform assigned tasks. Does the person have up-to-date skills? If not, he or she is out the door. Attitude, communication, and teamwork skills complete the set. Employers want a reliable person who will come to work with a positive, can-do attitude. Following the conclusion of a task, supervisors and managers expect employees to move onto the next activity without having to be coaxed to do so.

Some time ago, a newspaper advertised for Web masters and Web designers:

> We need a variety of risk taking, fun loving, creative people who will thrive in a start-up environment. If you are looking for a traditional or comfortable place to work 9-to-5, FORGET IT! We need cutting edge, off-the-wall, 24/7 type people who don't worry about job descriptions to become a part of our team.[2]

The emphasis in the advertisement is attitude, enthusiasm, and a willingness to work. The employer expects technical capability, but clearly, that is not the only job qualification. Employers may take the zeal and raw talent that a person exhibits and, if the person shows promise, train him or her to do the job.

---

[2] *Connecticut Post* (September 3, 2000): 12.

FIGURE 1–1

Employer expectations for a desirable employee: Remain on the TACT target

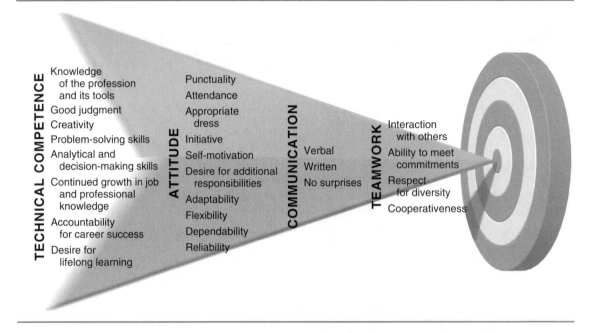

Businesses depend on accurate and complete verbal and written communication skills when working with customers, clients, colleagues, subordinates, and supervisors. They expect prompt information transfer so that managers and supervisors remain informed of all major issues. Customer reports, manufacturing and production difficulties, vendor delays, engineering problems, and purchasing issues must be quickly documented so that people take appropriate actions and make timely responses.

The days of the "lone wolf" are gone. Businesses and industries work in teams, operating with interdepartmental groups, cross-functional teams, "tiger teams," "skunk works," joint ventures, and corporate teams. Companies place a premium on people skills, because teams must meet regularly to share information and discuss the resolution of common issues. Members depend on one another to meet commitments that support design, development, and production schedules. Teams consist of a broad spectrum of ethnic, racial, regional, and international personnel, so employees must be able to work comfortably and compatibly with a diverse mix of individuals. People must respect gender and age differences. A diverse workforce provides the wide range of skills and insights demanded by the modern global marketplace. Unprecedented challenges confront American companies: They must be faster, smarter, and more flexible than the competition. Companies must take advantage of all of the knowledge inherent in a diverse workforce, and individuals must respond by welcoming the opportunity to maximize the benefits derived from working with people from a wide range of cultures, ages, and backgrounds.

Selecting the best employees requires a detailed review of their previous efforts. The human resource department maintains an archive of employee performance evaluation records. Examining this information will permit managers to assess each employee's potential for contributing to future activities.

EMPLOYEE EXPECTATIONS

Employees are an organization's greatest asset. Their performance has a direct effect on profitability. Performance reviews and evaluations not only give employers an opportunity to shape the development of employees, improve work standards, and define areas of responsibility, but also promote accountability and identify future goals and expectations.

Employees are judged on their contributions to their assigned projects. Employee performance reviews usually consist of two parts. The first part includes a review of the ongoing, informal oral or written communication that takes place throughout the year between the employee and his or her supervisor. The second part includes a formal discussion between the employee and the supervisor about the written results of a periodic employee evaluation report.

The periodic evaluation report should be seen as a communication tool for the employer and employee. The document informs the employee of the supervisor's expectations and provides an opportunity to establish or identify employee goals and the tools necessary for attaining them. In cases of subpar performance, the review identifies areas for improvement that will enable the employee to reach a satisfactory level of job performance. The supervisor should inform employees of the company's professional expectations at the same time he or she tells them about their performance relative to these indicators. On the basis of this evaluation, the employer frequently makes decisions about employee salary increases, promotions, and training. The review measures on-the-job performance and may indicate the employee's future job direction. It clarifies the employee's duties, summarizes major accomplishments since the last review, and discusses training and development needs for current and future assignments.

Frequently, employers evaluate new employees more often during the first year than those employed for a longer term. New employees may receive reviews three months, six months, and one year following the date they are hired. The reviews enable supervisors and managers to understand their employees' capabilities while clarifying expectations. Long-term employees may receive only an annual review.

The employee review forms in Appendix 1 show that technical capability is important, but is not the sole criterion of long-term success. Companies value and measure many different aspects of an individual's contributions:

- Quality of work produced (work should be accurate, complete, timely, and consistent)
- Quantity of work produced (work should keep pace with workload, and employee should provide extra effort when needed)

- Dependability (consistent attendance, punctuality, reliability)
- Independence (ability to work with a minimum of supervision)
- Organizational ability (ability to set priorities and meet commitments)
- Teamwork (employee should be cooperative and interact well with customers, suppliers, and colleagues)
- Communication (employee should have good verbal and written communication skills and should share information with coworkers)
- Motivation (commitment to work and to one's profession, as evidenced by being a self-starter and maintaining a positive attitude)
- Judgment (tact, sensitivity, sound decision-making skills)
- Ability to handle stress (ability to work under pressure to meet deadlines, remain calm, and control temper)
- Problem-solving ability (quick insight into problems, offering of appropriate solutions, and ability to analyze complex interdependencies)
- Creativity (willingness to try new solutions and develop new ideas)
- Decisiveness (ability to make decisions and take action)
- Dress (proper attire for work and clean appearance)

An employee's salary and salary increase will reflect his or her total performance as perceived by managers and supervisors. Selecting people for a promotion or a layoff is a complex decision that depends on a broad range of factors, only one of which is technical competence. Because all companies keep records of employee performance appraisals, managers may use them as the basis for employment decisions. Over time, the employee's "complete picture" becomes clear, and the company can take action based on the overall performance record.

The following excerpt from an article that appeared on the Web illustrates the importance of an employer's perception of each individual's capabilities and attitude:

FedEx May Cut 200 Information Technology Jobs

FedEx Corp could cut 200 jobs by next month from its information technology operations, a company spokesman said Tuesday.

"Some of our projects are not adding value," said Jess Bunn, a FedEx spokesman in the [company's] Memphis headquarters. "We're looking for better ways to serve our customers and add values, so there's the possibility of about 200 layoffs."

Layoffs will probably begin by mid-September.

In the next two weeks employees will be evaluated based on their contributions to short-term tasks and objectives as well as long-term goals and strategies, their contribution to leadership, cooperation in teamwork and performance, other FedEx officials said.

The information technology workers develop and maintain computer software and hardware to help FedEx run its operations. [3]

---

[3] *http://biz.yahoo.com/rF/000816/1688665.html* (August 16, 2000), from *Reuters* (August 16, 2001).

FedEx intended to lay off employees on the basis of a variety of characteristics. Technical performance is necessary, but is not a sufficient reason to keep an employee. Social skills and willingness to "do whatever it takes" will help an employee keep his or her job and advance in the organization.

PROFESSIONALISM

The ideas of technical competence; responsibility to clients, customers, and employers; lifelong learning; the proper attitude; and appropriate behavior stem from the broad concept of professionalism. The Institute of Electrical and Electronic Engineers (IEEE) define a profession as "a learned occupation requiring systematic knowledge and training, and commitment to a social good."[4] Every profession has a specialized body of knowledge that is unique to it and that is, in some identifiable manner, intellectual in character. In its initial stages, this body of knowledge can be developed by a group of people, but educational institutions must transmit it to succeeding generations of practitioners.[5]

A profession may have any or all of the following characteristics:

- Work is predominantly intellectual and varied in character, as opposed to routine, menial, manual, mechanical, or physical.
- Members of the profession share common training, values, and skills.
- Competencies require knowledge of an advanced type in a particular field or discipline.
- Recognized educational institutions of higher learning provide necessary course work.
- The profession participates in the establishment and maintenance of educational institutions that meet minimum acceptable standards and teach necessary skills.
- Learning is continuous.
- Members carry out activities that require the consistent exercise of discretion and judgment.
- A well-defined and growing body of literature is available to all members of the profession.
- Research articles are peer reviewed before publication in journals.
- Members are motivated by a desire to perform public service.

The community of people who share common training, values, and skills create and participate in an organization that authenticates and promotes the profession.

---

[4] Wujeck, J. H., and D. G. Johnson, *How to be a good engineer*. Notes prepared for the Ethics Committee of The Institute of Electrical and Electronics Engineers. (January, 1992).

[5] Adams, J. R., and N. S. Kirchof, *Project Management, Professionalism, and Market Survival* (paper presented at a 1983 symposium of the Project Management Institute).

Dissemination of Information

Every professional organization defines itself by its mission, guiding philosophy, and unique occupational body of knowledge. Dissemination of information is sometimes the primary vehicle used to promote the organization and the profession. Journals publish peer-reviewed research-and-development results. In the peer-review process, professionals with similar backgrounds first read and review their colleagues' papers and then respond to the authors with comments intended to improve or clarify the work. In turn, the authors make corrections or clarifications and resubmit the manuscript. Publication of the article may take up to a year while it is being reviewed and modified. Monthly publications offered by professional organizations sometimes print articles of general interest that do not pass through such an extensive review process. Even so, it may take three to six months before they are published.

An organization frequently distributes newspapers or newsletters that contain articles of passing interest, announcements of conferences or awards, election information, and advertisements for employment. Editorial comments that reflect members' opinions about national political issues may appear in the newspapers that relate to an organization's mission. Local chapters of national organizations may also publish monthly or quarterly newsletters.

Service Activities

Professional organizations have a wide range of activities. While individuals receive compensation for work provided to customers, they seldom receive payment for service to their professions. Service activities include volunteering for local chapter or regional activities and supporting national seminars or symposiums. Authors of papers submitted to professional organizations do not usually receive financial compensation, but do receive the appreciation and accolades of their colleagues. Professionals serving on accreditation committees that review the quality of programs offered by educational institutions do so on a voluntary basis because they seek to support and further their chosen profession. Many companies endorse and provide financial support to educational programs, seminars, and symposiums offered by professional organizations in order to improve the knowledge of the practitioners in their employ.

Education

Professional organizations seek to promote the quality of education and training received by prospective members and students. As an example, IEEE, the American Society of Mechanical Engineers (ASME), and other engineering organizations collaborate under the umbrella of the Accreditation Board for Engineering and Technology (ABET) in order to improve the education of technical personnel in engineering and related disciplines. Upon request, ABET representatives visit colleges that offer engineering and technology programs. The team conducts a detailed review of the programs to ascertain that the institutions meet minimum standards established by ABET and its member bodies (the engineering societies). Periodic follow-ups encourage institutions to maintain quality programs. ABET accreditation is a voluntary process that helps graduates of an accredited program prepare for careers in engineering and engineering technology. With support from organizations like ABET, institutions are encouraged to provide education that meets a career's changing needs, modernize institutional facilities, employ competent faculty who participate in lifelong learning, and introduce new technology into the courses.

Managing Oneself

"Success in the knowledge economy comes to those who know themselves— their strengths, their values, and how they best perform."[6] We no longer enjoy the days of job security in exchange for moderate performance and corporate loyalty. We each must manage our careers to maintain our employability. Lifelong education is perhaps the most important factor in developing a workforce.

Some authors refer to the new professional as a person who is dedicated to the idea of continuous learning and who takes responsibility for his or her own career management. For each individual, this means staying knowledgeable about market trends and learning and maintaining the skills that the company may eventually need.[7] With constant changes in technology, professionals must assess their skills regularly and take action to upgrade themselves and direct their careers so that they can function with a maximum of effectiveness. A well-known author advises, "The best way to stay employed, today and in the future, is to look upon yourself as being in business for yourself, even if you work for someone else."[8]

For the most part, professional employees are engaged in *at-will* employment. That is, the employer can terminate the employee at any time, and the employee can likewise leave the employer at any time. Business and industry constantly asks the question *What have you done for me lately?* or *Are you worth paying for?* Professionals must engage in lifelong learning to enable them to respond affirmatively.

Professional Ethics

Professions want the public to perceive their members as following a principled standard of behavior in dealing with clients, customers, and colleagues. Consequently, professional organizations define a standard of behavior in the form of a code of ethics to which members must adhere. Ethics deals with a person's behavior toward others. Ethics attempts to arrive at acceptable principles of obligation and general value judgments that prescribe behavior that is morally right, good, and responsible. Several professional organizations'

---

[6] Drucker, P. F., "Managing oneself," *Harvard Business Review* (March/April, 1999): 65–74.

[7] Waterman, R. H., Jr., J. A. Waterman, and B. A. Collard, "Toward a career-resilient workforce," *Harvard Business Review* (July/August, 1994): 87–95.

[8] Koonce, R., "Becoming your own career coach," *Training & Development* 49, no. 1 (January, 1995): 18–25.

ethical codes are shown in Appendix 2. A common thread among these ethical codes requires a practitioner to accept responsibility for actions taken while conducting professional activities. The professional then must demonstrate responsibility to the public, the employer, customers, clients, colleagues, and him- or herself. Professional organizations require practitioners to exercise good judgment. Ethical discussions are particularly relevant to the development of a new technology such as the Internet or a network of computers in the office. Ethical questions arise continuously with regard to product safety, worker safety, privacy in the workplace, employee and consumer rights, a corporation's moral responsibility, obligations of employers to their employees, employment at will, a business's social responsibilities, and corporate regulations vs. government regulations.

During the course of their work, technologists will undoubtedly confront ethical dilemmas. The decisions they make could affect a user's health and safety, their own prospective promotion, or even their job. Technologists must make decisions even in situations that contain ambiguities or uncertainties. Consider, for example, the following situations:

- Space Shuttle *Challenger* engineers suspected a safety problem with the low-temperature performance of a gasket on the spacecraft. Failure to act on this suspicion resulted in the loss of several lives and was a major setback for NASA.

- Automotive engineers suspected that the location of a gas tank in at least two vehicles could lead to an explosion on impact. The automotive organization's failure to act quickly on this possibility also cost lives.

- From time to time, engineers discover deficiencies in a building's structural integrity. However, they might choose not to act on their knowledge because reporting the information to a third party would breach client confidentiality.

- Other ethical dilemmas have to do with identifying conflicts of interest between oneself and a client. Suppose, for instance, that someone witnesses employees or contracted laborers charging more hours than they actually work on a job. Does the person report the workers? Or, to put the shoe on the other foot, if someone knew that no one would report his or her indiscretion, would that person be tempted to charge more hours?

Ethical dilemmas frequently confront us, and we must recognize them and decide on a course of action.

Sometimes the questions are not easily resolved, and a professional may undergo substantial inner turmoil in making decisions. (See Figure 1–2.) Decisions could result in significant consequences relating to the employee's future. Employees have resigned from their job because of ethical conflicts, and some have lost their job because of them. The federal government has created the False Claims Act, or "Whistleblowers Act," to protect the job of a federal employee who charges his or her employer with a breach of ethical conduct. Many states have passed similar laws.

FIGURE 1-2

A cauldron of difficult decisions that confront employees

Practicing members of a profession have responsibilities to a wide range of people. Employers, customers, clients, and colleagues have concerns and expectations about the professional's performance and ethical standards, even in the sports arena (which is not a profession in the sense that we use it in this book). For example, upon assuming the position of president of basketball operations for the Washington Wizards, Michael Jordan commented, "It's my job to make sure they [the team's players] put the effort on the court to show respect for the people paying to watch them."[9]

Professional organizations spell out their members' ethical responsibilities. If a conflict arises between an employer's requests and demands, on the one hand, and the professional organization's code of behavior, on the other, the professional is expected to review the organization's code of ethics and talk with a colleague to clarify matters and resolve the conflict. New members of a profession are often advised to consider joining and supporting one or more of the profession's organizations.

Certification and Licensure

In an effort to promote quality professional service, some organizations require their members to be licensed or certified by a state agency or a private organization. Certification and licensure guarantee that a profession's members will

---

[9] Sandomir, R., "His airness laces up some new shoes." *The New York Times* (January 23, 2000): Section 4, 1.

be competent in the general discipline or in specialty areas. Professional organizations frequently establish committees that accept complaints from the public regarding members' performance or behavior. This internal self-policing program has the power to discipline the member, and the results of a disciplinary review may extend from no action, to censure, or even to revocation of the license or certification.

TRADES AND CRAFTS

The foregoing discussion does not intend to demean the competency, importance, or quality of trades and craft workers. In fact, there are a number of similarities between those workers and professionals. For example, just as professionals seek to further their education, trades and craft workers participate in training and apprenticeship programs. Also, just as professions promote their endeavors, some trades and crafts have organizations that promote their vocations. But there are differences between the two. First, a trade emphasizes manual dexterity and physical skills rather than intellectual activity. Second, although some trades require a license or certification to practice, few trade organizations monitor their members or have a code of conduct. Third, few trades and crafts monitor the quality of their educational programs via accreditation committees. Finally, unlike professions, trades and crafts tend not to have peer-reviewed publications.

Some students confuse the word *expert* with the word *professional*. A professional should be an expert, but an expert need not be a professional. The two words are not synonyms. Plumbers, carpenters, electricians, machinists, auto mechanics, and cabdrivers perform vital services, and some people practicing those occupations earn more money than lawyers, engineers, teachers, or physicians. Still, although they can be experts in their discipline, in the strict sense used in this book, we don't call trades and crafts workers professionals.

REVIEW QUESTIONS

1. Explain the statement, *Paradoxically, the selfish attitude of looking out for "number one" makes you a great resource for the company.*
2. Do you consider people who practice the following occupations to be professionals? Explain your answer.
   a) electrician
   b) plumber
   c) nuclear physicist
   d) social worker
   e) electrical or mechanical engineer
   f) stockbroker
   g) librarian
   h) physician
   i) lawyer
   j) teacher
   k) union member
   l) locomotive engineer
   m) welder
   n) military officer
   o) police officer
   p) politician

3. We sometimes hear the phrase, "That person did (or did not) behave professionally." Write a short essay describing your concept of *professionalism*.
4. Chapter 1 describes characteristics of a profession. With which characteristics do you agree or disagree? Explain your answer.
5. What are the common features of the ethical codes of conduct shown in Appendix 2? With which principles do you agree or disagree? Explain your answer.
6. Explain the statement: The end justifies the means. Do the ethical codes of conduct in Appendix 2 permit this philosophy? Describe circumstances under which this statement would be appropriate.
7. Do you agree or disagree with limiting personal phone calls at work to emergencies only? Explain your answer.
8. Morning social discussions with work associates
   a) improve morale and should be engaged in every day.
   b) reduce company productivity.
   c) should not be conducted in front of a manager.
9. Examine the three employee evaluations in Appendix 1.
   a) What are the common characteristics found in each?
   b) What are the major differences among them?
   c) What additional job performance criteria would you include in an evaluation?
   d) Describe your view of a perfect employee performance evaluation.
10. An article about John Rocker of the Atlanta Braves describes him as a 25-year-old, hard-throwing, 6'4", 225-pound left-handed relief pitcher. In the article, Rocker bashed African-Americans, Asians, Koreans, Vietnamese, Indians, Russians, Hispanics, single mothers, Asian drivers, AIDS patients, gays, and those people of a race or sexual orientation different from his. He called an overweight black teammate a "fat monkey."[10]

    Bud Selig, the commissioner of baseball, ordered Rocker to undergo psychological evaluation and then punished him for his comments with a $20,000 fine and a two-month suspension and ordered him to undergo sensitivity training. According to one source,

    > Perhaps without the added burden of tabloid headlines, many businesses face similar situations: A star employee's privately tolerated "idiosyncrasies" spin out of control, and management must respond publicly. "In the business world, there's a very good chance that somebody like this would be fired immediately," said Joseph L. Badaracco Jr., professor of business ethics at the Harvard Business School. "The hideous content of his views would badly damage the company's reputation, so they'd want to disassociate themselves."[11]

---

[10] Pearlman, Jeff, "At Full Blast," *Sports Illustrated* (December 27, 1999).

[11] Seglin, Jeffrey L., "The Right Thing: Throwing a Beanball in Business." *The New York Times* (January 16, 2000): Section 3, p. 4.

In a subsequent chance meeting with Rocker, reporter Jeff Pearlman said the pitcher threatened him and tried to get him banned from the Atlanta Braves' clubhouse. Neither the team nor Major League Baseball took further action against Rocker. Outfielder Brian Jordan said, of Rocker, "You've got one guy being a cancer time and time again. Eventually, it's going to have an effect on the team."

The Braves traded Rocker to the Cleveland Indians in June of 2001.

a) Comment on the statements made by John Rocker.
b) Should Rocker be penalized for exercising freedom of speech as outlined in the first amendment to the U.S. Constitution?
c) Suppose you were Rocker's manager. What would you do to stabilize the situation? In your discussion, consider the impact of his statements on his teammates, other teams, the sport, and the public.
d) Suppose a "star employee" working at a company voices derogatory comments about some other employee? In your opinion, what position should the company take?

11. Suppose the Rekcor Company manufactured the finest Framistans (a fictitious component) at the lowest prices. If you were a purchasing agent from another company, and you discovered that several employees from the Rekcor Company were intolerant of some of your personal beliefs, would you purchase Framistans from Rekcor? Explain your position.

12. The human resource department at Magna-Net has a policy requiring all nonunion technical employees to work one unpaid overtime hour daily. Tundra Industries permits flexible hours and does not have a formal policy to track the coming and going of its employees.

a) For which employer would you prefer to work? Why?
b) What are the advantages and disadvantages of each policy? Formulate your response first from the employer's viewpoint and then from the employee's perspective.
c) Which employer treats its staff in a more professional manner? Explain your answer.
d) Why would Magna-Net institute such a policy?

13. Do you agree with the argument that personal ethical practices and business ethical practices have little in common? Explain your answer.

14. **Class Exercise** As stated in Chapter 1, organizations emphasize cooperation among team members. This class exercise examines both an individual's and a group's responses to an unusual set of questions. At the end of the exercise, compare your individual score with that of the group. Divide the class into groups of three or four people and follow the directions. Do not peek at the answers shown in Appendix 3 until the group has completed the worksheet. Correct the worksheet once each group has responded.

Wilderness survival worksheet [12]

Following are 12 questions concerning personal survival in the wilderness. Your first task is individually to select the best of the three alternatives given under each item. Try to imagine yourself in the situation depicted. Assume that you are alone and have a minimum of equipment, except where specified. The season is autumn. The days are warm and dry, but the nights are cold.

After you have completed this task individually, consider each question again within your small group. Your group will have the task of deciding, by consensus, the best answer to each question. Do not change your individual answers, even if you change your mind in the group discussion. Both the individual and group solutions will later be compared with the "correct" answers provided (in Appendix 3) by a group of naturalists who conduct classes in woodland survival.

Question	Your answer	Your group's answer
1. You have strayed from your party in trackless timber; you have no special signaling equipment. The best way to attempt to contact your friends is to a. call for help loudly, but in a low register. b. yell or scream as loud as you can. c. whistle loudly and shrilly.		
2. You are in snake country. Your best action to avoid snakes is to a. make a lot of noise with your feet. b. walk softly and quietly. c. travel at night.		
3. You are hungry and lost in wild country. The best rule for determining which plants are safe to eat (among those you do not recognize) is to a. try anything you see the birds eat. b. eat anything except plants with bright red berries. c. put a bit of the plant on your lower lip for five minutes; if it seems all right, try a little.		
4. The day becomes dry and hot. You have a full canteen of water (about 1 liter) with you. You should a. ration it (drink about a cup per day). b. not drink until you stop for the night, and then drink what you think you need. c. drink as much as you think you need when you need it.		
5. Your water is gone. You become very thirsty. You finally come to a dried watercourse. Your best chance of finding water is to a. dig anywhere in the streambed. b. dig up plant and tree roots near the bank. c. dig in the streambed at the outside of a bend.		
6. You decide to walk out of the wild country by following a series of ravines where a water supply is available. Night is coming on. The best place to make camp is a. next to the water supply in the ravine. b. high on a ridge. c. midway up the slope.		

---

[12] Printed with permission from the New York State, Monroe County Parks Department, Nature Center at Mendon Ponds Park.

(continued)

Question	Your answer	Your group's answer
7. Your flashlight glows dimly as you are about to make your way back to your campsite after a brief foraging trip. Darkness comes quickly in the woods and the surroundings seem unfamiliar. You should a. head back at once, keeping the light on and hoping that the light will glow enough for you to make out landmarks. b. put the batteries under your armpits to warm them, and then replace them in the flashlight. c. shine your light for a few seconds, try to get the scene in mind, move out in the darkness, and repeat the process.		
8. An early snow confines you to your small tent. You doze with your small stove going. There is danger if the flame is a. yellow. b. blue. c. red.		
9. You must ford a river that has a strong current, large rocks, and some white water. After carefully selecting your crossing spot, you should a. leave your boots and pack on. b. take your boots and pack off. c. take off your pack, but leave your boots on.		
10. When crossing through waist-deep water with a strong current, you should face a. upstream. b. across the stream. c. downstream.		
11. You find yourself at a rimrock; your only route is up. The way is full of mossy, slippery rock. You should try it a. barefoot. b. with boots on. c. in stockinged feet.		
12. Unarmed and unsuspecting, you surprise a large bear prowling around your campsite. As the bear rears up about 10 meters from you, you should a. run. b. climb the nearest tree. c. freeze, but be ready to back away slowly.		

Score:

Number you have correct: _____

Average score for your group (sum of individual scores ÷ number
   of group members): _____

Group score: _____

Difference between group score and average: _____

CHAPTER TEST

1. Which of the following are services?
   a) mail delivery
   b) valet parking
   c) teaching
   d) taxi ride
   e) wedding pictures
   f) newspaper
2. Which of the following are products?
   a) physician's diagnosis
   b) life insurance
   c) fruits and vegetables
   d) tire
   e) tire changer
3. What are some characteristics of modern organizations?
   a) stable
   b) specialized
   c) accountable
   d) stressful to employees
   e) dynamic
4. Identify expectations that employers have of good employees.
   a) excellent attitude
   b) excellent communication skills
   c) limit personal activities (personal telephone calls, Web surfing, etc.) to 30 minutes during the workday
   d) ethical
   e) ready and willing to contribute to a team effort
   f) sexy dresser
   g) come late and leave early
   h) outstanding technical capability
5. How often do most long-term employees receive formal written employee evaluations?
   a) daily
   b) weekly
   c) monthly
   d) annually
6. Which are not examples of professional organizations?
   a) a trade union
   b) AFL-CIO
   c) Automobile Workers Union
   d) American Management Association
   e) American Medical Association
   f) American Bar Association
   g) Institute of Electrical and Electronic Engineers

7. Characteristics of a profession include
   a) predominantly intellectual activity
   b) learning a skill that will last a lifetime
   c) common body of knowledge that is taught in institutions of higher education
   d) code of ethics
   e) journals that publish peer-reviewed articles
   f) uniform
   g) use of specific tools
8. Select the best answer that describes a professional code of ethics.
   a) a principled standard of behavior in dealing with the employer, customers, and colleagues
   b) a standard of behavior that deals with customers
   c) a set of rules to be used at the discretion of the professional
   d) a certification that permits a person to practice a profession

CHAPTER 2

THE ORGANIZATION

You miss 100 percent of the shots you never take.
Wayne Gretzky, professional hockey player

OBJECTIVES

After studying this chapter, you should be able to

- Understand an organization's core identity
- Explain the difference between objectives and goals
- Explain the idea of "strength, weakness, opportunity, threat" (SWOT)
- Apply the SWOT concept to your own personal life
- Understand organizational standards, policies, and procedures

INTRODUCTION

The word *organization* is used throughout this book to mean a group of people working together for a common purpose. The group creates a structure in which individuals cooperate in the conduct of their activities. An organization may have a profit or nonprofit financial orientation and may consist of voluntary or paid workers (or a combination of both). An organization may operate in the public sector (e.g., it may be a federal, state, or local government agency) or the private sector. It may have a religious or a secular purpose. It may consist of professionals or of amateurs pursuing a hobby. It may employ people represented by a labor union, may instead be made up of nonunion workers, or may even be a group of consultants. The organization may exist in a local geographic area only or may be multinational. The project management ideas discussed in this book apply to all organizations, whatever their scope, purpose, demographics, or financial orientation—from organizations consisting of a single small independent contractor to the large international corporation with multimillion-dollar contracts.

CORE IDENTITY

An organization's core identity consists of a mission, an ideology, and a vision. Not all organizations think about and intentionally create an identity. If management does not articulate a core identity, the corporate culture will. However, without leadership, the identity that evolves may or may not inspire and guide the employees in the direction that management prefers.

Mission

The mission statement explains the organization's purpose; it is a statement of why the organization is in business. The mission is the organization's raison d'être, not its goal or business strategy. The mission statement serves as the basis for establishing the organization's strategic objectives. According to one source,

> I want to discuss why a company exists in the first place. In other words, why are we here? I think many people assume that a company exists simply to make money. While this is an important result of a company's existence, we have to go deeper and find the real reasons for our being. As we investigate this, we inevitably come to the conclusion that a group of people get together and exist as an institution that we call a company so they are able to accomplish something collectively that they could not accomplish separately—they make a contribution to society, a phrase which sounds trite but is fundamental.... You can look around [in the general business world] and see people who are interested in money and nothing else, but the underlying drives come largely from a desire to do something else: to make a product, to give a service—generally to do something which is of value.[1]

---

[1] Attributed to David Packard, cofounder of Hewlett-Packard Corporation, in Collins, J. C., and J. I. Porras, *Built to Last* (New York: Harper Business, 1997), p. 56.

Thus, Hewlett-Packard exists, not to make electronic test and measurement equipment, but to make technical contributions that advance the welfare of humanity. This mission will last for as long as Hewlett-Packard's senior management regards it as important. Some other corporate missions are as follows:

Konosuke Matsushita (Panasonic): to foster the progress and development of society and the well-being of people through the company's business activities, thereby enhancing the quality of life throughout the world.

Mary Kay Cosmetics: to enrich women's lives.

Sony: To experience the joy of advancing and applying technology for the benefit of the public.

ExxonMobil: to provide quality petrochemical products and services in the most efficient and responsible manner in order to generate outstanding customer and shareholder value.

Staples: to slash the cost and hassle of running your office!

New Jersey Transit: to provide safe, reliable, convenient, and cost-effective transit service by means of a skilled team of employees dedicated to customers' needs and committed to excellence.

Samsung: to create superior products and services that contribute to a better global society.

Reader's Digest: to create products that inform, enrich, entertain, and inspire people of all ages and cultures around the world.

Southwest Airlines: to provide the highest quality of customer service, delivered with a sense of warmth, friendliness, individual pride, and company spirit.

Kellogg: to build long-term volume and profit and to enhance the company's worldwide leadership position by providing nutritious food products of superior value.

3Com: to connect more people and organizations to information in more innovative, simple, and reliable ways than any other networking company in the world.

Adolor Corporation: to develop, on the basis of recent advances in proprietary medicinal chemistry and recombinant opiate receptor technology, the next generation of novel analgesics and related therapeutics for the treatment of pain.

Abbott Laboratories: to improve lives worldwide by providing cost-effective health care products and services.

Millennium Restaurant (San Francisco, California): to offer a gourmet dining experience created out of vegetarian, healthy, and environmentally friendly foods.

Core Ideology

An organization's core ideology is the glue that holds the organization together as it grows, decentralizes, diversifies, expands globally, and incorporates diversity into the workplace.[2] The core ideology represents a company's under-lying values and beliefs. For example,

- The Walt Disney Company is famous for its values of imaginativeness and wholesomeness.
- Hewlett-Packard emphasizes a respect for the individual and a commitment to the community.
- Merck's core ideology embraces corporate social responsibility, honesty, and integrity, and profit from work that benefits humanity.
- Sony's values include elevating the Japanese culture and national status and being a pioneer—not following others, "doing the impossible," and encouraging individual ability and creativity.

The values and beliefs that make up a company's core ideology should be so fundamental that the company should follow them, even if at some point one or more of them were to put the firm at a competitive disadvantage.

Vision

"A company's vision articulates what the company would like its future to be." An "organizational dream," the vision stretches the company's imagi-nation and motivates its people to rethink what is possible.[3] The vision represents something the organization aspires "to become, to achieve, to create—something that will require significant change and progress to attain."[4] Microsoft's vision is "a computer on every desk and in every home, all run-ning Microsoft software in every computer." This is certainly a lofty ideal. In the 1960s, everyone knew and understood the mission of the National Aero-nautics and Space Administration (NASA): Get to the moon and back before the end of the decade. Martin Luther King's most famous speech is labeled "I have a dream," because he elucidated his vision of a nonracist America.[5]

Vision statements often incorporate four elements: a customer orientation, a focus on the employee, organizational competencies, and standards of excel-lence.[6] A vision should be vivid and evoke emotion. It should motivate people and be powerful enough to persuade all those in the organization to take part in the effort to achieve the mission. In addition, the vision should be[7]

- Clear, concise, and easily understandable
- Memorable

---

[2] *Ibid.*, 1977. Chapter 3.

[3] Belgard, W. P., K. K. Fisher, and S. R. Rayner, "Vision, Opportunity, and Tenacity: Three Informal Processes That Influence Transformation, in R. Kilman & T. Covin, eds., *Corporate Transformation* (San Francisco: Jossey-Bass, 1988), p. 135.

[4] Collins & Porras, *Op. cit.*, p. 221.

[5] Jick, T. D., "The Vision Thing," *Harvard Business Review* (September 26, 1989), reprint no. 9-490-019, p. 1.

[6] *Ibid.*, p. 3.

[7] *Ibid.*, p. 2.

- Exciting and inspiring
- Challenging
- Centered on excellence
- Stable, but flexible
- Implementable and tangible

Know the Organization's Core Identity

Before joining an organization, investigate its core identity. Ask questions and make certain that you feel comfortable with the organization. Ascertain whether it shares your values and beliefs. Find out whether the organization accepts a diversity of people and opinions. If you join an organization, don't expect to create a new core ideology. If the organization's values are compatible with yours then press on. If not, look to another organization. Sometimes you cannot determine whether employees actually practice the values described in the company's literature. If, after joining an organization, you discover that a value gap exists with which you cannot live, then look for a new opportunity.

GOALS AND OBJECTIVES

Once an organization establishes its mission, core ideology, and vision, its employees can establish and pursue goals and objectives. The organization's *goals* reflect its general purpose and direction; they do not set specific targets (objectives). Goals may be strategic (long term) or tactical (short term). Upper management determines an organization's long-term strategic goals, which will guide the organization over perhaps three to five years. One type of aid used in determining an organization's direction is called a *SWOT* (*S*trengths, *W*eaknesses, *O*pportunities, *T*hreats) analysis.

Strengths, Weaknesses, Opportunities, Threats (SWOT)

A SWOT analysis helps find the best match between an organization's external trends (opportunities and threats) and internal capabilities:

- A *strength* is a resource the organization can use to achieve a desired result.
- A *weakness* is a limitation that will keep the organization from achieving a desired result.
- An *opportunity* is a situation that will, or at least is likely to, increase demand for a product or service that the organization offers.
- A *threat* is a potentially damaging situation in the organization's environment. The threat may be a political or economic restriction, barrier, or constraint that could prevent the organization from delivering its products or services.

An effective set of strategic goals takes advantage of opportunities by using the organization's strengths and wards off threats by overcoming them or by correcting weaknesses.

A SWOT analysis involves an impartial examination of the organization and its environment. SWOT analysts review markets; competition; technological, political, social, and environmental issues; economic trends; and the organization's marketing and distribution system, research-and-development (R&D) capabilities, reputation, and resources, including financial resources, the labor pool, computing resources, facilities, employee competencies and credentials, inventories, and management skills. The SWOT team categorizes the information it finds into strengths, weaknesses, opportunities, and threats. Sometimes, information can be considered both a strength and a weakness. On the basis of the SWOT analysis, management creates strategic goals, such as those illustrated in Figure 2–1.

Middle managers develop tactical goals to meet near-term demands. Typical tactical goals include increasing the dollar volume of sales, reducing fixed costs, increasing the number of pounds of material produced, upping enrollment, and increasing worker productivity. Following the establishment of general goals, managers develop a *plan* to establish objectives in order to achieve a desired result.

Objectives are observable and measurable results that contribute toward meeting the general organizational goals shown in Figure 2–1. Measured in terms of what, when, where, and how much, objectives describe conditions that will exist after the work is performed. In many organizations, managers establish objectives. In others, the people doing the work participate in setting objectives, recognizing that approval of the objectives rests with their immediate supervisor or manager. One organization had as an objective challenging a salesperson to increase the sales of books in Bergen County, New Jersey, from $5,000 per month to $8,000 per month by the end of the year. Another demanded that an office reduce its mobile telephone costs in the Fairfield County, Connecticut, area from $5,000 per month to $3,000 per month by the end of the first

FIGURE 2–1

SWOT process

quarter. Organizations use the acronym SMART to help establish objectives. Each objective identified should be

Specific,	encompassing a single task
Measurable,	establishing a clear indicator of progress
Assignable,	given to someone as a task to be completed
Realistic,	expressing what can actually be achieved with the time and resources budgeted
Time related,	stating the duration in which the task is expected to be completed

SIDEBAR: A PERSONAL SWOT ANALYSIS

Organizations frequently use SWOT analyses to evaluate their past efforts and determine their future. Because the process requires a great deal of soul-searching, the organizations send their executives away from the hustle and bustle of the office in which they work, to a neutral ground devoid of daily business interruptions. At this retreat, the executives begin a no-holds-barred brainstorming session, examining all ideas with no consequences or repercussions following the meeting.

Each of the participants brings different life experiences to the session. They interpret their experiences differently, of course, and not all will agree with each other. However, all participants must agree to respect each other and give one another the opportunity to articulate their thoughts and perspectives. Many of the comments will be of a sensitive nature, and the participants agree to respect the information revealed at the meeting and not seek retribution afterward. Sometimes, organizations cannot really recognize or accept honesty and genuine open thought.

As it happens, individuals can benefit from a similar analysis. Everyone can profit from a self-examination of his or her life. Think about your vision. Put it down in on paper. If you have not thought about it before, do it now. Does the vision relate to self-satisfaction, marriage, education, money, your career, or something else? Categorize your strengths and weaknesses. Consider the opportunities in your life. Identify situations that might prevent you from attaining your vision. Be brutally honest, and don't show what you have written to anyone else.

Now think about several broad actions that you need to take to pursue your vision. Perhaps it involves the development of a certain set of skills, a college education, or a move to a new location. If so, those are your goals.

If you have reached this point, you've done the hard part. Only the specific tasks remain. For each of the goals identified, you have to identify objectives that will assist you in achieving the goals. List the actions you think are required to achieve the goals. Those actions are the tasks. Associate with each task some way of recognizing that you have accomplished it. Each task should have a well-defined outcome that clearly indicates when it will be deemed to have been completed. Ideally, you should be able to accomplish each separate objective

TABLE 2–1

Personal Action Plan

Personal Vision:

Goal or Broad-based Endeavor #1:

Objectives Involved in Achieving Goal #1:

Specific Objective	Measured Outcome	Time for Completion
_____	_____	_____
_____	_____	_____
_____	_____	_____

Goal or Broad-based Endeavor #2:

Objectives Involved in Achieving Goal #2:

Specific Objective	Measured Outcome	Time for Completion
_____	_____	_____
_____	_____	_____
_____	_____	_____

within a month or less: It's too easy to postpone the start of objectives that take longer than a month. An overall sequence of objectives may take many months.

Table 2–1 can aid in developing a personal action plan. Add more goals if required, every so often examine your progress toward achieving your objectives, and make needed corrections.

ACTIVITIES

Activities are work steps that must be accomplished before an objective or a standard can be achieved. Some examples of activities are preparing a specification, getting a specification approved, completing a design, purchasing a component, and installing a telephone.

Resources represent the raw material used by the organization to complete activities. Resources include the people, money, materials, machine, facilities, information, technology, time, and energy needed to accomplish the activities. People *control* an activity by comparing the current performance with the expected performance and making required changes. Many managers create a model for what is expected by collecting data on similar previous activities.

They record information about the resources used to complete the earlier activity at a given level of quality and use that information as the basis for their estimate of the resources required to complete the new activity.

STANDARDS

Setting an expected performance leads to the idea of standards. The International Organization for Standardization (ISO) *(http://www.iso.ch/iso/en/ ISOOnline.frontpage)* defines standards as

Documented agreements containing technical specifications or other precise criteria to be used consistently as rules, guidelines, or definitions of characteristics, to ensure that materials, products, processes and services are fit for their purpose. For example, the format of the credit cards, phone cards, and "smart" cards that have become commonplace is derived from an ISO International Standard. Adhering to a size standard such as optimal thickness (0.76 mm) means that the cards can be used worldwide.

The ISO further states, "International standards contribute to making life simpler, and to increasing the reliability and effectiveness of the goods and services we use."

Managers and supervisors usually have an idea of the resources required to complete an activity. The estimates for these resources stem from either a performance *standard* based on the organization's experience or a generally accepted industry practice. If a standard doesn't exist, then the organization establishes it. As an example, suppose organized baseball wants to create a batting standard of performance. The baseball industry assembles a committee with outstanding knowledge about batting and impeccable baseball credentials. The committee meets, and it creates and adopts the standard of batting excellence shown in Table 2–2.

On the basis of the new standard, baseball players are categorized in terms of their hitting ability. Table 2–3 illustrates the categories as applied to the 1999 New York Yankees baseball team. Each team member is assigned a quality rating. If, after using this standard for some time, the sports community decides

TABLE 2–2

Standard of Batting Excellence[a]

Last Season's Batting Average	Hitting Ability	Hitting Quality Rating
.326 or higher	Outstanding	A
.301 to .325	Excellent	B
.276 to .300	Good	C
.251 to .275	Fair	D
.250 or below	Poor	F

[a] The player must have had at least 150 turns at bat to qualify for a rating.

TABLE 2–3

New York Yankees Batting Averages, 1999

Player	1999 Batting Average	No. of Times at Bat	1999 Hitting Quality Rating
D. Jimenez	.400	20	NR[a]
D. Jeter	.349	627	A
B. Williams	.342	591	A
D. Cone	.333	3	NR[a]
O. Hernandez	.333	3	NR[a]
D. Strawberry	.327	49	NR[a]
A. Watson	.300	10	NR[a]
C. Knoblauch	.292	603	C
P. O'Neill	.285	597	C
R. Ledee	.276	250	C
C. Davis	.269	476	D
T. Martinez	.263	589	D
C. Curtis	.262	195	D
L. Sojo	.252	127	D
S. Brosius	.247	473	F
J. Posada	.245	379	F
J. Girardi	.239	209	F
J. Leyritz	.235	200	F
S. Spencer	.234	205	F
C. Bellinger	.200	45	NR[a]
A. Pettitte	.200	5	NR[a]
J. Manto	.182	33	NR[a]
T. Tarasco	.161	31	NR[a]
A. Soriano	.125	8	NR[a]
R. Clemens	.000	4	NR[a]
H. Irabu	.000	4	NR[a]
M. Stanton	.000	1	NR[a]

[a] Not rated due to an insufficient number of times at bat.

that the standard does not reflect its needs, then the committee members would meet again to modify the standard. All professional communities examine and update old standards continually and create new standards as technology and general expectations change.

Many types of standards exist. The baseball batting example may be considered a production standard. The size, shape, form, and weight of sporting equipment follow prescribed standards. Technical standards define electrical, mechanical, and software interfaces. There are standards that establish requirements for the composition and structure of materials. Workmanship standards detail methods for evaluating welds, soldering connections, wiring harnesses, and more. Documentation standards clarify the formats used for submitting manuscripts. Standards establish expectations. If the items that organizations use meet established standards and the standards meet the requirements set forth by the customer, then the product or service will likely be adequate. Independent organizations such as the U.S. military, U.S. Department of Agriculture,

IEEE, ANSI, Software Engineering Institute, Underwriters Laboratory, and International Organization for Standardization (ISO) publish standards for a variety of applications.

POLICY, PROCESS, PROCEDURE, RULE

Policies are broad guidelines created to help an organization achieve its plans. A *process* is a method of reaching a desired outcome within an organization— "a structured, measured set of activities designed to produce a specified output for a particular customer or market. It implies a strong emphasis on how work is done within [the] organization."[8] A *business process* has been defined as "a set of logically related tasks performed to achieve a defined business outcome" and characterized as having internal or external customers and crossing departmental boundaries.[9] Recall that a person or group delivers a product or service. If the product or service is delivered to someone or some group within the same organization, the person or group is referred to as an *internal customer*. A person or group that performs work and that is unaffiliated with the buyer of the product or service is an *external customer. Procedures* outline the steps required to achieve a goal. *Rules* are definite, specific instructions.

Policies, processes, procedures, and rules are necessary to implement plans. As shown in Figure 2–2, senior managers create policies that establish a process. Managers then create procedures to implement the process. Rules are the specific detailed instructions that support the procedures. The entire *planning process* enables managers to determine the goals and actions needed to achieve the desired results. Throughout any organization, all components associated with the planning process must be in harmony at each level of management. The planning process is dynamic and requires periodic review and adjustment to accommodate changing circumstances.

SIDEBAR: PUBLIC VERSUS PRIVATE COMPANIES

Pat and Sarah believed they had a wonderful idea for a fast-food Middle Eastern restaurant. Into the pockets of pita bread they wanted to insert a mix of chopped vegetables with balls of spiced falafel (ground chickpeas) and a special family-devised blend of hummus and tahini sauce. As an unusual dessert treat, they wanted to offer baklava, a pastry covered with honey and filled with ground pistachio nuts. The mint tea accompanying the pastry would include real peppermint leaves and could be served iced or hot, depending on the season.

Pat and Sarah took their life savings together with some money they borrowed from their parents and opened Sa-pa's Middle Eastern Restaurant in the

---

[8] Davenport, T. H., *Process Innovation* (Boston: Harvard Business School Press, 1993).
[9] Davenport, T. H., and J. E. Short, "The New Industrial Engineering: Information Technology and Business Process Redesign," *Sloan Management Review* (Summer 1990): 11–27.

FIGURE 2–2

Organizational Continuum from Policy to Rule

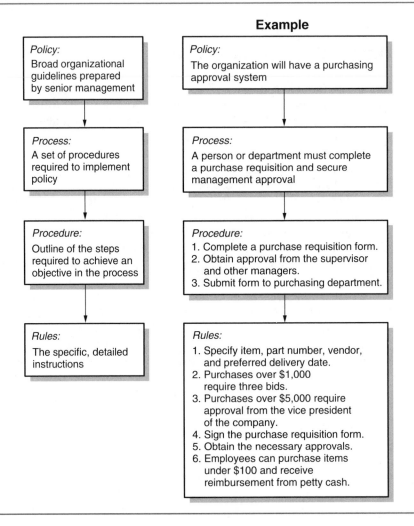

Example

| Policy: | Policy: |
| Broad organizational guidelines prepared by senior management | The organization will have a purchasing approval system |

| Process: | Process: |
| A set of procedures required to implement policy | A person or department must complete a purchase requisition and secure management approval |

| Procedure: | Procedure: |
| Outline of the steps required to achieve an objective in the process | 1. Complete a purchase requisition form.
2. Obtain approval from the supervisor and other managers.
3. Submit form to purchasing department. |

| Rules: | Rules: |
| The specific, detailed instructions | 1. Specify item, part number, vendor, and preferred delivery date.
2. Purchases over $1,000 require three bids.
3. Purchases over $5,000 require approval from the vice president of the company.
4. Sign the purchase requisition form.
5. Obtain the necessary approvals.
6. Employees can purchase items under $100 and receive reimbursement from petty cash. |

city. The people in the business district enjoyed the fresh high-quality food, the excellent service, the unique background music, and the clean surroundings. In less than a year, the business earned a profit, and Pat and Sarah repaid the loan.

On the basis of their accomplishment, Pat and Sarah decided to open Sa-pa's Too, a second restaurant in another part of town. With established credit, a proven successful idea, pluck, and contagious enthusiasm, they convinced a local bank to lend them the funds to open Sa-pa's Too. After a great deal of hard work finding a good location and setting up the restaurant, they again earned a profit within a year. They repaid the new bank loan within two years. Pat and Sarah demonstrated that they had good business sense in addition to wonderful recipes.

Pat and Sarah owned and operated the restaurants privately. Their success convinced them to expand the business and open other Sa-pa's Too in nearby towns and cities. The expansion effort required a great deal of money. In order to convince prospective backers, Pat and Sarah had to develop a good business plan. They began thinking strategically: They needed a long-term vision, goals, objectives, and values. They needed plans for recruiting and training staff, obtaining standard cooking equipment, standardizing the restaurant décor, legally protecting their ideas and recipes, identifying other prospective locations, and developing a food distribution plan so that new Sa-pa's Too restaurant patrons would enjoy the same quality of food that those eating at the established restaurants enjoyed. But the plans would take them away from direct involvement in the first two restaurants they started. They would change their careers from restaurant proprietors to restaurant executives.

Pat and Sarah decided to sell a portion of their business and go public. They chose not to borrow the money from a bank, because they didn't want to have monthly principal and interest payments. Instead, the founders decided to give up part of their ownership. Financial organizations, investment bankers, and venture capitalists assist people in raising money for starting a new business or expanding an existing business. In return for the funding to expand Pat and Sarah's restaurants, the investment organization demanded two-thirds of the business. The investment counselors divided the business into 30,000 shares. Pat and Sarah would keep 10,000 shares and set aside 20,000 shares for investors. After examining the industry, similar businesses, and their restaurant's financial record, the investment counselors, Pat, and Sarah agreed to value each share at $25. The investment organization prepared the documents associated with an initial public offering and attempted to sell the shares to people that had confidence in the future success of other Sa-pa's Too restaurants. If the organization successfully sold 20,000 shares, it would raise $500,000, which the business would use to expand.

Pat and Sarah now led a publicly owned and publicly traded company. Accordingly, Sa-pa's Too shareholders could sell their stock to anyone at anytime. A stockbroker would handle the transaction by arranging the sale of stock from seller to buyer. In a publicly traded company, the public determines the value of a share of stock through its perception of the company's future prospects. The company's profits or earnings provide a good guideline for estimating the price of a share of its stock. Suppose that Sa-pa's Too restaurant earns a profit of $300,000, or $10 per share, after the first year of operation. The price-to-earnings ratio is a commonly used method for valuing stocks. Many companies have a price-to-earnings ratio of 15 to 20. That ratio would value Sa-pa's Too restaurants at $150 to $200 per share, which would represent a very healthy profit to the company's shareholders. Of course, if the restaurant did not earn a profit—or worse, if it lost money—then the value of the shares could plummet to pennies.

Very often, newly formed companies (also known as start-ups) choose to compensate key employees with a lower salary, plus shares of stock as a "sweetener." The employee exchanges immediate income for potential future profits. If the company does well, then the employee will do well, because the stock price will likely increase. This arrangement serves to motivate managers and other executives to focus on company profits so that the value of the stock will increase.

REVIEW QUESTIONS

1. If you were to start a new organization tomorrow, describe the core values you would build into it.
2. Most large organizations have a corporate persona or identity that they share with the public. This identity becomes the public perception of the organization and is often used to shape government policy, as well as to convince the public to believe in the organization and use its services or products.
    a) Use the Internet to find the names of the 30 companies upon which the Dow–Jones industrial average is based.
    b) Visit the Web site of two of the companies you found listed in part (a). Try to discover their corporate identity by searching for their mission, values, and vision statements. The information may not be explicitly termed the company's mission, values, and vision, so you will have to make a judgment about the data.
    c) Repeat part (b), using two of the following organizations:

American Red Cross	Avon Products
Boy or Girl Scouts of America	Colgate-Palmolive
Eastern Mountain Sports	Lands' End
Liz Claiborne	Patagonia
Procter & Gamble	Reebok International, Ltd.
Salvation Army	W. W. Norton & Company

    d) Compare the results of parts (a) and (b). Describe the similarities and differences in the information that you obtained.
3. Use the Internet to determine the winners of the most recent Malcolm Baldrige award.

CHAPTER TEST

For each of the following questions, circle the correct answer or fill in the blanks:

1. An organization's core identity consists of _____, _____, and _____.
2. Select the best answers.
    a) The mission statement explains an organization's purpose.
    b) A mission statement describes specific, time-limited activities.
    c) A mission statement represents the values and belief systems underlying an organization.

    d) The vision statement represents something an organization aspires "to become, to achieve, to create—something that will require significant change and progress to attain."

3. Select the phrase that best defines an organization's goals.
    a) An organization's goals represent a general statement of purpose and direction.
    b) An organization's goals represent specific targets.
    c) An organization's goals represent its strengths, weaknesses, opportunities, and threats (SWOT).

4. Which statement characterizes an organization's objectives?
    a) Objectives are observable and measurable results that contribute toward meeting the general goals of an organization.
    b) Objectives are measured in terms of what, when, where, and how much.
    c) Objectives describe conditions that will exist after work is performed.
    d) Objectives represent an organization's strengths, weaknesses, opportunities, and threats (SWOT).

5. The acronym SMART represents the following:
    i) S   _____
    ii) M   _____
    iii) A   _____
    iv) R   _____
    v) T   _____

6. True or False? A SWOT analysis relates external trends (opportunities and threats) to internal capabilities (strengths and weaknesses).

7. Examples of resources are
    a) people   b) land
    c) machines   d) materials
    e) money   f) a train ride

8. True or False? The fundamental premise behind controlling an activity is a comparison of current performance with expected performance and then making required changes.

9. Which of the following can trace their assigned value to an accepted standard?
    a) a team's won–loss record
    b) U.S. Grade A meat
    c) distance in miles
    d) temperature
    e) shoe size
    f) a container of milk purchased in a store
    g) lumber

CHAPTER 3

PROJECT MANAGEMENT: ORGANIZATIONAL OVERVIEW

If I am not for myself, who will be?
If I am not for others, what am I?
And if not now, when?
Hillel, "Ethics of the Fathers"

OBJECTIVES

After studying this chapter, you should be able to

- Define a project
- Explain the difference between a program and a project
- Understand and create an organization chart
- Understand the different types of organizational structures
- Explain a matrix operation

INTRODUCTION

General management concerns itself with the leadership and management of the organization as a whole. At a minimum, general management encompasses planning, organizing, staffing, coordinating, executing, communicating, and controlling the operations of an ongoing enterprise. However, general managers go beyond the basics of management, to deal with the processes, systems, and technologies that integrate the organization and enable it to carry out its mission. Of necessity, general managers also frequently involve themselves with the broader community's external constituencies, jointly developing philosophies, values, and strategies that create a successful enterprise.

Project managers have a narrower view than general managers. To be sure, they employ general management skills, but they use the processes and procedures developed by others to accomplish a specific effort. Project managers work on *projects*—endeavors undertaken to create a unique product or service. Nowadays, almost all industries from defense, information technology, and construction to the pharmaceutical and chemical industries, commonly use the project management methodology. Typically, projects begin after the customer signs a contract. Alternatively, they are initiated internally, with the intent of introducing a new product to the marketplace.[1] The organization uses internally funded projects either to leapfrog the competition with a new product or service or to "play catch-up" and just stay abreast of competitors.

Projects do not go on forever: Every project has a definite beginning and a definite end. Projects start with an identifiable need. Staff members prepare a requirements list or perhaps a detailed specification document. The organization's purchasing department distributes the list of requirements to internal or external suppliers. Organizations usually demand a response from prospective suppliers within 30 to 90 days. Interested suppliers respond to the organization with a bid—a proposal describing the equipment they will deliver and the price they will charge. The organization reviews the bids, selects a winner, and awards a contract. Figure 3–1 summarizes the process.

After the contract is awarded, a project manager assembles a team that develops the product or service embodied in the customer's idea and distributes the work and the associated budget to the organization's departments. The product or service is developed and tested, and then technicians install it at the customer's site and confirm that the system operates. Often, the customer requires the organization to train the customer's staff in the correct way to use and maintain the product. This project *life cycle* summarizes the steps associated with a project. The bell-shaped pattern shown in Figure 3–2 depicts the money spent or the labor hours worked on a large project. Funding for the project starts slowly and increases progressively. The design-and-development effort expends the majority of the funds, because the largest number of people work on that aspect of the job. Fewer people perform installation, and the chart shows less spending in that direction. Projects usually end with an acceptance test at

---

[1] Shenhar, A. J., "From Theory to Practice: Toward a Typology of Project-Management Styles," *IEEE Transactions on Engineering Management* 45, no. 1 (February 1998): 33–48.

FIGURE 3–1

The bidding process

XYZ Company identifies a need.

XYZ Company prepares a list of requirements or a specification.

The XYZ Company purchasing department distributes a specification to various suppliers.

Suppliers prepare and submit a bid to the XYZ Company.

XYZ Company evaluates the supplier's bids.

XYZ Company awards the contract to the ABC Company.

FIGURE 3–2

Project life-cycle phases

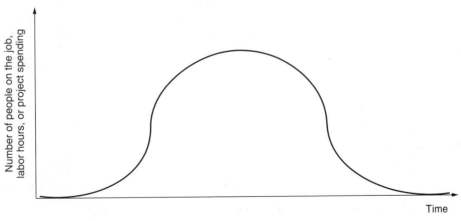

Number of people on the job, labor hours, or project spending

Time

| Contract award | Planning: Assembling team and disbursing work | Design, development, and testing | Installation | Training | Transfer to maintenance |

the customer's site, after which the customer's staff is trained in the use of the product or service. At this point, the remaining people on the project return to their respective departments for reassignment. Naturally, labor hour distributions and spending patterns vary among projects.

A software or hardware product may require ongoing maintenance, but that is not considered part of the original project's activities. Indeed, many organizations have a separate group concerned with product maintenance. Customers usually receive annual payment notices for periodic hardware or software maintenance and product updates.

A product or service provided by a project differs from previously delivered products or services. The Project Management Body of Knowledge (PMBOK)[2] defines *project management* as the application of (certain specialized) knowledge, skills, tools, and techniques in order to meet or exceed stakeholder needs and expectations from a project. *Project managers* use many of the same techniques and tools employed by general managers. After negotiating for the resources the organization requires for a project, the project manager assigns those resources with the intent of completing specific objectives and goals. The project manager has complete responsibility for the success or failure of the project. Frequently, however, he or she lacks the authority to insist that the organization's staff support the completion of the required activities. (We will discuss the ramifications of this apparent paradox in the next section.)

Table 3–1 illustrates a family of microprocessors developed by Intel. Each of these internally funded microprocessors started as the aim of a project with a set of requirements. Each project required a large number of software and hardware engineers and technicians to develop a design that supported a machine code that software designers could use to program the microprocessor.

TABLE 3–1

Thirty Years of Intel Microprocessor Projects[a]

Microprocessor Device Number	Year of Introduction	Number of Transistors
4004	1971	2,250
8008	1972	2,500
8080	1974	5,000
8086	1978	29,000
286	1982	120,000
386™ processor	1985	275,000
486™ DX processor	1989	1,180,000
Pentium® processor	1993	3,100,000
Pentium II processor	1997	7,500,000
Pentium III processor	1999	24,000,000
Pentium 4 processor	2000	42,000,000

[a] Data from *http://www.intel.com/research/silicon/mooreslaw.htm*.

[2] Project Management Institute Standards Committee, *A Guide to the Project Management Body of Knowledge* (Upper Darby, PA: Project Management Institute, 1996).

Engineers and technicians built a prototype and tested it extensively. After the test results showed that the prototype was satisfactory, the design group completed the drawings and documentation and transferred the product to the integrated-circuit-manufacturing department for large-scale production. The design, fabrication, and testing of each of the microprocessors in the table constitute a project.

A *program* is a group of projects managed in a coordinated way in order to obtain benefits that would not be available from managing them individually. The projects making up a program share some common features, in any or all of the areas of application or purpose, components, development or fabrication tools, developer labor pool, training, and maintenance. The organization desires to take advantage of these common features and thus creates a program. The effort represented by Table 3–1 was in behalf of the Intel microprocessor program conducted over a 30-year period. The development of many of the projects overlapped. Possibly, a single person managed two or more projects simultaneously. A *program manager* has responsibility for several related projects. After a project team gains experience on one of the projects in a program, the program manager is inclined to assign the team to other projects in the program. The members of a team that successfully completes a project understand each other's strengths and weaknesses, as well as the major technical aspects of the old and new projects. From the old project, the team members have acquired a knowledge of the development tools required to perform the job, so they will not require extensive training on the new project. The program manager meets with the various project managers to determine which project(s) the team would benefit most. The customer benefits as well, because combining projects saves money.

Consider this example of the difference between a project and program. Over a 50-year span, the U.S. Navy's Blue Angel acrobatic flight team used eight aircraft: the Grumman F6F Hellcat, Grumman F8F Bearcat, Grumman F9F Panther, Grumman F9F-8 Cougar, Grumman F11F-1 Tiger, McDonnell Douglas F-4J Phantom II, McDonnell Douglas A-4F Skyhawk II, and McDonnell Douglas F/A-18 Hornet. Each aircraft represents a separate project that went through several phases, including the initial conceptualization, aircraft development, prototype manufacture, and testing and evaluation, before the aircraft went into production. Keep in mind that production manufacturing and aircraft maintenance are not part of a project. From the U.S. Navy's perspective, all of the aircraft represent the Blue Angel aircraft program.

WHY PROJECT MANAGEMENT?

Organizations divide into four broad management categories (Figure 3–3). Upper management establishes the policy and future direction of the organization, middle management focuses on planning, supervisory levels deal with distribution and scheduling the work, and the large nonsupervisory workforce completes and delivers the product or service. As shown in Figure 3–4, *functional managers* take responsibility for activities in specialized departments or

Stratified organizational levels

Upper management: Policy
Middle management: Planning
Supervisory: Scheduling
Nonsupervisory worker: Product or service

Functional department view of the organization

	Engineering	Manufacturing	Purchasing	Human Resources	Customer Service	Sales and Marketing	...
Upper management							
Middle management							
Supervisory							
Nonsupervisory worker							

functions (e.g., engineering, purchasing, manufacturing, management information systems, information technology (IT), sales, marketing, human resources, publications, and customer service). Most managers concentrate on their area of expertise. For example, an engineering manager has little interest in the issues that are relevant to the manufacturing or publications department. Most organizations impose constraints, if not outright restrictions, on employees from one department involving themselves in the activities of another department.

Combining the stratified organizational levels with the functional departments creates a patchwork of "fiefdoms" (Figure 3–5). Few managers in the organization take a broad view. In fact, upper management usually prefers functional managers to tend solely to their activities. Accordingly, a close examination of an organization reveals a vast "sea" of operational "islands" on which highly territorial supervisory and nonsupervisory personnel closely guard those regions in which they are especially interested. This arrangement of turf leads to the need for a manager who can integrate and meld the parts of the independent "fiefdoms" into a cohesive group that takes an interest in completing a particular job or project. That person is the project manager.

The project manager also provides a focal point of responsibility: The buck stops at his or her desk. All of the organization's stakeholders bring their questions, comments, complaints, and issues to the project manager, who speaks for the organization. This does not, of course, mean that the project manager acts unilaterally without seeking guidance and assistance from other stakeholders.

FIGURE 3–5
Operational islands

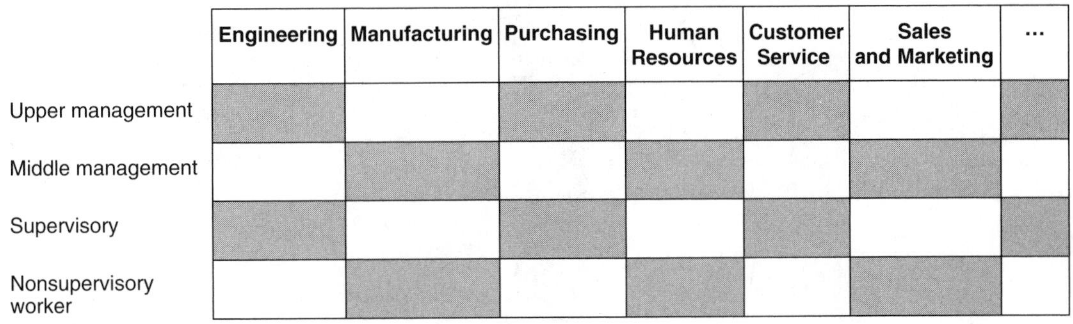

	Engineering	Manufacturing	Purchasing	Human Resources	Customer Service	Sales and Marketing	...
Upper management	▓		▓		▓		
Middle management		▓		▓		▓	
Supervisory	▓			▓		▓	
Nonsupervisory worker		▓		▓			

However, it is the project manager who makes decisions after consulting with the technical, financial, purchasing, manufacturing, and sales communities; suppliers; and, if necessary, senior management.

PROJECT MANAGER'S RESPONSIBILITIES

The essential goal of project management is to make the most effective use of resources such as labor, equipment, facilities, materials, money, information, and technology so that the goals of a project can be achieved within budget, on schedule, while meeting performance requirements, and with the approval of customers. The project manager takes into account the changing legal, social, economical, political, and technological environments. Upper management holds the project manager accountable for all project activities. The project manager must coordinate strategies and resources across the organization's functional interfaces, resolve conflicts, and apply integrated planning and control techniques. The project manager crosses organizational boundaries continually in an effort to acquire and deploy resources and to develop the project team into a harmonious group as quickly as possible. Undoubtedly, a major responsibility of the project manager involves securing a customer's commitment to a firm and realistic set of requirements. A good specification defines the scope, schedules, and quality controls associated with the job. The requirement definition has an immense impact on the resources selected and the profitability of the project. A successful project manager must have administrative expertise and an understanding of human behavior and must act as an integrator, a communicator, a leader, and an environment enhancer.

The project manager is the focal point of the organizations's *stakeholders*, which include the customer, the upper-level-managers, the functional managers, and other individuals and organizations involved in or affected by a project (Figure 3–6). Project managers strive to meet or exceed stakeholders' needs and expectations. Some project managers believe, not entirely with tongue in

FIGURE 3–6

The project manager is pulled in all directions

Functional
department
Managers

Upper-level
Managers

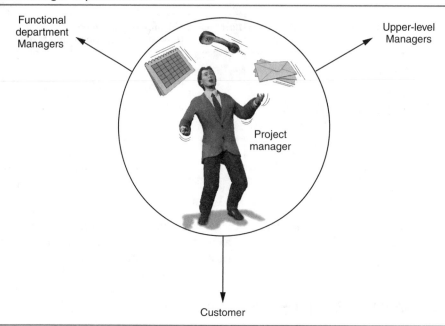

Project
manager

Customer

cheek, that without a project manager in charge, a project will operate within the following seven phases:

1. Wild enthusiasm
2. Disillusionment
3. Chaos
4. Search for the guilty
5. Punishment of the innocent
6. Promotion of the nonparticipants
7. Definition of the requirements

ORGANIZATION CHARTS

All organizations formally divide management responsibility into layers, represented by organization charts. Figure 3–7 illustrates a traditional top-down organization chart. Organization charts are not one size fits all; there simply is no "best" organization chart. An organization structure used successfully for a Fortune 500 industrial company may not be suitable for the operations of a smaller business or a different industry. Nor are organization charts cast in concrete: They change, depending on business, economic, and labor conditions. Organization charts frequently reflect the chief executive's personality and preferred way of conducting operations.

FIGURE 3–7

Traditional management structure: Functional organization

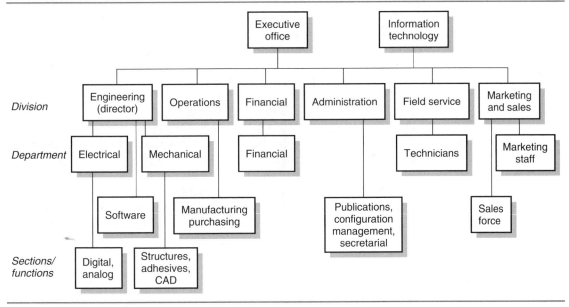

In Figure 3–7, the executive office may consist of the organization's president, vice presidents, legal staff, and administrative staff. The organization's staff provides advice and support and maintains control over their resources. The vice presidents report to the president and are responsible for one or more functional or support departments.

Depending on the organization's size, either a vice president or a director reporting to the vice president leads the functional and support departments. Frequently, there are vice presidents of engineering, manufacturing, sales and marketing, information technology, human resources, and other functional departments, to whom midlevel managers report. Nonsupervisory employees report to the midlevel managers.

Functional Organization

The functional organizational chart shown in Figure 3–7 identifies the disciplines required to develop and produce a product or service. Each department manager can trace a line back to the organization's president. Everyone understands where he or she stands in the "pecking" order. When a special project comes into the "house," no particular person receives responsibility for its completion. Instead, the managers meet and agree to divide the work according to a plan that they have devised. Each midlevel manager establishes priorities. A dispute among departments would likely work itself up the chain of command and require intervention by vice presidents—probably not a very efficient way to attack a project. Each department manager tries to maximize the usage of personnel within his or her department, assigning tasks to individuals and establishing priorities among the tasks.

The functional organization structure is based on specialization. Individuals in each specialized department, such as engineering, production, marketing, accounting, and logistics, report to one superior. In a multiple-project environment, conflicts may develop over the relative priorities of different projects that are competing for limited resources. If the organization's policy does make use of a project manager, the project manager has little formal authority and is compelled to rely on negotiation, the informal power structure of the organization, and interpersonal skills in order to realize the project's goals. Project team members then place more emphasis on their functional specialties, which can work to the detriment of the project. According to some managers, it is easier to manage specialists if they are grouped together and supervised by an individual possessing similar skills or experiences. The functional organization centralizes similar resources and provides mutual support to group members by keeping them in close physical proximity. A functional organization structure can define career paths for employees.

Project-Structured Organization

Figure 3–8 illustrates a project-structured organization. In this kind of structure, established to manage a variety of large, long-term projects, employees are dedicated to specific projects and work in one of several large project groups.

FIGURE 3–8

Project-structured organization

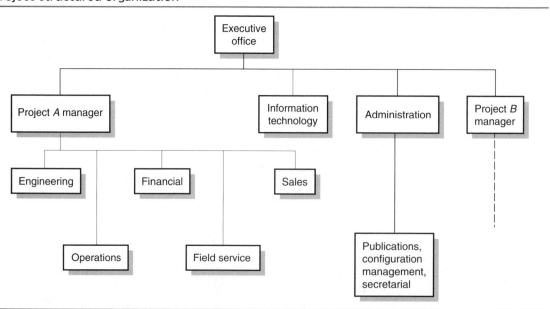

Each such group contains a complement of engineers, technicians, administrators, and other professional and nonprofessional personnel. Functional managers do not have to make project-level decisions; they work only on a single project. All managers report to the assigned project manager, who has both the authority and the responsibility for the project. The project manager requests functional managers to hire personnel to work on the project. Upon completion of the project, employees may find themselves looking for a new job, unless they can obtain a position in another project organization.

The project manager has unfettered authority over the project and retains the flexibility to acquire resources from within or outside the parent organization. A project structure promotes informal channels of communication between the project manager and the team, but it may not promote the efficient use of resources, and facilities may be duplicated. Because every project has a beginning and an end, project team members inevitably work themselves out of a job, whereupon they may be laid off. Some fortunate employees may find a new position on another project within the same organization.

Matrix Organization

Many organizations prefer not to duplicate personnel for each project. Instead, they attempt to create a single "world-class" functional organization and share their talented workers among the various projects. This approach leads to the matrix organization shown in Figure 3–9. On initiating a new project, the organization assigns a project manager, who then assembles a team comprising personnel from the various functional groups that make up the organization.

FIGURE 3–9

Matrix organization

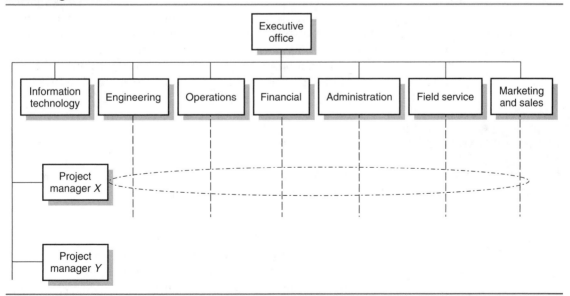

Naturally, project managers negotiate with the functional managers to obtain the best people for the project. Project managers who are familiar with the functional departments' personnel have the best chance of recruiting a capable staff. Toward that end, project managers cultivate relationships with functional managers so that they can obtain people suitable for the projects entrusted to them.

The project manager plans and coordinates a project by working with and integrating all groups within the organization. Relying on his or her organizational and people skills more than technical ability, the project manager works with the team to identify and address the needs of all stakeholders. The project manager's focus is on work relationships and leadership; he or she motivates the team members, delegates tasks, builds team spirit, and manages and resolves conflicts. The project manager negotiates a suitable working relationship with the functional manager to reward and discipline employees. Using his or her communication skills and problem-solving ability, the project manager influences stakeholders.

The matrix organization is a combination of the functional and project management structures. It attempts to maximize the benefits and minimize the weaknesses of the two structures. The matrix maintains functional or vertical lines of authority, while establishing a relatively permanent horizontal structure to support new projects. It is designed to work with all functional departments that support a project and to reduce or eliminate duplication of effort on the project team. The matrix design enables the organization to manage several projects simultaneously, even when it lacks the resources to staff each project separately.

Because each worker has two "bosses"—the project manager and the functional manager—in the matrix system, it may create conflicts among the workers. To reduce the likelihood of conflicts, the roles and responsibilities of each worker must be clearly defined before work on the project begins. In a strong matrix, the project manager enjoys greater authority, whereas in a weak matrix, authority passes to the functional manager. The functional department's employee is at a disadvantage if he or she is placed on a long-term project, because the time the worker spends away from the department may affect his or her chances of receiving a promotion or a "choice" assignment. Table 3–2 summarizes the relationships among the functional, project, and matrix organizational structures.

LINE ORGANIZATION

Most workers contribute directly to an organization's product or service. For example, in a company that manufactures computers,

> engineers design the computer's circuit boards,
> technicians and engineers test prototypes,
> technicians fabricate the printed circuit boards,
> factory workers stuff the boards with electronic components,
> factory technicians assemble the components into the finished computer,
> testing technicians test the fabricated system,

TABLE 3–2

Comparison of Project Leadership in Different Organization Structures

	Traditional Functional Organization	Project-Structured Organization	Matrix Organization
Project leadership responsibility	May use a project coordinator	Uses a project manager	Uses a project manager
Project priorities	Established by executive management	Established by project manager	Established by project manager
Stakeholder disputes	Resolved by functional or designated manager	Resolved by project manager	Resolved by project manager
Personnel selection	Functional managers recruit personnel	Project Manager designates managers to recruit personnel	Functional managers recruit personnel
Project manager responsibility	None	High	High
Project manager authority	None	High	Weak
Personnel at end of project	Remain in functional organization	Possible forced organizational leave (layoffs)	Return to functional groups

salespeople sell the product, and

field technicians install the equipment in the buyers' facility or home.

Without all of these people doing their jobs, customers will not receive the quality of products or services they demand. In contrast, some employees at the firm have little to do with the final product or service. For example, lawyers protect and advise the company about legal matters, nurses care for a person injured on the job, librarians assist people in obtaining information, marketing personnel develop advertisements and create ideas for future products, and senior managers guide the organization. Important as they might be, none of these people has anything directly to do with the actual product or service provided to the customer.

Organizations use the term *line manager* to describe managers who actually contribute to making a product or performing a service. In a line organization, direct, straight-line relationships exist between different levels within the company that are involved with a product line. The members of the line organization perform or manage functions essential to the existence of the firm and product or service. A line organization has a clear chain of command and promotes fast decision making. Most of the people assigned to a project manager are line workers. All the people mentioned in this section's first paragraph are line workers. Lawyers, nurses, librarians, marketing personnel, and senior managers support the organization, but do not perform work required to get the product or service to the customer and therefore are not line workers.

REVIEW QUESTIONS

1. Explain the difference between a project and a program.
2. What is an organizational chart? What is its purpose?
3. Think of a company, religious organization, charitable organization, or college with which you have some familiarity. Perform a SWOT analysis. That is, identify the strengths, weaknesses, opportunities, and threats confronting the organization. On the basis of your analysis, identify two strategic goals appropriate to the organization.
4. Describe the advantages and disadvantages of functional, project, and matrix organizations.
5. What may happen to the members of a project team when the organization completes the project?
6. Describe a functional manager and a line manager. Can they be the same? Explain.
7. Do you believe that a project manager must have technical expertise in the organization's specialty areas? Explain.
8. Sketch a project life cycle. Describe the meaning of the term.

CHAPTER TEST

For each of the following questions, circle the correct answer or fill in the blanks:

1. True or False? A project is an endeavor undertaken to create a unique product.
2. Every project has a definite _____ and a definite _____.
3. True or False? Project management is the application of knowledge, skills, tools, and techniques in order to meet or exceed stakeholder needs and expectations from a project.
4. True or False? The project manager has responsibility for the success or failure of a project.
5. True or False? A program is a group of projects managed in a coordinated way to obtain benefits not available from managing them individually.
6. True or False? A line organization describes the direct, straight-line relationships between different levels within a company involved with a product.
7. A project manager is concerned about which of the following goals?
   a) effective use of resources
   b) completing the project within budget
   c) completing the project on schedule
   d) meeting performance requirements stated in the contract
   e) receiving customer acceptance
   f) achieving state-of-the-art performance
   g) giving the customer everything he or she asked for.

8. Which of the following are examples of stakeholders?
   a) external customer
   b) functional departments
   c) IRS auditors
   d) suppliers
   e) senior management
9. Select the employees that contributes to making a product or performing a service:
   a) line manager
   b) legal staff
   c) librarian
   d) company nurse
   e) purchasing staff
10. The functional organization is characterized by
    a) specialty personnel
    b) colleagues sharing a common work area
    c) manager with the authority to make decisions regarding the priority of tasks
    d) technical problem-solving skills
11. Morning social discussions with work associates
    a) improve morale and should be engaged in every day.
    b) reduce company productivity.
    c) should not be conducted in front of a manager.
12. Characteristics of a functional organization include the following:
    a) specialty skills
    b) minimal skills
    c) a broad cross section of the organization's disciplines
    d) outstanding writing skills
13. True or false? The matrix organization is designed to manage several projects simultaneously, even though the organization may lack the resources to staff each project separately.
14. True or false? Because there are two "bosses" for each worker, the matrix organization may create conflicts among workers on a project.
15. The project manager focuses on work relationships and leadership and uses the following techniques:
    a) motivation
    b) delegation
    c) supervision
    d) building of team spirit
    e) conflict management and resolution
    f) superior technical skills
16. A project manager's primary goals involve delivering a product or service and satisfying the following conditions (choose all that apply):
    a) within budget
    b) on schedule
    c) meeting the performance requirements
    d) exceeding the performance requirements described in the specification
    e) receiving customer acceptance
    f) with employee satisfaction

CHAPTER 4

MANAGEMENT CONCEPTS

> *There is nothing more difficult to handle, more doubtful of success, and more dangerous to carry through than initiating changes. The innovator has for enemies all those who have done well under the old conditions, and lukewarm defenders in those who may prosper under the new.*
> Machiavelli, *The Prince*, Chapter 6

OBJECTIVES

After studying this chapter, you should be able to

- Understand the difference between a manager and a supervisor
- Understand fundamental management theories
- Define *efficiency* and *productivity*
- Discuss the functions of management
- Discuss management styles
- Explain the types of power used by managers
- Compare a group with a team
- Explain the difference between a manager and a leader

INTRODUCTION

Before reading this chapter, students in the class should perform a little exercise. The purpose of this exercise is to stimulate your thinking regarding the nature of a manager's job. Many students have held one or more jobs. Recall your supervisors or managers in these jobs. Take a few minutes to answer the following questions:

1. List the broad supervisory responsibilities that you believe this person had.
2. List the reasons that you took the job.
3. Identify the actions taken by the organization and the supervisor or manager that would motivate you to pursue your tasks with greater diligence.
4. What did you like least about the job?
5. What did you like best about the job?

Now join with other members of the class to form small groups consisting of three or four students. Discuss your individual responses to each question with your group. Then have the group evaluate the responses and select the best five answers to each question. Discuss the results of your deliberations in class.

MANAGEMENT

What does a manager do? What makes a good manager? Practitioners and theorists alike have wrestled with these topics at length. Most agree that management is the process of getting activities completed efficiently and effectively, with and through other people. The manager's goal is to get the job done in the shortest time with a minimum of cost and resources expended. Resources consist of people, places, and things. From the organization's perspective, they include time, labor, material, facilities, land, tools, money, equipment, and other resources. An organization has (1) people that do the work, (2) people that plan and distribute the work, and (3) people that plan for the organization's future. The second category includes the day-to-day managers and supervisors. The last group consists of upper management.

Management is not a new idea. Consider the management skills required by the ancient Egyptians to build the pyramids (Figure 4–1a). Depending on which historian you believe, the pyramids required from 20,000 to 100,000 laborers, an impressive workforce. The Chinese built the Great Wall (Figure 4–1b), which stretches to a length of 4,000 miles across the border between China and territories in the north. The 4,000-year-old Stonehenge (Figure 4–1c) structure in the United Kingdom is a set of concentric rings and horseshoe shapes. The construction of this monument likely involved moving stones weighing as much as 25 tons from a quarry more than 20 miles away. Once in place, the inner stone circle was one of the earliest structures to align with sunrise during the summer

FIGURE 4–1

(a) A pyramid. (b) The Great Wall. (c) Stonehenge. (d) A Roman aqueduct. (e) The Temple of the Inscriptions

(a)

(b)

(c)

(d)

(e)

Photographs courtesy of the following:

(a) Sphinx and Great Pyramid. Printed with permission from the New York State Archives Glass Lantern Slide Collection, Albany, New York.
(b) The Great Wall. Printed with permission from the New York State Archives Glass Lantern Slide Collection, Albany, New York.
(c) Stonehenge, Salisbury Plain, England. Printed with permission from Cristina Hernandez-Olsson, © 1997.
(d) Roman Aqueduct, Segovia, Spain. Printed with permission from Cristina Hernandez, © 1989.
(e) Temple of the Inscriptions, Palenque, Mexico. Printed with permission from Cristina Hernandez-Olsson, © 2001.

solstice. Roman engineers built aqueducts (Figure 4–1d) that crossed mountains, valleys, and plains. Eleven major aqueducts that were built over a period of more than 500 years and stretch over hundreds of miles supplied water for the city of Rome. The Romans even built aqueducts in numerous other parts of their empire, notably, France, Spain, and northern Africa. In Chiapas, Mexico, the Mayan civilization constructed the Temple of the Inscriptions (Figure 4–1e), a pyramid covering a subterranean tomb that still houses the sarcophagus of the Mayan ruler Pakal. The temple stands 30 meters high and is approximately 60 meters wide at the base. These technically sophisticated projects must have required enormous amounts of human labor, as well as planning, controlling, and coordination. In each project, the leaders likely established a vision and motivated the workforce to accomplish the desired goals. Managers just below the leadership level presumably worked with the "technical experts" to integrate their thoughts and ideas into feasible plans of action. We can just picture these managers preparing and monitoring schedules, planning how they would obtain and distribute raw materials and other resources, and resolving conflicts among workers. Finally, they must have concluded the job by defining success with an acceptance test: water flowing, troops marching, or high priests conducting a religious ceremony. In short, the jobs required management skills.

Employees receive supervision at work, and some workers will become managers sometime during their careers. A prospective employee's decision to work or not to work for a certain company is based in part on his or her perception of the quality of the organization's management. An understanding of basic management principles aids the prospective employee in making informed decisions about the organization. Such an understanding brings forth the right questions at the interview and helps years later, when the employee is deciding whether to pursue a management opportunity. Finally, effective project management requires the manager to understand and use many of the fundamental management concepts discussed in this section.

MANAGERS AND SUPERVISORS

The difference between *managers* and *supervisors* varies among organizations. Both a manager and a supervisor represent the employees in their charge to a management level above them. In most organizations the hierarchy ends with a supervisor, preceded in turn by a manager, a middle manager, and a senior manager. The supervisor must have a good command of the technical skills required by the workers because the supervisor is so close to the "hands-on" work performed by the employees. As the person moves up the management hierarchy, technical skills become less important and interpersonal skills assume greater importance. A project manager is at the level of a middle manager.

Managers make broad decisions with potentially wide organizational impact, whereas supervisors make decisions about a particular work unit. Frequently, a manager has an external role and may visit stakeholders such as customers and suppliers; a supervisor has a more limited role that is confined to the unit or department. Supervisory management is a combination of the two functions that is more focused and has a short-term outlook.

The supervisor maintains the routine flow of work. Both the manager and the supervisor receive, collect, and transmit information, but the manager receives and transmits more information from people outside the organization than does the supervisor. In effect, the manager is one of the organization's spokespersons to the outside world. Acting at the center of organizational decision making, the manager disseminates the organization's information into its environment. The manager initiates change, deals with threats to the organization, decides on organizational priorities, and negotiates on behalf of the organization.

HISTORICAL OVERVIEW

Management thought has evolved over the years. An evolutionary continuum is shown in Figure 4–2. As researchers conducted social experiments and performed studies, organizations began to modify their management processes and procedures and adopt new methods. Abrupt changes were rare; rather, organizations "eased" into new ideas.

FIGURE 4–2

Selected contributors to management thought

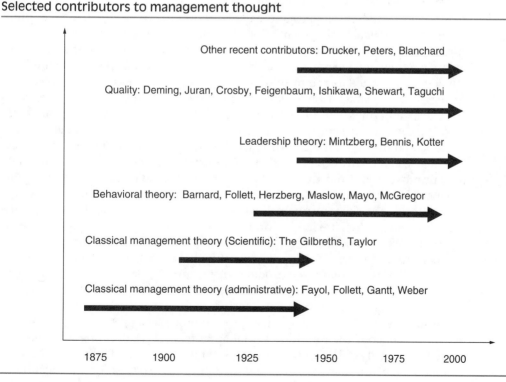

Not everybody agrees on the titles of the schools of management thought discussed next. Certainly, practitioners (managers working in business, in industry, for profit and nonprofit organizations, and in the public and private sectors) do not care about management categories. A senior executive cares about meeting the planned quarterly financial targets and strategic goals. The midlevel executive or project manager is concerned about meeting the customer's demands through well-defined objectives. These managers' interests lie in using techniques to motivate their staffs to provide a product or service that satisfies the stakeholders. Managers mix and match ideas and theories to help them get the job done. Recognizing that distinct categories blend into one another and do not have sharply defined edges, the next section nonetheless separates and classifies the various schools of management thought in an effort to gain insight into the subject.

CLASSICAL MANAGEMENT

During the Industrial Revolution (1750–1850), the United States moved from an agrarian society to a nation of urban factory-based centers. Dramatic changes in the social and economic structure took place as new technology created the factory system of large-scale production. Managers emphasized the division of labor and the importance of machinery to assist labor.

Classical management theory developed during the Industrial Revolution and continued into the first half of the 20th century. Theorists believed that money motivated employees and called a worker thus motivated "economic man." The classical period focused on efficiency and relied on bureaucratic, scientific, and administrative concepts. A common assumption held that improvements in efficiency led to increases in productivity. With respect to technology, efficiency is defined as the ratio of output to input, expressed as a percentage. As regards the organization, *efficiency* is defined as the resources spent to complete a specific task, compared with a reference standard. Based on previous projects, the resources normally used to complete a task may be an acceptable reference point. Reducing the time to complete the task improves efficiency, which also can result from a worker's gaining experience on the job. Efficiency may improve, too, from the use of a new tool or piece of equipment that will produce more product within a given period. Often, a new tool *reduces* efficiency during the short term, until workers learn how to use it effectively. Efficiency ensues when tasks are ordered in a way that uses a minimum of resources. When production processes are made more efficient, organizational productivity improves. *Productivity* is defined as a worker's output over a specified period of time. Increased productivity results when an increased amount of product is produced during a given period, compared with the amount of product produced during a previous period.

Managers expect workers to use specific processes, procedures, and methods in carrying out their activities. Managers rely on (1) a set of guidelines and procedures or rules, (2) a hierarchy of tasks and workers, and (3) a clear division of labor. Scientific management focuses on the way to do a job that results in the highest productivity. Administrative management emphasizes the flow of information in the organization's operation. According to administrative management, the worker acquires information and then performs the operations required to achieve organizational goals. Among the leading classical management theorists are Frederick Taylor (the "father of scientific management"), Henri Fayol, Henry Gantt, Max Weber, and Frank and Lillian Gilbreth (the originators of time and motion studies).

Henri Fayol identified five functions of management: planning, organizing, commanding, coordinating, and controlling. These functions revolutionized management thinking and continue to serve as a basis for administrative actions. *Planning* requires an understanding of the work so that the supervisor or manager can identify the tasks to be performed and then develop a schedule to perform the work. *Organizing* requires the manager to identify and assemble the resources needed to perform the work. *Commanding* entails assigning people to the work and making sure that the job gets done. *Coordinating* involves unifying the activities and resources in a logical manner so that the work can get done. *Controlling* implies directing the operation so that the work is performed and completed in accordance with the organization's established policies and procedures. Controlling the work operation yields consistency in output from worker to worker. A list of management functions presented as an alternative to Fayol's (although the two overlap in three functions) is the following:[1]

- planning
- organizing
- staffing
- directing
- coordinating
- reporting
- budgeting

The addition of staffing, reporting, and budgeting to Fayol's original list adds tasks for which managers frequently have responsibility. Replacing commanding is directing, a softer, less militarylike word. In the modified list, formal authority and the role of direct supervision are emphasized. Later studies found that successful managers spend a great deal of time communicating, cultivating networks and personal contacts, and delegating work to subordinates.[2]

Fayol embellished his baseline five management responsibilities with the following 14 management principles, which characterize all organizations:

1. *Division of work through labor specialization.* Specializing encourages the development of expertise associated with the performance of specific tasks.

---

[1] Gulick, L., and L. Urwick, **Papers on the Science of Administration** (New York: Columbia University Press, 1937).

[2] Mintzberg, H., **The Nature of Managerial Work** (New York: Harper & Row, 1973).

—; Kotter, J. P., **A Force for Change: How Leadership Differs from Management** (New York: The Free Press, 1990).

2. *Authority and responsibility.* Authority should reside with the people having the responsibility for the task. Recognized personnel should have the right to give orders and the power to demand that the employee comply. One individual is charged with the responsibility for making certain that activities associated with a given job get done. Project managers frequently have the responsibility, but not the authority, for completing a job.

3. *Discipline.* The manager expects and insists that employees obey the rules. The manager has the means of enforcing this demand.

4. *Unity of command.* Each employee should report to one supervisor.

5. *Unity of direction.* A single project is controlled by a single individual.

6. *Subordination of individual interests to the organization's needs.* Only work-related activities are to be pursued at work.

7. *Employee compensation.* Employees receive fair payment for the services they perform.

8. *Centralization.* Management functions are consolidated so that decisions are made from the top.

9. *Scalar chain (line of authority).* A formal chain of command is used from the top to the bottom of the organization, creating a pyramidlike top-down structure that is standard operating practice in today's organizations.

10. *Order.* All materials and personnel have a designated location. The six-sigma quality concept implemented by Motorola and other major organizations used this principle as a starting point. (Refer to Chapter 9 for information about six-sigma.)

11. *Equity.* All personnel receive equal (but not necessarily identical) treatment.

12. *Personnel stability.* Turnover in personnel is minimized, because changing personnel requires retraining and lowers productivity. In good economic times, people tend to change jobs more often than in business slumps.

13. *Initiative.* Managers make things happen. Many use the credo "Do it now and ask for forgiveness later."

14. *Esprit de corps.* The manager encourages harmony and cohesion among personnel.

Principles 1, 2, 4, 5, and 9 are the most widely known. Classical theorists believed that understanding and applying all 14 principles in a rational manner would lead to the successful resolution of management problems.

Henry Gantt is best known for developing a chart used for scheduling tasks over time. Modern managers use the *Gantt chart* more extensively than most other project management tools. Microsoft Project and Primavera are two software products commonly used to develop schedules. Gantt also recommended motivational schemes that emphasized rewards for good work rather than penalties for poor work. He advocated a compensation incentive system with a guaranteed minimum wage and bonus systems for people on fixed wages. Gantt believed in the importance of leadership and management skills in building effective industrial organizations.

At about the same time that Fayol described the manager's job, Frederick Taylor introduced scientific management.[3] Both Fayol and Taylor were task and thing oriented, rather than people oriented. Scientific management focuses on the worker–machine relationship. Taylor's scientific model evolved from his experience with mass production and relied on standardization of work, control of quality, the division of labor, and a structural hierarchy. He analyzed work that had to be completed and broke down organized work activities into a group of basic operations. The concept worked reasonably well with repetitive industrial tasks. Taylor strongly believed that managers and supervisors should cooperate with their staffs and motivate them to perform. With an eye toward improving production efficiency, he advocated improving the tools employees used to perform the work and then selecting and training personnel in the proper use of those tools. He argued that good working conditions and the use of economic incentives to motivate employees would help earn their cooperation.

Frank and Lillian Gilbreth further advanced the scientific model by performing detailed time and motion studies. They identified the fundamental motions in a work activity, studied the way the motions combined to perform a task, and assigned a duration for each separate motion. Frank Gilbreth collected data by filming individual physical-labor movements during the performance of a worker's job. The Gilbreths then analyzed the worker's movements. They showed managers how to break down a job into its component motions and reassemble the motions so as to minimize the time required to perform certain tasks. Using the resultant information, the manager prepared a more efficient procedure that, if followed by the employee, not only reduced the time to complete a job, but helped to make the time consistent from worker to worker. The Gilbreths' work enabled managers to accurately estimate the time required to complete a job, a result that, when implemented in the workplace, customers appreciated. Workers, however, found this mechanized method for performing work highly restrictive and boring.

Max Weber promoted *bureaucracy* as the most logical form for large organizations. During the early part of the 20th century, the word did not have the negative connotation with which we now associate it. Documented processes and procedures and a hierarchical structure governed by an impersonal authority typify a bureaucracy. Authority stems from an individual's position in the organization's hierarchy and is not based on the individual's personality or charisma. The worker's title defines his or her authority. The following are some characteristics of a bureaucracy:

- well-defined and specialized jobs
- testing of job qualifications
- formal rules of behavior
- a hierarchical system of supervision
- unity of command

---

[3] Taylor, F. W., *Principles for Scientific Management* (New York: Harper & Row, 1911).

- written processes and procedures [e.g., an employee handbook, industrial safety directions, and directions on handling hazardous materials (HAZMAT)]
- skill-based training
- work assignments and personnel recruitment based on technical expertise
- continuity of operations despite changes of personnel
- promotions based on competence
- continued employment based on merit

Weber believed that organizations would become successful by applying these bureaucratic rules. Historically, bureaucracies established concepts of fairness and equality of opportunity. Bureaucracies excel at businesses involving routine tasks that can be specified in writing and do not change quickly.

The Industrial Revolution and the progress made by science and technology in the 1900s gave credence to the idea of a single best way to manage. Scientific management seemed to reinforce this idea. The training that engineers and scientists receive leads them to expect a single answer to a problem. In mathematics, science, and technology courses, students tend to present a single number as the solution to a question. They are comfortable with the existence of a single, best way to accomplish an objective. During the 20th century, it was common for engineers and scientists to move up the ranks and become managers, and the idea of a single best way to accomplish a task moved with them. In the real world, however, there frequently exists an array of solutions to business and management problems, some better than others, but many perfectly acceptable because they lead to the completion of the job. One of Mary Parker Follett's important contributions to management theory was the "law of the situation," which emphasizes that there is no one best way to do anything—it all depends on the situation. Contingency theory, or situational theory, uses Follett's concepts and is now considered mainstream management thinking.[4] Precise management formulas do not exist; if they did, far more managers would be successful. The techniques recommended by the classical theorists should be used as guidelines in managing organizations.

HUMAN BEHAVIORAL MANAGEMENT

Human behavioral management studies began in the 1920s. Based on psychological concepts, the studies dealt with the human aspects of organizations. The philosophy of "social man" began to compete with the concept of "economic man." The movement began when researchers T. N. Whitehead, Elton Mayo, George Homans, and Fritz Roethlisberger conducted a series of industrial psychological experiments at the Hawthorne Plant of the Western Electric Company in Cicero, Illinois, from 1924 to 1933. One study examined the effect of changing the electric lighting illuminating the employees' work area. The

---

[4] Fielder, F. E., *A Theory of Leadership Effectiveness* (New York: McGraw-Hill, 1967).

researchers established two groups: a control group for which the workplace lighting was held at a constant level and an experimental group that had varying illumination. The researchers expected that the group of workers receiving improved illumination would be more productive. The surprising results showed that the productivity of *both* groups improved. The researchers concluded that the increased attention given to the two groups made each feel special and led to the improved productivity. Mayo identified the "Hawthorne effect," which is the improvement in productivity that results when people know they are being studied.

The researchers at the Hawthorne plant conducted many experiments relating worker and group output to working conditions. Their efforts highlighted the importance of *informal groups* (i.e., groups arising out of the formal organization, but not specifically created by management) and the benefits of listening to employees' feelings and opinions. Work breaks, the freedom to talk, and approved requests for supervisory changes influenced individuals' work behavior in a positive manner. Over a period of years, the researchers found that workplace changes other than increased wages also affected productivity. Among these changes were varying the length of the workday and workweek, varying workers' starting and stopping times, and providing lunches paid for by the company. Nowadays, concerns about families' complicated lives have forced organizations to seek methods of improving worker satisfaction while improving productivity. One company had a problem with mandatory overtime on weekends. "Taking the suggestion of its manufacturing employees, the company switched to a schedule where workers put in a full workweek over four days. That allowed the company to schedule overtime, when needed, on Fridays, and let employees save weekends for family activities and, occasionally, have a three-day weekend."[5] Similarly, Hewlett-Packard (H-P) decided to reconsider its traditional eight-to-five workday thinking:

> Self-directed work teams in one H-P financial-services center opted to switch to a four-day-week, 10-hour-day schedule to process the high number of transactions. The results: Overtime dropped 50%, workers had more "quiet" time to develop process improvements, and the number of transactions processed daily per person increased by 70%.

The Hawthorne studies did not find a direct cause-and-effect relationship between working conditions and productivity; the worker's attitude was important. The researchers found that employees' complaints might be a symptom of some underlying problem on the job, at home, or in the workers' past. These findings led to the consideration of the psychological and group dynamics aspects of group productivity. People are not the rational economic beings assumed by classical theorists. Social interaction also is important in the workplace, and people work well if they feel valued. The studies at the Hawthorne plant gave birth to the human-relations movement and behavioral science approaches to management. In the 1940s, group dynamics studies encouraged

---

[5] Verespej, M. A., "Human Resources: Flexible Schedules Benefit All," *Industry Week.com* (August 21, 2000): 25.

increased individual participation in decision making, and as a result, group performance improved.

Scientific management promotes a way of thinking about managing that is appropriate for an assembly line operation. This approach, however, may not work for other kinds of jobs. In particular, industries characterized by rapidly changing technology or not-well-understood processes require a different management approach. Managing technology and technologists, for example, demands solutions that use unconventional or "out-of-the-box" thinking.

HUMAN RESOURCES SCHOOL

During the 1950s, researchers began to examine employees' motivations in an effort to increase their productivity and efficiency. Because the behavioral approach did not always increase productivity, motivation and leadership techniques became a topic of great interest. Viewing workers and managers as human beings with social and emotional needs, modern theorists such as Abraham Maslow, Douglas McGregor, Frederick Herzberg, Chester Barnard, W. Edwards Deming and Warren Bennis emphasize the importance of social relations in organizations. The human resources school believes that employees are creative and competent and that much of their talent is largely unused by employers. Employees want meaningful work, desire to contribute to the organization's success, and wish to participate in decision-making and leadership processes.

Herzberg's "Hygiene Factors"

Herzberg proposed a theory for motivating workers that introduced the following organizational motivating agents, which he called "hygiene factors":

- administrative policies
- working conditions
- salary
- personal life
- peer, superior, and subordinate relationships
- status within the organization
- security

Herzberg concluded that positive hygiene factors are necessary, but not sufficient, to produce a contented worker. Also, although poor hygiene factors may destroy an employee's motivation, an improvement in those factors likely will not increase the worker's motivation. Positive results stem from the opportunity to achieve and experience self-actualization or personal fulfillment. For a worker to achieve maximum productivity and efficiency, the worker should experience a sense of self-worth or personal growth and responsibility from his or her work. The following are some positive motivating agents:

- recognition for a job well done
- work that is meaningful to the employee and to the employer

Maslow's hierarchy of motivational needs

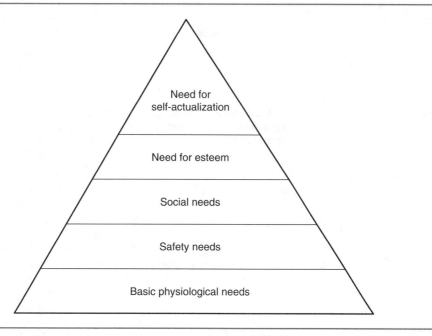

- delegation of responsibility
- ongoing professional growth

Maslow's Hierarchy

Abraham Maslow formulated the theory of human motivational needs depicted in Figure 4–3.[6] He argued that people seek to satisfy an orderly progression of needs, from physiological and safety needs to social needs and the need for esteem, before they can achieve self-actualization. Each layer in the pyramid builds upon the one that precedes it. Table 4–1 extends this concept to the workplace, wherein we note that workers, too, have a hierarchy of fundamental needs.

Maslow suggests that people follow a track extending from the lowest element in the hierarchy (satisfying physiological needs) to the highest (realizing self-actualization). The pursuit of self-actualization is an ongoing activity in which people attempt to attain perfection through self-development. Integrity, responsibility, high-mindedness, simplicity, and naturalness characterize the highest state of self-actualization. Self-actualizers focus on problems external to themselves. According to the table, people reach the highest level of motivation only after achieving some measure of accomplishment.

---

[6] Maslow, A., *Motivation and Personality* (New York: Harper, 1954).

TABLE 4–1

Workplace Equivalents of Maslow's Hierarchy of Basic Needs

Basic Human Needs	Life Examples	Workplace Environment Examples
Physiological	Air, water, food, housing, and clothing	Adequate wages; satisfactory work; environment: light, temperature, and ventilation
Safety	Protection from danger (security), stability, and freedom from threat of physical harm	Freedom to change positions; complaint system; protection from hazards (e.g., government work regulations, Occupational Safety and Health Administration (OSHA) rules, and environmental protection (EPA) regulations; collective bargaining agreement; health and disability insurance; retirement packages
Social	Love, affection, approval, friends, and affiliations	Social interaction; company-sponsored functions; team or work groups; professional, trade, or craft organization functions
Esteem	Respect, dignity, attention, and appreciation	Signs of accomplishment (college degree, titles, awards, honors, peer recognition, and publications)
Self-actualization	Self-fulfillment, growth, learning, and realizing one's potential through competence, creativity, and achievement	Participation in decision making; creating something; participation in lifelong learning

McGregor's Theory X and Theory Y Worker

Examining the attitudes and perceptions of managers and workers, Douglas McGregor posed the idea that, in a company, two diametrically opposed belief systems coexisted among both the managers and the workers.[7] He called the different sets of beliefs theory X and theory Y. McGregor compared two workers and the resulting management implications. The theory X worker, he said, held the following views:

- People are inherently lazy and require supervision.
- People dislike work and prefer to avoid it whenever possible.

---

[7] McGregor, D., *The Human Side of Enterprise* (New York: McGraw-Hill, 1960).

- To induce the worker to exert adequate effort, the supervisor must threaten punishment and exercise careful supervision.
- The average worker avoids increased responsibility and seeks to be directed.

This view of people pertains to managers, too. Theory X managers rely on an authoritarian style or a top-down approach. They use external motivation techniques that include strict rules, performance incentives, rewards, and threats to the worker's job security.

In contrast, McGregor's theory Y worker holds the following beliefs:

- People are creative.
- People want to do the job they are assigned and do not need continuous supervision.
- People want to be active and wish to find the job physically and mentally rewarding.
- People participate willingly in a task.
- People not only accept, but actively seek, responsibility and authority.
- People are not necessarily resistant to the needs of the organization. Indeed, they are concerned with self-growth and fulfillment within the organization's rules.
- People seek opportunities for personal improvement and circumstances in which they can gain self-respect.

Like his or her worker, the theory Y manager believes that people are self-starters and advocates worker participation in decision making. He or she expects that employees will tend to work toward objectives without having to be coerced or controlled. Theory Y managers try to establish cordial worker–manager relationships. They develop an environment in which the workers can achieve their objectives by directing their efforts toward the organization's goals. Theory Y managers permit workers to design their own jobs, a type of freedom required and appreciated by highly trained and creative workers such as scientists and engineers. These managers understand that using a coercive or dictatorial management style causes employees to leave the organization for other job opportunities. Nonetheless, caution is advised: Some professionals will want to "tweak" a design or improve the operation of a system beyond what the organization requires; others insist on finding a better way to achieve a desired result or simply exercise scientific curiosity, regardless of cost. Happily, these people take great pride in their work and desire to express their individualism and talent, but project managers must balance the completion of the task within schedule and budgetary constraints with the employee's ego and personality.

In recent years, many of the ideas advanced by Maslow, Herzberg, and McGregor have been corroborated.[8] A challenging project has been found to be the single most important factor influencing the behavior of project team

---

[8] Sotiriou, D., and Wittmer, D., "Influence Methods of Project Managers: Perceptions of Team Members and Project Managers," *Project Management Journal* 32(3): 12–20.

members. Other factors, ranked in order of importance, are having authority for the project, possessing project management expertise, the prospect of similar future work, an increase in salary, friendship, and coercion. The project manager's leadership role includes negotiation, the use of his or her personality, persuasion, and management competence. Finally, team members value professional integrity—fairness, honesty, consistency, and trustworthiness in leaders whom they can count on for the duration of the project.

Acceptance Theory of Authority

Chester Barnard, a former CEO of New Jersey Bell Telephone, developed the concepts of strategic planning and the acceptance theory of authority.[9] Strategic planning guides the organization in its pursuit of major goals. Barnard believed that the most important functions of the executive were to (1) establish and maintain an effective communication system, (2) hire and retain productive personnel, and (3) motivate those personnel. He advanced the idea that managers have only as much authority as employees allow them to have. The employees' acceptance of authority depends on the following four conditions:

- an understanding of what the manager wants them to do.
- the ability to comply with the directive.
- the belief that the request is in line with the organization's goals.
- the belief that the manager's request does not conflict with their personal objectives.

Barnard believed that each individual accepts orders without consciously questioning them, but only up to a point. Accordingly, the organization must provide inducements to raise each employee's threshold of acceptance so that the manager's orders will be followed.

Management by Objective

Peter Drucker has interpreted management theory for more than 50 years. During the 1940s and 1950s, he advanced the ideas that management would have to treat workers as individuals, that an organization's culture would influence its production, and that foreign competition would become a significant factor in U.S. business. Since the 1960s, Drucker has stressed management fundamentals, including strategic management ideas, and has introduced the phrase *management by objective* (MBO), also known as managing by results. MBO is the annual process of selecting a set of objectives [targets that meet the SMART criteria (see Chapter 2)] that an employee would attempt to achieve during the year. Organizations used MBO to establish objectives for their staffs in an effort to assess what they have accomplished. Technical and business managers frequently believe that only what is measurable can be improved. Among the indicators of performance that can be measured are financial margins, revenue

---

[9] Barnard, C., *The Functions of the Executive* (Cambridge, MA: Harvard University Press, 1938).

per employee, price-to-earnings ratio, asset turnover, debt-to-equity ratio, current ratio, working capital, unit costs, inventory turns, manufacturing cycle time, forecast accuracy, units produced, win–loss rates, service margins, service call response rates, customer retention, number of new customers, head counts, retention rate, hiring cycle time, learning rate, recruitment, labor costs, skills learned, absenteeism, and overtime. The annual objectives that employees develop usually include some combination of these performance measurement indicators.

MBO gained popularity because (1) it was designed to produce tangible outcomes, (2) it could be used at any or all levels in the organization, and (3) it was relatively simple and inexpensive to implement following training. As a measure of performance, MBO attempted to keep people focused on producing results, which are evaluated against outcomes. The supervisor meets periodically with each of his or her workers to review their progress in achieving the stated objectives. Some organizations link the manager's salary increments to MBO success.

Drucker further emphasized that management must be tough both outside (focused on its mission and on the aims of the organization) and inside (focused on the structure, values, and relationships that enable each worker to excel).[10] Drucker asserts that management is a discipline—a practice—and not a science.

Deming's Ideas

During the 1950s, Japanese industry exported a variety of products to the United States, many of poor quality. Then the Japanese embraced W. Edwards Deming's ideas of statistical quality control. Deming stressed both the human factors and the technological aspects of production. His concept of total quality management (TQM) was intended to, and did, actively involve workers in discovering ways of improving the quality of the products and services they delivered in an ongoing manner. Deming encouraged industry to continually examine its products at the various stages of production and gather data to determine whether and when the production process was showing signs of veering away from predetermined limits. If it was, the worker and management together were to identify and implement appropriate changes to fix the problem. In the 1970s, the quality of Japanese cars became almost legendary and forced the U.S. auto industry to wake up and improve. In part, improvements came when Deming's and operations research analyst Joseph M. Juran's ideas of statistical process control were implemented. Forty years after Japanese industry began to use Deming's recommendations, the ideas of involving workers in the production process and of statistical process control were accepted and introduced into U.S. industry.

In the 1980s, Deming consulted with executives from Ford Motor Co. and General Motors about their decision to adopt the philosophy of continual improvement. In Deming's system of management, continual improvement becomes a way of life in which everyone—the organization and its people,

---

[10] Drucker, P. F., *The Frontiers of Management: Where Tomorrow's Decisions Are Being Shaped Today* (New York: Truman Talley Books, 1986).

suppliers, and customers—wins. Managers and workers cooperate on process-improvement teams and try to change adversarial attitudes. Using statistical methods that involve collecting and analyzing data, they help the organization determine whether a problem is occurring randomly or is embedded in the production process. Then they analyze and act on the data to resolve the problem.

Interestingly, Deming strongly opposed MBO. Although he cared about results, he was equally concerned about the method used to try to achieve those results. He believed that working to meet quotas, fulfill numerical objectives, and otherwise manage by numbers was destructive to the overall organization, an approach that is decidedly different from the views of many management theorists and practitioners.

Deming formulated 14 managerial points that describe controversial fundamental philosophy and represent his program for improvement. The Deming–Shewhart cycle ("plan, do, check, act"), discussed further in Chapter 9, describes their joint approach toward continuous improvement. According to its tenets, management selects areas for improvement and develops measurement strategies and planning goals. Using a TQM format, cross-functional teams coordinate improvement in each area of interest. The teams develop tests and gather data to confirm the presence or absence of problems. Where needed, they generate and then implement action plans to make improvements. Afterward, the teams evaluate the results of their efforts, fine-tune corrections, and continue fine-tuning and evaluating until they achieve satisfactory results. In this manner, the team attacks newly recognized issues and problems as they are discovered. Deming's 14 points are summarized below:

W. Edwards Deming's 14 points for management[a]

1. Create constancy of purpose toward the improvement of product and service, with the aim of becoming competitive, staying in business, and providing jobs.
2. Adopt the new philosophy. We are in a new economic age. Western management must awaken to the challenge, learn its responsibilities, and take on leadership for change.
3. Cease dependence on inspection to achieve quality. Eliminate the need for inspection on a mass basis by building quality into the product in the first place.
4. End the practice of awarding business on the basis of the price tag. Instead, minimize total cost. Move toward a single supplier for any one item, on a long-term relationship of loyalty and trust.
5. Improve constantly and forever the system of production and service, to improve quality and productivity and thus constantly decrease costs.
6. Institute training on the job.
7. Institute leadership. The aim of supervision should be to help people, machines, and gadgets do a better job. Supervision of management is in need of overhaul, as is supervision of production workers.
8. Drive out fear, so that everyone may work effectively for the company.
9. Break down barriers between departments. People in research, design, sales, and production must work as a team to foresee problems of production and use that may be encountered with the product or service.
10. Eliminate slogans, exhortations, and targets for the workforce that ask for zero defects and new levels of productivity. Such exhortations only create adversarial relationships, as the bulk of the causes of low quality and low productivity belong to the system and thus lie beyond the power of the workforce.

11. a. Eliminate work standards (quotas) on the factory floor. Substitute leadership.
    b. Eliminate management by objective. Eliminate management by numbers and numerical goals. Substitute leadership.
12. a. Remove barriers that rob the hourly worker of his right to pride of workmanship. The responsibility of supervisors must be changed from sheer numbers to quality.
    b. Remove barriers that rob people in management and in engineering of their right to pride of workmanship. This means, *inter alia*, abolishment of the annual merit rating and of management by objective.
13. Institute a vigorous program of education and self-improvement.
14. Put everybody in the company to work to accomplish the transformation. The transformation is everybody's job.

---

[a] Excerpted from Chapter 2 of Deming, W. E., *Out of the Crisis* (Cambridge, MA: MIT Center for Advanced Engineering, 1986).

Recent Management Views

In the mid-1960s, the contingency view of management, or situational approach, emerged. This view integrated management thought by advocating that managers use any approach that they deem appropriate to the situation at hand. In effect, the manager is an actor and should assume a behavior that deals with the circumstances before him or her.

New management viewpoints have emerged during the last 20 years. *Total quality management* emphasizes achieving customer satisfaction by providing high-quality goods and services. *Reengineering the organization* redesigns the processes that are crucial to customer satisfaction.

Another relatively recent idea is *managing in chaos*.[11] According to this idea, the starts, stops, spurts, and other movements of the technological revolution demand both personal and corporate flexibility. The outpouring of information and data and the constant flow of governmental, personnel, and technological changes require a "flat" (i.e., nonhierarchical) organization wherein people have the authority to respond quickly to competitive pressures.

In the future, managing will face some unusual challenges. AT&T, IBM, and other organizations are experimenting with alternative workplaces.[12] Nontraditional work practices include a variety of techniques. In one such technique, "*hoteling*," workspaces include shared space, equipment, and services. People working in companies with many offices located in different geographic areas use "hotel" workspaces in satellite offices. Another nontraditional practice, made possible by the telecommunications revolution, is *telecommuting*, wherein employees work at home. Managers and organizations accustomed to face-to-face interaction have to adjust to these new ways of operating. Nowadays, "managers and employees are moving up the curve toward information-age literacy, which is characterized by flexibility, informality, the ability to change when necessary, respect for personal time and priorities, and a commitment to

---

[11] See Peters, T., *Thriving on Chaos: Handbook for a Management Revolution* (New York: Perennial Library, 1988).

[12] See Apgar, M., IV, "The Alternative Workplace: Changing Where and How People Work," *Harvard Business Review* (May–June 1998): 121–136 (reprint no. 98301).

using technology for improving performance."[13] To meet the challenge, managers will have to adjust their way of monitoring employees and the progress of projects. Employee evaluations and salary reviews may be affected, and customers, suppliers, and other stakeholders will require education in this new approach.

Managers are still learning to manage diversity. Cultural, ethnic, and gender differences require special management considerations. Not long ago, I attended an annual corporate status review for a privately held technology company. The chief executive officer (CEO) addressed the assembly of employees. The company consisted of about 400 employees, with a minority population of perhaps five percent. The executive, known for his sense of humor, decided to break the ice by telling a joke that made fun of a certain ethnic group. The only reaction to the joke's punch line was some nervous laughter. The CEO was clearly surprised that his joke did not get the expected response, and he remarked, "Well, if you didn't get it, see me in private." After the meeting, several upper managers commented in private on the insensitivity of the CEO's joke. It was clear that they had lost respect for him. Ultimately, the joke contributed to a decision by one of the handful of employees who was a member of the ethnic group that was the butt of the joke to leave the company. Because that individual was a key manager, the loss was deeply felt by the company.

The global organization with transnational operations requires new management approaches. Managing in tomorrow's environment will require a new set of rules, which have yet to be formulated.

MANAGEMENT STYLES

Four generic management styles have evolved: *autocratic, laissez-faire, democratic,* and *participative.* The autocratic manager is the traditional figure of a boss who exercises tight control over employees. This manager expects the employee to follow through on a directive, regardless of the employee's thoughts or wishes. His or her philosophy is "I call the plays and don't bother me with facts." In today's environment, this stereotypical theory X manager could demoralize the organization. Perhaps such a manager could successfully manage a low-risk project with an inexperienced staff that will execute a project plan as presented to them. Still, the autocratic style could lead to resentment if the staff's contribution is not recognized. Highly skilled people desire and expect managers to listen to their voices. Not considering or continually rejecting employee's opinions may lead to dissatisfied employees and poor decisions.

Applied to organizational management practice, the French term *laissez-faire* means that the manager provides little guidance to employees, who are free to pursue almost anything they wish. Projects that require considerable creativity such as people involved in research and development, laboratory research, or a university environment require a freethinking, tolerant, hands-off

---

[13] *Ibid.,* p. 125.

atmosphere and will benefit from a minimum of management oversight. By contrast, a laissez-faire management style will prove disastrous for high-visibility, schedule-driven projects that require quick decisions and fast actions.

A democratic management style invites employee involvement. Managers and their staffs collectively discuss and evaluate issues and reach decisions. This management style aligns itself with American tradition and culture. Democratic managers empower employees by giving them more decision-making power and by seeking ideas from every worker. A democratic manager lets the forces within the group work toward a decision. Since the employees participate in the decision-making process, they will assume ownership of, and responsibility for, the final plan of action. Democratic leadership implies majority rule or rule by consensus. Sometimes, majority rule may not lead to the best solution, especially if a vocal, but uninformed, person takes a leadership role. A further disadvantage of the democratic style involves time: If full discussions of issues take place, decisions may take longer to be reached.

Like the democratic manager, the participative manager encourages employee involvement in making decisions. The participative manager asks for and receives input from the group in an atmosphere of trust, honesty, and open communication. Such a manager demonstrates to his workers that their inputs are valued. However, unlike the democratic manager, the participative manager makes the final decision. Because most managers are unwilling to give up that right, there are more participative managers than democratic managers.

A person's management style depends on his or her personality and on the situation. Rarely does a manager use one style all the time. A manager must be flexible and use a style appropriate to the stakeholder and the situation.

POWER

Managers use power both to influence the success of a project and to elicit employees' cooperation. Power is based on the worker's perception of the leader and can be categorized as follows:[14]

- *Reward power.* The worker believes in the manager's ability to obtain rewards (e.g., financial compensation, a promotion, recognition, or various privileges) for those who comply with specific requests.
- *Coercive power.* The worker believes in the manager's ability to punish him or her (e.g., by withholding raises in salary or promotions or by reprimanding the employee).
- *Formal power.* The manager has the right to exercise power because of his or her designated position in the organization.
- *Referent power.* The worker identifies with the manager because of his or her attractiveness, reputation, or charisma.

---

[14] The first five categories are after French, J. R. P., and Raven, B. H. "The bases of social power." In D. Cartwright (Ed.), *Studies in social power* (Ann Arbor: University of Michigan, 1959), pp. 150–167.

- *Expert power.* The manager has competence, special knowledge, or expertise in a well-defined discipline.
- *Power through control of information.* The manager can either communicate information or withhold it at will.

The three "legitimate" forms of power (formal, reward, and coercive power) stem from the person's position within the organization. Referent, expert, and information forms of power may come from factors outside the organization. Although the project manager exerts legitimate power, it sometimes may not influence workers' behavior as much as expected. In particular, creative people and workers with technical knowledge frequently respond better to expert power rather than to "bureaucrats."

Expert power results from the internal or external recognition that a person has achieved. Employees recently transferred to a project management role as a consequence of demonstrating outstanding technical ability will discover a very uncomfortable lesson: A project manager cannot both stay technically current and manage a project. In any project of some complexity, the project manager will regularly interact with customers, suppliers, functional managers, upper-level managers, and other stakeholders. There is much to do, and there will never be enough time to stay technically current. Accordingly, technical analyses and designs must be left to the functional personnel. People coming to project management from a technical background find it frightening to leave that background behind them. Up to that point, they have spent their careers accumulating, developing, and honing their technical skills. Exchanging technical expertise for management competencies may be a sufficient reason to discourage some people from making such a career change.

Table 4–2 illustrates how others might view the project manager's power from their organizational perspective. The evaluations listed represent subjective conclusions. A technical functional manager may have little regard for a project manager's technical ability, but high regard for that person's ability to

TABLE 4–2

Impact of a Project Manager's Power

| | GROUP POWER EXERTED ON | | | | | |
Type of Power	Upper Management	Project Manager's Direct Reports	Functional Managers	Functional Department Personnel	External Customers	Suppliers (Vendors)
Formal	None	Maximum	Moderate	Minimal	Maximum	Maximum
Reward	None	Maximum	Minimal	Minimal	Minimal	Maximum
Coercive	None	Maximum	Minimal	Minimal	Minimal	Maximum
Expert	Minimal	Maximum	Minimal	Minimal	Moderate	Moderate
Referent	None	Maximum	Maximum	Maximum	Moderate	Moderate

Adapted from Adams, J. R., and B. B. Campbell, "Roles and Responsibilities of the Project Manager in Principles of Project Management," in J. S. Pennypacker (editor in chief), *The Global Status of the Project Management Profession* (Upper Darby, PA: Project Management Institute, 1996), pp.69–122.

control a customer. Upper management may value a project manager's ability to plan and coordinate efforts and to motivate people. Suppliers believe that the project manager, as the primary contact between the organization and external stakeholders, wields great influence in the selection of organizations for future contract awards. Suppliers who are hungry for new work will make great efforts to deliver goods and services in a timely fashion to impress the project manager.

TEAMS

During the 1980s and 1990s, managers discovered the benefits of using teams to get a job done. A team is a small number of people with complementary skills who are committed to a common purpose, set of performance objectives, and approach for which they hold themselves mutually accountable. [15]

Teams are empowered by the organization to establish objectives within the framework of the project's objectives. Competitive demands require quick decisions by knowledgeable employees who work close to the source of problems. Empowered teams can make decisions fast. The team has the approval, trust, and encouragement of the organization to make the decisions necessary to accomplish the job. Successful teams depend on good communication methods to share information, and they demand that their members have outstanding problem-solving skills. Effective supervisors empower employees by giving them more decision-making power and by seeking ideas from every worker.

Not all groups are teams. A team may be differentiated from a group in the following ways:

Characteristics of a Working Group	Characteristics of a Team
• Has a strong, clearly focused leader.	• Leadership roles are shared.
• Accountability rests with the individual.	• Accountability is both individual and mutual.
• The group's purpose is the same as that of the broader organizational mission.	• The team has its own specific purpose, apart from that of the organization.
• Work output is individual.	• Work output is collective.
• Runs efficient meetings.	• Encourages open-ended discussion and active problem-solving meetings.
• Measures its effectiveness indirectly by its influence on others (e.g., financial performance of the business).	• Measures performance directly by assessing collective work output.
• Discusses, decides, and delegates.	• Discusses, decides, and does real work together.

In a sense, the leader of the team acts as a facilitator. A group achieves *synergy* (an effect greater than the sum of the effects into which it is broken) if its members become a team. A team begins as a collection of individuals brought

---

[15] Katzenbach, J. R., and D. R. Smith, "The Discipline of Teams," *Harvard Business Review* (March–April 1993): 111–120 (reprint no. 93207).

together in a work situation. For a group to unite and form an effective team, the group members must successfully move through the following four stages of development:[16]

1. *Forming.* The members of the group come together and begin to get acquainted. Depending on their personalities, some are eager to meet and work, some act formally and tentatively, some are hostile, some focus on the task, and others focus on people. The group decides and agrees on its objectives and the basic operational ground rules, such as dates and times of meetings, requirements for attendance, how decisions will be made, and so on.

2. *Storming.* Members still view themselves as part of their parent department rather than part of the team. Individual personalities surface and generate interpersonal conflict. Individuals begin to compete for attention and influence. Emotions are stirred, and depending on the personalities of the team members, conflicts may arise. Individuals reveal their personal agendas as they assert their feelings, ideas, and viewpoints. Interpersonal skills are critical. Members learn to appreciate each other's capabilities. The group must agree on the distribution of power, responsibility, and authority among its members. A sense of humor helps at this stage of low morale and productivity. Success cannot begin until the next stage.

3. *"Norming."* The individuals blend together into a project team and realize that they can perform if they accept other viewpoints. The project manager can help this process along by establishing an esprit d' corps and a cohesive group. Individuals begin to think of one another. They become more sensitive to each other's needs and begin to share ideas, information, and opinions. Fewer conflicts arise, and members expend less energy engaging in them. Task considerations start to override personal objectives and concerns. Plans develop. Both formal and informal procedures for solving problems, making decisions, and resolving conflicts develop. Productivity increases.

4. *Performing.* The group emerges as a team. Flexibility is the key and hierarchy is of little importance. Team roles are strongly connected to the task that is performed. Members work and solve problems together. Structural and interpersonal issues have been resolved. Members trust, support, and feel comfortable with each other. Everyone cares about doing a good job. If any of the previous phases did not terminate satisfactorily, the team will return to them, resulting in wasted time and energy.

In 1983, General Motors began to plan the Saturn Corporation, which, using an entirely new set of employment practices, would build and sell small cars. Saturn decided to compete with Japanese auto manufacturers by using self-directed work teams of 10 to 15 members who were cross trained and who

---

[16] Tuckman, B. W., "Developmental Sequence in Small Groups," *Psychological Bulletin* 63 (1965): 384–399.

rotated responsibility for the tasks in their units. Each team would hire new members and elect its leaders. Teams had responsibility for quality assurance, job assignments, record keeping, safety and health, material and inventory control, training, supplies, and housekeeping.

Saturn's self-governing work teams would follow the construction of an automobile through the entire assembly line. The objective of the changes was to increase the quality of the product, decrease boredom, and increase worker job satisfaction. Saturn incorporated robots and other forms of automation into the production line to help reduce boredom and fatigue and to ensure high standards of quality.

Ultimately, Saturn's successful approach helped to alter the rigid departmental boundaries within the auto industry. The team-based structure consisting of knowledgeable employees who worked close to the source of problems promoted quick decisions. Labor and management leaders had to learn to overcome their resistance to sharing power. The team concept forced management to redefine the organization's mission, objectives, and hierarchical structures.

Project Managers Lead Teams

Teams succeed if thay are taken seriously, are given a clear purpose, are given authority to make decisions, and have the appropriate technical mix of skills and if their members can work together. Effective teams have clear and well-understood objectives that are accepted by their members. Frequently, organizational outcomes benefit from teamwork, and individual member satisfaction improves. Nonetheless, implementing a team-building program is far from easy.

The project manager assembles and leads a team, sharing project-related knowledge and information so that the team can solve problems. The team members possess technical knowledge and skills. Using his or her ability to communicate to, and on behalf of, the team, the project manager acts as the liaison with stakeholders such as upper management, other internal teams, customers, and suppliers. The project manager represents the team's interests, obtains needed resources, clarifies expectations, gathers information, and keeps the team informed.

Implicit to the success of any team is the mutual trust and respect between it and the project manager. Each must have credibility, integrity, character, and reliability. Lacking any of these elements will cause unneeded tension in the group and may cause it to return to the storming stage.

The elements of an effective team may be summarized as follows: [17]

- Contributions made within the group build upon each other.
- The group moves forward as a unit; there is a sense of team spirit and high involvement.
- Decisions are made by consensus.
- Most members have a strong commitment to the team's decisions.

---

[17] Argyris, C., *Organization and Innovation* (Homewood, IL: R. D. Irwin, 1965).

- The group evaluates itself continually.
- The group is clear about its goals.
- Conflict is brought out into the open and dealt with.
- Alternative ways of thinking about solutions are presented.
- Leadership of the group tends to go to the individual who is best qualified for the post.
- Feelings are dealt with openly.

Dealing with and implementing these elements turns the group into a team.

LEADERSHIP

Management and *leadership* are intertwined. Indeed, nowadays managers must know how to lead as well as manage.[18] Questions arise: What is leadership? How does it relate to management? Leadership means different things to different people. The following quotes present various thoughts and opinions on leadership:

Getting the job done using whatever means required!—1999 Fairfield University leadership class.

Damn the torpedoes—full speed ahead!—Vice Admiral David Glasgow Farragut at the Battle of Mobile Bay in August 1864

Leadership is the ability to inspire other people to work together as a team, following your lead, in order to attain a common objective, whether in business, in politics, in war, or on the football field . . . . Leadership cannot really be taught. It can only be learned.—Harold Geneen.[19]

Leadership is the capacity and will to rally men and women to a common purpose and the character which inspires confidence.—Bernard Montgomery, British field marshal

Leadership is a dynamic relationship based on mutual influence and common purpose between leaders and collaborators in which both are moved to higher levels of motivation and moral development as they affect real, intended change.—Kevin Freiberg and Jackie Freiberg[20]

Take the course opposite to custom and you will almost always do well.—Jean Jacques Rousseau

There are many elements to a campaign. Leadership is number one. Everything else is number two.—Bertolt Brecht

A leader is a man who has the ability to get other people to do what they don't want to do and like it.—Harry Truman

Coaches who can outline plays on the blackboard are a dime a dozen. The ones who succeed are those who can get inside their players and motivate them.—Vince Lombardi

---

[18] See Kotter, J. P., *A Force for Change: How Leadership Differs from Management* (New York: The Free Press, 1990).

[19] Geneen, H., and A. Moscow, *Managing* (New York: Avon Books, 1985), p. 133.

[20] *Nuts! Southwest Airlines' Crazy Recipe for Business and Personal Success* (Austin, TX: Bard Books, 1996), p. 298.

Leaders have a significant role in creating the state of mind that is the society. They can serve as symbols of the moral unity of the society. They can express the values that hold the society together. Most importantly, they can conceive and articulate goals that lift people out of their preoccupations, carry them above the conflicts that tear a society apart, and unite them in the pursuit of objectives worthy of their best efforts.—John Gardner

We herd sheep, we drive cattle, we lead people. Lead me, follow me, or get out of my way.—George S. Patton

Pull the string, and it will follow wherever you wish. Push it, and it will go nowhere at all.—Dwight D. Eisenhower

Leadership is an influence relationship among leaders and followers who intend real changes that reflect their mutual purposes.—Joseph C. Rost

A leader is responsible for lean and simple statements of policy consistent with beliefs and values, vision and strategy. Policy gives practical meaning to values. Policies must actively enable people whose job it is to carry them out.—Max De Pree

Leadership is the art of accomplishing more than the science of management says is possible.—General Colin Powell

Plainly, many great minds have different views of leadership, and defining the term is not easy:

Never have so many labored so long to say so little. Multiple interpretations of leadership exist, each providing a sliver of insight but each remaining an incomplete and wholly inadequate explanation. Most of these definitions don't agree with each other, and many of them would seem quite remote to the leaders whose skills are being dissected. Definitions reflect fads, fashions, political tides and academic trends. They don't always reflect reality and sometimes they just represent nonsense.[21]

There are almost as many definitions of leadership as there are persons who have attempted to define the concept.—Ralph M. Stogdill[22]

The following definition, which emphasizes the idea that a leader promotes change, is used in the pages that follow:[23]

Leadership refers to a process that helps direct and mobilize people and/or their ideas.... Leadership does not produce consistency and order; it produces movement.... Leadership

1. Establishes direction—develops a vision of the future along with strategies for producing the changes need to achieve that vision
2. Aligns people—communicates the direction to those whose cooperation may be needed so as to create coalitions that understand the vision and that are committed to its achievement
3. Motivates and inspires—keep people moving in the right direction despite major political, bureaucratic, and resource barriers to change by appealing to very basic, but often untapped, human needs, values, and emotions.

The suggestion is that a leader must develop a future-directed orientation: Anticipate industry trends and challenge the status quo. Think about some of

---

[21] Bennis, W. and B. Nanus, *Leaders* (New York: Harper & Row, 1985), pp. 4–5.

[22] Bass, B. M., *Bass & Stogdill's Handbook of Leadership: Theory, Research, and Managerial Applications*, 3rd ed. (New York: The Free Press, 1990), p. 11.

[23] Kotter, *op. cit.*, p. 5.

the great leaders that have made their mark on the world. In biblical times, figures such as Moses, Jesus, and, later, Mohammed presented a vision, communicated ideas to people, and motivated their followers to effect change. Winston Churchill had a vision to save his country from the onslaught of tyranny and oppression. He rallied the British people during World War II against a horrific leader, Adolph Hitler. After September 11, 2001, U.S. President George W. Bush related his vision of ridding the world of terrorism. Toward that end, he communicated the vision to other world leaders, as well as the American people, in an effort to build a coalition to attack terrorist forces. Modern business leaders such as Jack Welch (retired from General Electric), Steve Jobs (Apple), Michael Dell (Dell Computers), and Bill Gates (Microsoft) had visions of where to take their organizations. They communicated their visions to their employees and then motivated them to implement the vision.

After defining a vision, leaders set out to inform and persuade others to follow their beliefs and philosophy. During the 1960s, Martin Luther King had a vision of a nonracist America that he communicated to the American populace through speeches, marches, sit-ins, and his writings. He mobilized his "troops" to action by inspiring them. King motivated the American people and their political representatives to take action and pass legislation in support of his vision.

Leadership applies to everyone—not only political, military, and business figures. At the very least, people lead their lives by creating a vision of where they want to go and then communicating that vision to others who need to know it. People then need to motivate and inspire themselves to pursue and attain their goals.

LEADERSHIP VERSUS MANAGEMENT

Are managers leaders? The following is one distinction between management and leadership:[24]

- Management is more formal and scientific than leadership. It relies on universal skills such as planning, budgeting, and controlling. Management involves an explicit set of tools and techniques, based on reasoning and testing, that can be used in a variety of situations.
- Leadership, in contrast to management, involves having a vision of what the organization can become.
- Leadership requires eliciting cooperation and teamwork from a large network of people and keeping the key people in that network motivated, using every manner of persuasion.

Management theorists draw an important distinction between leadership and management. The leader creates a vision for the organization and gains support among its personnel. The leader specifies the organization's objectives, as

---

[24] *Op. cit.*, p. 39.

TABLE 4–3

Organizational Approaches of Leaders and Managers[a]

Category	Leader	Manager
Creating an agenda	Establishes direction: Develops a vision and the strategies needed for its achievement.	Plans and budgets: Establishes detailed steps and timetables for achieving needed results; allocates necessary resources.
Developing a network for achieving the agenda	Involves aligning people: Communicates direction by words and deeds to all those whose cooperation may be needed to help create teams and coalitions that understand the leaders' vision and strategies and that accept their validity.	Organizes and staffs: Establishes a structure for achieving the plans; staffs the organization; delegates responsibility and authority for implementing the plans; develops policies and procedures to guide people; creates monitoring systems.
Execution	Motivates and inspires: Energizes people to overcome major political, bureaucratic and resource barriers to change by satisfying basic human needs.	Controls and solves problems: Monitors results, compares them with plans, and then plans and organizes to close any gaps.
Outcomes	Produces change, often to a dramatic degree. Has the potential for producing extremely useful change, such as new products desired by managers.	Produces a degree of predictability and order: Has the potential to consistently produce key results expected by various stakeholders (such as meeting deadlines for customers and paying dividends to stockholders).

[a]From Kotter, J. P., *A Force for Change: How Leadership Differs from Management* (New York: The Free Press, 1990).

well as the strategy for attaining them. In contrast to the leader, the manager's key function involves implementing the leader's vision by establishing supporting objectives and using skills such as planning, organizing, directing, and controlling. The manager chooses the means to achieve the end that the leader formulates. Leadership deals with change, inspiration, motivation, and influence; management deals more with carrying out objectives. Table 4–3, compares the leader's and manager's organizational approaches.

Some researchers believe that a leader's orientation differs fundamentally from a manager's. Table 4–4 compares the beliefs and attitudes of an administrator, a manager, and a leader. In each case, does the leader's response follow the maxim "Managers are people who do things right, and leaders are people who do the right thing"?[25]

---

[25] Bennis, W., and B. Nanus, *Leaders* (New York: Harper & Row, 1985), p. 21.

TABLE 4–4

Primary Beliefs and Attitudes

	Administrator	Manager	Leader
Rewarding subordinates	Get just what the policy provides	Fair pay for fair work	Major rewards for major results or accomplishments
Decision-making basis	Decision is made by the policy or procedure	Stick with policy, except where exceptions are fully justified	Special circumstances require different decisions
Strategic orientation	Internal	Internal, except when major external events intervene	External
Innovation and creativity	Change is threatening	Tries to plan out major changes	Improvements come through change
Handling variables	One variable at a time	Handle multiple variables if not too complex	Balances and blends multiple, complex variables
Efficiency and effectiveness	Covers every detail in depth	Doing things right	Doing the right things
Time frame for thinking	Short range, month to month or year to year	Medium range, 2–4 years	Strategic, 5–10 years
Big vs. small picture	Concentrates on details	Concentrates on details as they fit into a system	Sees the "big picture"
Organization structure	Bureaucratic, many levels	Traditional	Flat, few levels
Security level	Low, protect my rear	Average, except when things go wrong	Very secure and confident
Management atmosphere	You can't fight city hall	Your progress depends upon you	Win–win atmosphere
Policies	Cast in concrete, takes an act of God to change	Exceptions can be made, but must be strongly justified	Uses only as a guide to most actions
People	Emphasis on controls and time spent	Emphasizes team effort	Leads by example
Change	Seeks to maintain status quo; don't rock the boat or make waves	Changes made if major problems dictate or when pressure builds up	Change is encouraged continually
Conflict	Avoids conflicts at any cost	Addresses if they become major	Recognizes that they will occur; concentrates on resolving them for improvements
Subordinate loyalty	Is to the policy	Mixed between the policy and the manager	Is to the leader
Risk taking	Avoids at all costs	Accepts minimal risk	Encourages planned risk taking
Information sharing	Little	Need-to-know basis	Open and frank
Approach to problems	Avoids like the plague	Solves as they develop; reactive	Problems are normal part of the job; proactive
Handling mistakes	Protect my rear and offer excuses; pin the guilty	Emphasize why it happened, not who caused it	Learn from them, don't dwell on them once solved
Authority	Emphasizes formal authority and power	Authority goes with the position	Maximum use of informal authority

COMPETITIVE ADVANTAGE

Every year, *Industry Week* selects the 100 best-managed companies. "Each company is a leader in its industry and demonstrates superior management skills in areas such as financial performance, innovation, leadership, globalization, alliances and partnerships, employee benefits and education, and community involvement."[26] "All companies understand that the key to competitive advantage in this century will be the capacity of top leadership to create social architecture capable of penetrating intellectual capital.... The best managed companies are able to integrate and implement the new-economy virtues of speed and e-commerce with the old-economy virtues of generating profit, market share, and excellent customer service."[27] Major management challenges confront organizations in this century.

REVIEW QUESTIONS

1. What type of manager would a stereotypical ex–military officer make? Would this person be a good candidate to manage a drug research organization? Explain your answer.
2. Presidents Carter and Reagan had different management and leadership styles. Use the Internet to obtain examples of their styles. Which president would you rather work for? Why?
3. In their article, "Power is the Great Motivator," McClelland and Burnham state, "A high need for power is an important characteristic of successful managers."[28] Comment on the following statement: Managers with a high need for power frequently use it for the benefit of the organization rather than for self-aggrandizement.
4. How well does the following quote describe the managers that you know? Explain.

   Leaders articulate and define what has previously remained implicit or unsaid; then they invent images, methaphors, and models that provide a focus for new attention. By so doing, they consolidate or challenge prevailing wisdom. In short, an essential factor in leadership is the capacity to influence and organize meaning for the members of the organization.[29]

5. This chapter talks about accountability. Describe the difference between "the boss holds me accountable" and "we (I) hold ourselves (myself) accountable."

---

[26] Hasek, G., "The World's 100 Best," *Industry Week.com* (August 21, 2000): 46–68; quote from p. 49.

[27] Bennis, W., and R. Aggarwal, cited in *ibid.*, p. 49. Or see http://industryweek.com/currentarticles/asp/articles.asp?ArticleId=861

[28] McClelland, D. C., and D. H. Burnham, "Power is the Great Motivator," *Harvard Business Review* (January–February 1995): 2–11 (reprint no. 4223).

[29] Bennis and Nanus, *op. cit.*, p. 39.

6. In its evolution, management theory has been influenced by classical management, behavioral approaches, and quantitative methods. Many have contributed to the development of management as a discipline. Research and discuss someone who has contributed to the development of management theory. Limit the paper to 500 words. Examples include the following people:

Chester Barnard	Elton Mayo
W. Edwards Deming	Max Weber
Peter Drucker	Frederick W. Taylor
Henri Fayol	Max Weber
Mary Parker Follett	Henry Mintzberg
Henry Gantt	Peter Drucker
Frank Gilbreth	Warren Bennis
Lillian Gilbreth	John Kotter
Douglas MacGregor	David C. McClelland
Peter Block	Chris Argyris
James Kouzes	Barry Posner

7. What is meant by the statement "Managers are people who do things right, and leaders are people who do the right thing"?
8. What does leadership mean to you? Do you think there is a difference between management and leadership? Explain.
9. Use the Internet or go to the library to respond to this question.
   a) Compare and contrast the leadership and management (e.g., vision, planning, organizing, and controlling) styles exhibited by Al Dunlap (formerly of the Sunbeam Corporation) and Howard Schultz (Starbucks Corporation's CEO).
   b) Characterize Dunlap and Schultz according to McGregor's theory X and theory Y leadership styles. Explain your answer.

CHAPTER TEST

Answer each of the following questions. Multiple choice questions may have more than one correct selection.

1. When did classical management theory begin?
   a) 1200s   b) 1650s
   c) 1750s   d) 1850s
   e) 1950s
2. Define efficiency.
3. Define productivity.
4. What are characteristics of bureaucratic management?
   a) quick reaction to competitive issues
   b) wasting time
   c) written processes and procedures
   d) hierarchical structure
   e) impersonal authority
   f) large number of employees

5. Which type of work or worker is appropriate for a bureaucratic organization?
   a) installing tires on an automobile   b) bank teller
   c) designing jewelry   d) train conductor
   e) writer

6. Select the basic management functions established by Fayol?
   a) planning   b) organizing
   c) staffing   d) commanding
   e) directing   f) coordinating
   g) reporting   h) delegating
   i) budgeting

7. What are 3 of the 14 management principles discussed by Fayol?
   a) division of work through specialization
   b) time and motion
   c) authority should be equal to responsibility
   d) unity of command
   e) unity of direction
   f) the scalar chain of command

8. What is Fredrick Taylor known for?
   a) time and motion
   b) father of scientific management
   c) Hawthorne experiments

9. What is a time-and-motion study?

10. What is the Hawthorne Effect?

11. What are the five basic human needs described by Maslow? Give examples of each.

12. What are the characteristics of a theory X worker?

13. What are the characteristics of a theory Y worker?

14. What are four generic management styles?

15. What are the five types of power used by people in organizations?

16. What is the difference between a team and a group?

17. What are the four stages of development that a team passes through?

18. Is conducting a meeting an example of leadership or management? Explain.

CHAPTER 5

PROJECT PLANNING

> *Character cannot be developed in ease and quiet.*
> *Only through experience of trial and suffering can the soul*
> *be strengthened, vision cleared, ambition inspired, and success achieved.*
> Helen Keller

OBJECTIVES

After studying this chapter, you should be able to

- Understand the scope of a project
- Understand the use of a project charter
- Understand the components of a project plan
- Understand and prepare a project statement of work
- Understand and prepare a project work breakdown structure

INTRODUCTION

Planning is the process of establishing courses of action to accomplish predetermined objectives.[1] Establishing a plan for a project before committing the organization's resources maximizes the likelihood of developing and delivering a customer's product or service on time, within budget, and according to the technical specifications. The project manager oversees the preparation of a project plan and then manages in accordance with the plan. This chapter deals with the activities that precede the start of a project. The discussion applies to

- electronic, mechanical, electromechanical, and software-based products,
- small systems consisting of the integration of these components,
- the construction of facilities to house the components and systems, and
- services required to support the design, fabrication, installation, training, and maintenance of the components, systems, and services.

Planning lies at the heart of managing a project's scope. Without a thorough and mutually agreed-upon plan, *scope management* becomes impossible. Scope management encompasses the processes that will ensure that the project include all the work, and only the work, required to complete the project successfully.[2] Scope management extends the length and breadth of the job and encompasses all activities associated with the project. At some point in most projects, the buyer or seller requests changes. The changes may come about for several reasons: improvements in technology that occur after the project is conceived, but before it is approved; obsolete components or new versions of software; or changing customer requirements. Frequently, the discussions that take place while the proposal is being evaluated or during the initial development of the product itself improves the customer's understanding of the product's use. Following this increase in understanding, the customer sometimes requests the developer to incorporate "minor" product modifications without a corresponding change in price. Controlling the scope of the project then becomes paramount. The organization must employ a method for evaluating changes and determining their cost. Armed with the facts, the organization can make an informed decision; agreeing to changes—whether initiated by a customer or someone inside the organization—without thoroughly understanding their impact is the path to breaking the budget and delivering the product late.

REQUEST FOR (a) PROPOSAL AND REQUEST FOR (a) QUOTE

The process of acquiring a product or service begins with a customer (or a buyer) sending a description of its needs to several suppliers (also called a seller or vendor) in the form of either a *request for (a) proposal (RFP)* or a *request for (a)*

[1] Badiru, A. B., *Project Management Tools for Engineering and Management Professionals* (Norcross, GA: Industrial Engineering and Management Press, 1991).

[2] Project Management Institute Standards Committee, *A Guide to the Project Management Body of Knowledge* (Upper Darby, PA: Project Management Institute, 1996).

quote (RFQ). Frequently, organizations use an RFQ to seek bids for familiar, standard items and an RFP to procure consulting, advertising, or maintenance services or items requiring development. Many organizations establish a minimum dollar amount (e.g., $2,500), below which neither an RFQ nor an RFP is required. A customer distributing an RFP for a high-technology product or service may do so for any of the following reasons:

1. The customer believes that the product is not readily available off the shelf from suppliers and that it requires a special development effort,
2. If the product is readily available, it may require the addition of special features that the customer chooses not to develop, or
3. The product demands technical expertise during its installation or initial operation.

The planning process begins during the preparation of the response to the RFP or RFQ. The RFP response (i.e., the proposal) requires a detailed description of the deliverable items, including a technical discussion describing both the unique features of the design and the activities that the organization will perform to ensure delivery within the customer's requested time frame. The proposal frequently describes the product, its history, its unique technical features, and the organization's technical competencies, management philosophy, quality assurance approach, and training capabilities. The proposal also presents a *statement of work (SOW)* that includes a *work-breakdown structure (WBS)* and schedule, as well as a *specification compliance matrix*. The specification compliance matrix lists every requirement of the buyer, together with a statement by the seller agreeing to meet, or stating that it will not meet, the requirement. Sometimes the seller meets the intent of the specification requirement, but not its literal interpretation. In this case, the seller provides a brief description of the course of action it recommends. Larger organizations attach a set of *terms and conditions* to the proposal—a legal statement attached to the bid that, among other things, limits the organization's liability and establishes a return policy. Finally, the RFP or RFQ response includes a *cost proposal* that contains a price for each item on the list of deliverables. Often during the proposal process, a proposal team identifies several technical options that may enhance the baseline product or service. The proposal will then identify these options and their prices separately.

Managing the preparation of a proposal is itself a project. Responding to an RFP requires a significant organizational team effort, led by a project manager. The effort costs time and diverts resources that would otherwise be allocated to other activities. Suppliers interested in providing products or services for the buyer may spend as much as two percent of the final sales price on the preparation of a proposal. Organizations evaluate the likelihood that they will obtain a contract before deciding whether to respond to an RFP. No one wants to invest resources in a hopeless cause. Larger organizations use a formal evaluation approach sometimes called an *opportunity review board (ORB)* for this purpose. Senior executives make the decision to respond to an RFP for a variety of reasons. Most important, they believe that the organization has a greater than 50% chance of winning the bidding. Sometimes an organization submits a bid for strategic reasons: Perhaps the organization wishes to break into a new market and desires to establish a presence for name recognition purposes, or perhaps an important customer wants the organization to submit a bid. Most organizations will expend the effort to satisfy a good customer.

A response to an RFQ requires much less effort than a response to an RFP. The respondent prepares a price for each item on the list of deliverables, adds the organization's standard terms and conditions, and supplies a cover letter (also known as a letter of transmittal). While it is preparing a response, the supplier may decide that it must spend funds to develop new software or hardware (or both). If so, many departments must participate in the effort. The project manager then contacts the various departments, such as engineering (mechanical, electrical, chemical, software, networking, etc.), purchasing, training, service, quality assurance, and technical support. In responding to either an RFP or an RFQ, the project manager prepares a *responsibility assignment matrix (RAM)* that identifies the tasks required for the effort, the person responsible for each task, and the date the task is due to be completed. The project manager provides each functional department manager and other stakeholders with the baseline information required to perform his or her tasks; often, this information includes the customer's technical specification, the number of units required, documentation requirements, a schedule, installation needs, testing demands, special standards, and quality assurance requirements. For the work required to meet the customer's specification, each department furnishes a labor estimate in hours, hardware and software material costs, travel and living estimates, special tools or capital equipment required, consultant fees, and labor hours required to prepare documentation. The response to the RFQ sums up the costs in a manner that will be discussed later and provides a bottom-line number. The details are not usually given to the customer. The RFP response may provide bottom-line prices for the first and subsequent systems, plus support service prices or a detailed price breakdown that reflects the customer's demands.

PROJECT CHARTER

Projects funded by an external customer are automatically chartered by (i.e., receive automatic recognition from) the organization. In this regard, money is honey! Organizations react to cash. Following the awarding of a contract, senior management immediately assigns a project manager to the job and charges him or her with the responsibility to do whatever must be done to produce a product or service that meets the customer's technical specification, on time and within budget. Ideally, the person that led the preparation of the RFP or RFQ receives the project, because that person is most familiar with the effort. There is no need for a formal project charter if the contract includes a technical specification and an SOW.

A contract without a definition is like a car without a destination. The motor runs, and the car goes everywhere and nowhere at the same time. Accordingly, *a project should never be undertaken without either a written agree-*

ment that includes a specification and SOW or a project charter. Without a specification, people will "do their own thing." Designers will proceed with their interpretation of the customer's needs. The purchasing department will buy its customary material. The manufacturing department will build the product following its own standards. Invariably, the customer will have a different view, and the completed work will require modifications, wasting both time and labor. The absence of a project definition guarantees cost overruns and delays, dooming the project to failure.

Projects that receive internal funds *require* a project charter. As defined by the Project Management Institute, the charter (1) states the business need that the project addresses, (2) describes the product, and (3) includes the signature of a senior executive. A senior manager's signature implies that the organization accepts and is committed to the effort. An approved charter authorizes the project manager to proceed with the project and apply organizational resources to its activities.

The charter defined by the Project Management Institute is necessary, but not sufficient, to describe a project. To achieve sufficiency, the charter should also include a schedule, a budget, and a summary of the resources required to complete the project. Some have broadened the concept of a project charter,[3] and one source recommends the use of the following 10-part project charter template:[4]

- *Project description*: a brief explanation of the purpose of the project and the identity of the initial "owner" of the project.
- *Opportunity statement*: the business-related reasons for undertaking the project.
- *Impact statement*: the potential effect of the project on the organization's business, operations, schedule, other projects, current technology, and other systems.
- *Constraints and assumptions*: Limitations or restrictions placed on the project.
- *Project scope*: A precise definition of the project's boundaries. The scope may include the business areas or functions to be examined by the project (the domain of study), the work that will be performed (the domain of work), and the results that will be produced (the deliverables). A project scope should identify both what *is* and what *is not* within the purview of the project.
- *Project objectives*: a list of measurable criteria that define the aim(s) of the project and when they are deemed to have been met.
- *Project justifications*: The known costs incurred and benefits to be derived from performing the project. These financial parameters must be

---

[3] See, for example, Hayes, D. S., "Evaluation and Application of a Project Charter Template to Improve the Project Planning Process," **Project Management Journal** 31(1): 14–23.

[4] Tryon and Associates, "Project Charter Template," on-line at *http://www.tryonassoc.com/news/projchartertempl_asp*.

reforecast periodically during the life of the project and should be compared with the actual costs and benefits at the conclusion of the project.

- *Project approach*: the general strategy for carrying out the project, along with nontechnical descriptions of any methods, processes, or tools that will be used to complete the project.
- *Project organization*: Identification of the roles and responsibilities associated with the project.
- *Management commitment*: Signatures of senior managers signifying that they agree with the plan.

This template goes well beyond the traditional view of the project charter. Some organizations use it as the basis for a thorough internal project plan.[5]

Plans for internally funded projects differ from those associated with externally funded ones. The traditional project charter used for an internally funded project describes the job succinctly. Externally funded projects require far more extensive planning and preparation. Figure 5–1 compares internally funded versus externally funded efforts. The next section outlines a plan that establishes the baseline for project planning.

THE PROJECT PLAN

Whether a job receives internal organizational funds or external funds, the project plan answers the standard news reporter's questions of who, what, why, where, when, and how:

Who will do the work? Who is assigned to the project? Does the organization have the personnel to perform the tasks? Will consultants, permanent staff, or temporary workers need to be hired?

What must be done? What is the overall budget? What is the budget for each task? What resources are required to complete the project? What will the people assigned to the project do? What are the deliverables? What equipment has to be purchased? What documentation is required? What is the chain of command? What signifies project completion?

Why is the organization undertaking the project?

Where will the work be done?

When are the activities scheduled to start and finish?

How will the activities be done?

The project manager defines the project's scope by listing the technical requirements and objectives. The project manager prepares a schedule that identifies the dates for starting and completing activities and milestones. A *milestone* represents the identification of a significant event. Examples of milestones are the start or end of a project, the start or end of a design review, the

---

[5] Hayes, *op. cit.*

FIGURE 5–1

Project planning process

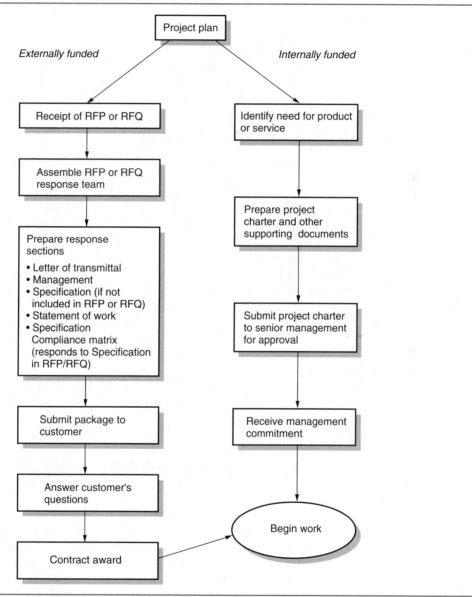

completion of a major system evaluation, the shipping of a product, and the installation of a product.

The plan identifies assumptions made by the different stakeholders. People make all kinds of assumptions while a proposal is being prepared. Managers realize that the organization may need to acquire various labor skills in order to complete a task. If so, they must inform senior management and the human resource department of the need. A department anticipates outsourcing tasks to other organizations, but senior management may have other plans. Designers may assume that the organization will purchase new software or hardware required for an analysis. Software developers may assume that an updated database application will be available. If a department purchases the latest and greatest equipment, did it also remember to update its training, maintenance, and support services? Managers may assume that the customer will furnish equipment to facilitate the installation and testing of a new system. The assumption may be correct, but the customer should be informed about what is expected. Often, there are internal "disconnects" due to a lack of communication. The project manager must obtain the information from stakeholders and put it into the plan.

The project plan identifies schedule, budget, and performance *constraints*. The schedule must clearly pinpoint which tasks precede which others. Sometimes, additional funding is contingent upon reaching a certain performance criterion. Functional managers should identify design, operational, or testing sequences; uninterruptible sequences represent important constraints.

All plans include reporting requirements. Periodically, stakeholders review the technical, financial, and scheduling progress of a project. Plans often schedule technical interchange meetings that clarify issues arising during the design and development phases of the project. The proposal specifies the frequency of reporting and the type of information provided to the customer. Usually, senior management wants to review the project's technical, financial, and scheduling progress on a monthly basis. Functional department personnel frequently participate in these status meetings, and the plan should make them aware of this need.

Although the project manager is responsible for creating the plan, he or she often requests functional managers to contribute to the process. Product or service expertise comes from the functional areas, not project management. The project manager depends on functional or department managers to provide him or her with particulars. As part of their input, technical personnel identify risk areas, uncertainties, and conflicts, which the project manager factors into the price and schedule during the preparation of the proposal. (See Chapter 10 for further information about risk.) At the outset of the proposal effort, the project manager creates a top-level schedule that complies with the customer's delivery requests. Functional managers provide detailed task descriptions to implement objectives, requirements, and milestones. They prepare detailed schedules and labor allocations consistent with the project's constraints. After reviewing the input from the functional areas, the project manager gains an understanding of possible scheduling conflicts arising from competing departmental demands. Internal stakeholders must resolve any scheduling or technical complications that surface. The project manager must inform senior management of likely troublesome technical, scheduling, or budgetary issues.

Ethical conflicts can arise during the preparation of plans for an RFP submission. Suppose a project manager receives draft proposal material from members of the organization that shows that the organization simply cannot meet the customer's requested delivery date. Or perhaps a technical requirement cannot be met. Does the project manager proceed without informing the customer? Does the project manager submit the proposal and agree to the customer's schedule or technical requirements, knowing that the likelihood of meeting the targets is slim? Does the fear that a competitor may agree to an impossible situation govern an organization's actions? These are not easy questions to answer.

Consider this actual scenario: A customer intentionally inserted several technical requirements into an RFP that were impossible to achieve. After discovering the questionable specifications during the proposal response phase, an organization that was contemplating responding to the RFP wrestled with what actions it might take. The organization ruminated over the answers to these questions:

Has the organization misunderstood the customer's requirement?

Does the customer realize what it requested?

What will competitors do?

Should the organization point out the problem with the RFP in its response thereto?

Should the organization submit an impossible-to-fulfill proposal and hope to renegotiate matters after the contract award?

The team members considering the RFP met and agreed upon a response strategy. They decided to state in their proposal that they could not meet certain technical and schedule requests and instead offered an alternative approach. The organization won the contract. During a kickoff meeting following the contract award, the organization raised the question, "Did the contractor realize that it inserted impossible conditions in the proposal document?" The customer's response was astonishing: The contractor intentionally inserted certain impossible-to-meet conditions in order to see the bidding organization's response. First, the contractor wanted to see if the bidders would recognize the issues. Were they technically savvy? Then the contractor looked at the response and eliminated companies that gave it a "line of goods." The moral of the story is that sometimes honesty prevails!

PLAN BENEFITS

A plan defines a project, clarifies stakeholders' expectations, reduces ambiguity and uncertainty, and eliminates conflict among functional managers. By describing the functional managers' roles, a plan improves an operation's efficiency. A plan defines the resources required by the organization to perform the work requested. A properly prepared plan distributes the expected labor and material expenditures over time, which provides a basis for monitoring and controlling work. A plan identifies the critical areas of a project and permits the organization to focus its efforts on monitoring them. Stakeholders use the plan embedded in the proposal as a communication tool. The project manager monitors the technical, scheduling, and budgetary status of a project on the basis of the agreed-upon plan.

The Project Plan Troika

So, how does a project manager create a project plan? All of the news reporter's questions are addressed in three documents: a formal product or system definition in the form of a list of requirements, or specification; a statement of work that includes a work breakdown structure and a schedule; and a budget for each task assigned to organization departments and to subcontractors. The project manager submits the system definition and the SOW to the external customer. Usually, departmental budget data remain within the organization and are not submitted to the customer.

Requirements or specification.   The list of requirements, or specification, is a quantitative definition of the deliverables, as delineated in the contract, the sales order, or an internal project agreement. The company that is awarded the contract agrees to deliver a product or service that meets the customer's requirements. Organizations call the list of requirements a product or service *specification*. The project manager assigned to the job distributes the specification to all stakeholders. The project manager monitors the project and continually reminds development personnel of the minimum technical requirements. The organization receiving the award has an obligation to deliver a product or service that meets the minimum requirements and not a bit more. Improving on the specification may be a challenge and great technical fun, but it expends labor effort and time for which the customer did not agree to pay. The project manager is interested in maximizing the organization's profit and, certainly, not losing money (especially in a nonprofit organization).

Exhibit 5–1 illustrates a typical hardware or software product specification. The specification includes critical performance factors describing the requested product or system: its speed, size, capacity, scalability, upgradability, reliability, and required software and hardware interfaces. Products delivered to environmentally unfriendly regions require special consideration. For example, a computing system that must operate at the North Pole or in the heat of a desert demands such consideration. Likewise, a system delivered to an offshore oil rig may have to withstand the rigors of high humidity and salt water. A medical product, such as a pacemaker, will require careful design and high-quality components to ensure that it is reliable. Morton-Thiokol, the developers of the space shuttle *Challenger* O-ring assembly, assumed that the ambient temperature in Florida would be greater than 50°F. On that tragic day in 1986, the temperature at Cape Canaveral dipped below 40°F. The rubber O-ring joining the two rocket sections became brittle. During the launch, a crack appeared and internal flammable gases escaped from the spacecraft and ignited a few seconds into the mission. The rocket exploded and lives were lost. The engineers built the system to a specification, but NASA officials and Morton-Thiokol executives chose to ignore its limitations. The tragedy points up the fact that customers and development organizations must define a product's design parameters and constraints carefully, taking into consideration all of the product's possible applications—especially critical life-critical ones.

Stakeholders involved in a sole-source contract (a contract in which only one supplier can furnish the required product or services) frequently develop a

EXHIBIT 5–1

Outline of a Typical Hardware or Software Product Specification

Specification title: **Date:**

Specification number (if required):

Specification revision no.:

Author(s):

Name and address of organization preparing document:

1. Description of product or service, including intended usage
2. Definition of terminology
3. Requirements
   3.1. System architecture
   3.2. Software required
   3.3. Components required
   3.4. Unique hardware or software features
   3.5. Test features
   3.6. Product or system self-test capability
   3.7. Factory test
   3.8. On-line test
4. Interfaces
   4.1. Software
   4.2. Hardware
   4.3. Equipment
   4.4. Operator
   4.5. Input/output devices
   4.6. Electrical
   4.7. Mechanical
5. Product or service characteristics
   5.1. Physical
       5.1.1. Size
       5.1.2. Weight
       5.1.3. Power
   5.2. Performance characteristics
       5.2.1. Speed
       5.2.2. Response time
       5.2.3. Data rates
       5.2.4. Electrical performance
       5.2.5. Mechanical performance
       5.2.6. Start-up and shutdown characteristics
       5.2.7. Capacities (e.g., electrical, mechanical, memory)
   5.3. Reliability
   5.4. Maintainability
   5.5. Environmental
       5.5.1. Temperature
       5.5.2. Humidity
       5.5.3. Vibration levels
       5.5.4. Shock
       5.5.5. Natural environments (e.g., earthquake levels)
       5.5.6. Electromagnetic interference
       5.5.7. Nuclear effects
   5.6. Safety considerations
   5.7. Quality assurance provisions

specification together and complete it before work begins on the project. The specification attempts to anticipate all questions that designers might ask.

If a product or system definition doesn't exist, one should be created and circulated among the stakeholders for approval. The stakeholders should be invited to comment on the draft document and the reviewers requested to complete their efforts within a reasonable time. Comments not received by that date will signify tacit approval of the definition. Granted, this is hardball, but if you are the project manager, it's your neck that's on the line. Developing a system or product without a definition guarantees breaking the budget and ensures late delivery. After the project starts, a stakeholder may complain, "I didn't realize that we were doing this." Well, if it's in the specification and the stakeholder didn't comment on it, he or she lost all rights to complain. We have all heard about the proverbial camel: a horse built by a committee without a specification. Everyone on the committee had a different view of the horse, and no one took the time to write it down. A product definition baseline must exist, and it's up to the project manager to create one if it doesn't.

Statement of Work.   The SOW is a detailed narrative description of the products and services supplied under the contract. The specification describes what will be supplied; the SOW states the quantity and describes the supporting material and services. The SOW also details any responsibilities for supplying material, products, and services that may not be explicitly included in the list of deliverables. A schedule accompanies the SOW and lists the tasks and the temporal relationships among them.

An SOW includes a methodology for proving to a customer that the product or service meets the specification. Where are the verification tests conducted, at the development site, at the customer's site, or at both locations? How extensive should testing be? The buyer and seller must agree on these issues during price negotiations.

Two examples serve to illustrate the importance of defining things clearly in the SOW. A medium-sized industrial company delivered a large system to a desert site in Nevada. Installation of the system required two employees to remain at the site for a month. The contract did not clearly identify which organization would supply utilities such as electricity and water, nor did it take into consideration basic human needs like a portable toilet and a cabin for protection from the intense sun. The resolution of this oversight delayed the schedule by two weeks until a portable generator, fuel, water, and a trailer were brought to the site. The lack of clarity in the SOW forced the company to pay for these items, which reduced its profit from the job.

On another occasion, a manufacturer delivered a water-monitoring system to a site in China. Technicians from the company installed the system on the bank of a river, but the SOW did not describe acceptance testing of the system at the customer's site. The seller and the buyer had two different ideas about a system acceptance test. The buyer wanted to confirm the operation of the system during a six-month evaluation period, and the seller expected to install the system and perform a three-day brief confirmation of its operation. Clearly, a disconnect had occurred—a very expensive disconnect for the seller because the customer expected the seller to participate in the six-month on-site evaluation. Even if the seller could provide a technician to live in a remote area of China for six months, the organization did not want to incur the costs and the loss of an employee for such an extended stay. The resolution of this dilemma required the seller to extend the product warranty for two years beyond the original warranty.

An SOW exists to clarify both the buyer's and the seller's expectations and, ideally, should anticipate all eventualities. During the preparation of the SOW, the project manager contacts all internal stakeholders to discuss the product. This enables the project manager to understand as many as possible of the problems that could arise during the development, delivery, installation, and operation of the product or service. The SOW reflects stakeholders' comments. Adding work or deliverables to the contract will have an upward influence on the price quoted to the customer.

The key elements of the SOW include the following:

- a general statement describing the scope of the work (refer to the functionality section of the specification)
- a list of deliverables, including hardware, software, construction items, documentation, utilities supplied, training, and others
- citations of related studies, documentation, standards, and commercial or military specifications that apply to the project
- data and documentation requirements
- a list of supporting equipment for the final deliverable
- a listing of material (e.g., property, facilities, equipment, services, and documentation) required by the contractor and furnished by the customer
- the overall schedule for the project
- a description of the testing that is to be performed (with expectations for the developer's location and the customer's site)
- a list of applicable governmental regulations and permit responsibilities
- an explanation of the method of shipping components or other products
- explanatory exhibits, attachments and appendices
- standard terms and conditions used by a supplier for all proposals

The detailed SOW template in Exhibit 5–2 outlines many of the items that define a product or service job. Exhibit 5–3 illustrates an actual SOW that describes a brief project with the objective of delivering and installing a standard database software package to a medical office. The document uses a subset of items described in Exhibit 5–2. The project manager takes responsibility for the preparation of the SOW, which may read like a legal document (because it is one!). In large organizations, the project manager frequently obtains assistance from the legal staff. If this is not possible, then the project manager must examine the agreement and confirm that it protects the organization while delivering the product or service the customer requires.

Exhibit 5–3 makes plain the customer's responsibilities. A typical area of confusion in this regard is software maintenance, which is customarily part of the buyer's responsibility. Unsophisticated customers frequently believe that

EXHIBIT 5–2

Outline of a Sample Statement of Work (SOW)

1. Top-level functional description (see specification for details)
2. List of required customer-supplied items
    a. Items required for development purposes
    b. Items required for factory acceptance test, installation, or site acceptance test
3. List of contractor-supplied deliverables and quantity
    a. Site construction equipment
    b. Hardware
    c. Software
    d. Manuals, documentation, and data
       No. of copies of documents
       Documentation examples include the following:
         i. Site architectural drawings
        ii. System interconnection drawings
       iii. Design review documentation
        iv. Functional design specification
         v. Assembly drawings
        vi. Electrical schematics
       vii. Intermediate and final product test results
      viii. Factory acceptance test
        ix. Site acceptance test
         x. System software specification
        xi. Software license rights
       xii. Software source-code rights (sometimes a provision exists to store source code in escrow)
      xiii. Software user manuals
       xiv. Maintenance manual
        xv. Block diagrams
       xvi. Installation and operating manuals
      xvii. Training manual
     xviii. Original equipment manufacturer manuals and documentation for items such as a computer, I/O devices (printer, bar code reader, display, etc.), and third-party software as received from the manufacturer
       xix. List of required or recommended spare parts
        xx. Reliability analysis
       xxi. Environmental analyses
      xxii. Performance bond
     xxiii. Certifications required
4. Customer/Subcontractor Reviews
    a. Quantity and location of technical interchange meetings, design reviews, etc.
    b. Preliminary list of items (schematics, drawings, hardware specifications, software specifications, documents, testing, quality assurance policies, etc.) for discussion at each meeting
    c. Contents and expected outcomes of preliminary design review and critical design review
    d. No. of times customer may review documentation
    e. Policy on travel and living expenses (who pays and at what price?) to attend reviews
5. Preferred vendors
6. Applicable reference documents and appropriate standards
    a. Quality assurance standards (e.g., ISO 9000, IEEE)
    b. Hardware standards (e.g., Underwriters Laboratories license, CE compliance, electromagnetic interference)
    c. Software standards (e.g., IEEE 730, Software Engineering Institute)
    d. Construction standards (e.g., building codes)

EXHIBIT 5–2

    e. Fabrication standards (e.g., for welding and soldering)
    f. Environmental standards (e.g., Federal Environmental Protection Agency and local requirements)
7. Schedule
    a. Create a work-breakdown structure.
    b. Link tasks.
    c. Assign starting and finishing dates.
    d. Identify critical dates.
    e. Specify customer approval dates.
    f. Identify the critical path.
8. Define task responsibility
    a. Contractor is responsible for the design, production, integration, calibration, factory testing, installation, and training for the proposed system.
    b. Customer is responsible for all site preparations needed for the installation and operation of the system. Customer personnel are responsible for ensuring the readiness of the installation site and for providing all heavy equipment and professional riggers required to receive, transport, and assemble the system at the installation site.
    c. Identify the party or parties responsible for the readiness of the installation site:
        i. Designate heavy equipment and professional riggers to unload system components from delivery trucks, transport system components through the facility, and reassemble system components at the installation site.
        ii. Ensure that floors, thresholds, loading dock ramps, freight elevators, cranes, forklifts, etc., have sufficient loading capacity to allow heavy equipment to unload and transport system components without exceeding maximum weight limits and to enable the system to be installed and operated.
        iii. Ensure that loading docks, doorways, hallways, rooms, etc., are of a size sufficient to allow heavy equipment to unload and transport system components through the facility and to enable the system to be installed and operated.
        iv. Examine and, if necessary, move ductwork, piping, security cameras, or other obstructions before delivery and installation to allow the unloading, transport, and assembly of system components.
        v. Ensure the readiness of all system facilities (e.g., electrical power, heating, and air-conditioning) for installation and operation.
        vi. Ensure that labor is available at the time of installation of the system.
    d. Define responsibility for site modifications in areas such as
        i. Plumbing
        ii. Electrical
        iii. Heating, ventilation, and air-conditioning
        iv. Gas lines
        v. Fuel storage and distribution
        vi. Chemical material storage and distribution
        vii. Hazardous material storage
9. Acceptance criteria agreement
    a. Subassembly acceptance testing
    b. System factory acceptance test
    c. Site acceptance test
10. Method of Shipment
    a. Air, train, truck, and courier
    b. Identify freight cost responsibility.
    c. Clarify FOB location.
    d. Identify customer responsibilities relating to off-loading, rigging, forklifts, overhead cranes, positioning, leveling, and placing of equipment positioned in the area.

EXHIBIT 5-2   (continued)

e. Identify the moment when title and risk of loss pass to the buyer. Is it at the factory, when the product is delivered to the transportation center, or when the product is delivered to the site?

11. Discuss site installation issues
    a. Required customer support
    b. Data migration for database products
    c. Product calibration

12. Training
    a. Course description
    b. Number of people attending
    c. Location of course
    d. Describe facilities and resources required.
    e. Describe supplier of facilities and resources.

13. Warranty and support
    a. Define equipment warranty term and coverage.
    b. State start of warranty (e.g., within two months of delivery to customer or following site acceptance test).
    c. Policy on software updates
    d. Prohibit buyer from installing user-written programs, upon penalty of nullifying warranty.
    e. Define specific warranty exclusions. (See Exhibit 5–3.)

14. Permits, licenses, and special training
    a. Identify responsibility for obtaining permits and licenses required for the installation and operation of the proposed system.
    b. Identify employee site training requirements.

15. Union and organized labor considerations
    a. Assign the customer responsibility for making in-house labor arrangements necessary for the installation and operation of the proposed system.
    b. Assign responsibility for special local, state, federal, and country requirements (e.g., OSHA)

16. Price and payment terms
    State that the final sale price may vary if the customer makes changes to the specification or makes other testing, documentation, training, or support service requests. Limit the term of the proposal to a comfortable period (e.g., 60 days). Beyond that time, changes in material or labor costs may necessitate a reexamination of prices. For quotes submitted to foreign customers, state that the quote is based on U.S. dollars. Identify responsibility for payment of local taxes, permits, and fees. Require payment for goods and services within 30 days of invoice. Consider using a payment milestone schedule, such as the following:

Approval of design	10%	of final fee
Procurement of materials	25%	of final fee
Completion of factory acceptance test	25%	of final fee
Delivery to site	30%	of final fee
Completion of site acceptance test	10%	of final fee

17. Ownership of data, etc.
    a. State that the contractor retains all ownership and rights to any contractor-manufactured software supplied. The buyer purchases a license to use the supplied software and cannot resell the product.
    b. State that specifications, drawings, manufacturing data, and other information given to the buyer by the seller remains the property of the seller. Without the seller's written consent, the information shall not be reproduced or copied.
    c. State that the contractor retains all ownership of patents and copyrights that may be issued as a result of the contract.

18. Penalities for late delivery or technical performance failure

19. General corporate terms and conditions

EXHIBIT 5–3

Example of a Statement of Work

The representative SOW that follows describes a fictitious software appointment scheduling and invoicing application entitled SoftApps designed for medical practice. The fictitious company SoftHuge developed and manufactured the software. Although complex, SoftApps is a standard off-the-shelf product. The document states that SoftHuge offers to install both the hardware and software, to transfer data from an existing legacy software application presently operating in the office to the new system, to test the resulting system, to train the staff, to deliver documentation, and to provide a warranty to the customer. The customer's name is MedPrac.

While the project is relatively brief, the SOW describes in detail both SoftHuge's and the customer's obligations and responsibilities. Most brand names used in this document to describe products are fictitious. The SOW establishes the deliverables and delineates the expectations so as to minimize surprises.

The author provides this SOW purely for educational purposes and does not advocate its use without obtaining appropriate technical guidance and legal representation. Every project and contract award requires unique tailoring.

Statement of Work

1. Description of Product
   SoftHuge Industries offers software and hardware to MedPrac that will perform billing, scheduling, document control, and patient history management for medical and dental offices. The software package called SoftApps developed by SoftHuge Industries provides full tracking of financial and receivables, electronic billing and claims submission, medical records, managed-care data, and appointments management. Following are some of the unique software features contained in SoftApps:

   - Relational database structure
   - Real-time data processing
   - Patient account retrieval by a variety of search criteria
   - Family billing capability
   - Preparation of a budget payment plan specific to each patient
   - Capacity for up to 50 insurance fee schedules
   - Sequential billing of up to six insurance carriers per patient
   - Open-item posting
   - Insurance payment accuracy audit against carrier fee schedules
   - Automatic reporting and resubmission of delinquent claims
   - Collection notes on patient accounts
   - User-defined billing cycles
   - User-defined linkage between procedure codes and appropriate diagnosis codes
   - Insurance-specific diagnosis and procedure codes
   - Insurance forms, itemized statements, and receipts on demand
   - Reprinting and resubmission of insurance forms or patient statements on demand
   - Electronic posting of payments
   - Treatment plans
   - Cross-checking between diagnosis and procedure codes
   - Reconciliation of actual payments with expected payments
   - Built-in automatic rebilling capability

   SoftApps calculates a practice's procedures and fees. The system can submit claims to major medical insurance commercial carriers electronically. There are multiple levels of system security, and the administrator or provider can designate each user's level of access. This feature protects patient confidentiality and limits clinical, bookkeeping, and financial data entry to authorized personnel.

EXHIBIT 5–3   (continued)

The following areas are of particular interest to mental health practices:

- Integrated word-processing and medical records features allow for recording treatment plans and progress notes and can generate letters and reports to referring physicians or other appropriate sources.
- Patient outcomes can be tracked and recorded.
- Multiple providers' schedules can be easily viewed at one time.
- Future appointments can be set up for patients who want the same times or days of the week.
- Referral sources can be tracked.
- Warnings are provided automatically when the number of remaining allowable visits is approaching the limit.
- Medications, dosages, and prescriptions can be tracked.
- Patients paying on sliding fee schedules based upon income, family size, etc., can be tracked.

2. Installation Schedule

Following the contract award, SoftHuge Industries will organize a meeting with MedPrac's personnel to conduct a detailed review of the project activities. The kickoff meeting will review MedPrac's detailed requirements, existing computer hardware and database software, schedule, prospective software customizations, initial software installation, data transfer from the practice's existing system, testing, and training.

The two organizations will develop a process to ensure prompt responses to questions arising as the project progresses, as well as to guarantee timely reviews of the hardware and software plans. The meeting will finalize the support that SoftHuge Industries personnel will need from MedPrac during the installation and testing periods. Following the meeting the SoftHuge Industries project manager will provide MedPrac with an in-depth schedule. Task priorities and the schedule may change as a result of discussions between MedPrac and SoftHuge Industries' personnel.

In general, the program will proceed according to the following phases:

	Task	Weeks after receipt of order
Phase I	Planning: Organization and review/agreement on plan	2
Phase 2	Hardware procurement	3–7
Phase 3	Hardware and software customization (if required)	None required
Phase 4	Hardware and software installation and testing	8–10
Phase 5	Data migration	11–12
Phase 6	Site acceptance test	13
Phase 7	Training	14–15
Phase 8	First-year warranty support	14–65

3. Deliverables

Deliverables include the following:

    Software

      SoftApps version 10.8 application software

      Report Writer

    Hardware

      1 Server computer, including

          Dual Pentium IV, 1.5-GHz processors

          256 Mbytes memory

          1 Mbyte cache memory

          40 Gbytes RAID hard drive

EXHIBIT 5–3

24X DVD
Ethernet interface
FAX Interface
56K modem interface
Printer interface
19" monitor
Laser printer, 20 PPM
Mouse
Keyboard
Documentation
  SoftApps user manual
  10 SoftApps System Operation training manuals
  10 SoftApps Database Administration training manuals
  Third-party-supplied hardware documentation
Services
  SoftApps installation resident on server
  Installation of MedPrac-supplied Elcaro database management system
  Creation of operational and test environments
  Migration of MedPrac data into new system
  Site test
  Verification of printer, network, modem, and FAX interfaces
  Verification of customer data transfer
  Verification of standard SoftApps screens
  One-year service and maintenance agreement for SoftHuge-provided hardware and software
  Two training courses with up to 10 students in each course:
    SSO-1234 [SoftApps System Operation]
    SDA-5678 [SoftApps Database Administration]

4. Installation and database security guidelines

The project includes the installation of SoftApps on MedPrac's computer, the creation of training and production environments, and the initial tuning of the relational database. SoftHuge Industries will install the system on MedPrac's server. At extra cost, SoftHuge personnel can install SoftApps on MedPrac's client computers. SoftHuge Industries personnel will require assistance from MedPrac's personnel on these tasks.

MedPrac must assist SoftHuge Industries personnel to ensure strict controls between the operational and test versions of the database. The data migration (transfer of existing data to the new system) phase requires that MedPrac establish a cutoff date after which data will not change. MedPrac will collect and store new data for future entry into the system. MedPrac must provide SoftHuge personnel a comma-delimited ASCII file of the data to be migrated to the new system. SoftHuge personnel will transfer MedPrac's data to the new database.

SoftHuge personnel will require a workplace area at MedPrac's faculty during portions of the project.

SoftHuge expects MedPrac to perform several tasks during and after the installation of the new system. These customer-performed tasks include the following:

- Maintain a copy of all operational databases.
- Ensure that all database software is backed up on a regular basis.
- Develop a database recovery policy.
- Develop and implement adequate office security features to protect the integrity, confidentiality, and availability of the database.
- Appoint a database administrator. This person should support SoftHuge personnel during the installation and data migration phases of the project.

The customer accepts responsibility for installing the network, attaching the computers to the network, and maintaining the network.

EXHIBIT 5–3 (continued)

5. Relational Database
The Elcaro relational database management system will be provided by MedPrac, unless otherwise arranged. SoftHuge Industries requires Elcaro version x.y.z and SQL*NET version v.w. Elcaro will be installed as part of normal system installation.

6. Manuals and Documentation
SoftHuge Industries will supply the SoftApps user manual, 10 SoftApps System Operation training manuals, and 10 SoftApps Database Administration training manuals. Additional user or training manuals may be purchased at a cost of $150 per copy. All third-party-supplied hardware documentation will be delivered to MedPrac as it is received by SoftHuge.

   SoftHuge Industries will provide one copy of the following SoftApps documentation:Software Requirements Specification (SRS), Software Design Documentation (SDD), Software Verification and Validation Plan (SVVP), Software Verification and Validation Report (SVVR).

7. Software Customizations
The baseline effort provides a standard off-the-shelf software product. SoftHuge Industries has a staff of outstanding software engineers and technicians dedicated to developing and maintaining database products. The technical database product support staff, database trainers, and project managers are supported by knowledgeable health practice and medical insurance professionals. Consequently, SoftHuge Industries engineers can provide software customizations as an extra cost option if requested to do so by the customer.

8. Factory Acceptance Test
Specific factory acceptance tests will not be performed on this product.

9. Site Acceptance Test
A standard SoftApps site acceptance test will be used to verify SoftApps installation and performance at MedPrac's site as part of the installation process.

10. Maintenance and Support
SoftHuge Industries provides upgrades to SoftApps as part of its annual maintenance program. The first-year warranty service, included in the price, begins following the completion of the SoftHuge Industries site acceptance test. During the software maintenance and support warranty period, the customer's staff may contact the SoftHuge Industries technical staff from 8:30 A.M. to 5:00 P.M. (Eastern time) on business days. The cost for subsequent years is detailed in the price quote. SoftHuge Industries can provide a quote for 24-hour, seven-day-per-week SoftApps support service.
   The SoftApps support software service agreement includes the following services:

   • Toll-free telephone assistance during the warranty period
   • SoftApps software and documentation updates
   • Immediate notification of critical software problems

As a courtesy to SoftHuge customers purchasing the service agreement, SoftHuge Industries software engineers can provide limited assistance on third-party software associated with the SoftApps package (e.g., Windows and Elcaro). Elcaro relational database maintenance support is not part of this service agreement. If requested, SoftHuge Industries will provide a quote for a separate Elcaro database maintenance service contract. As part of this extra cost option, SoftHuge Industries engineers will perform the following work on a periodic basis:
Monitor performance
   Monitor file I/O
   Monitor tables and Indices
   Monitor space utilization
Database tuning
   Distribute table spaces among different disks, based upon usage
   Resize table and index storage parameters, based upon statistics
   Add or remove indices for faster response to complex queries
   Adjust system parameters, based on changing needs

EXHIBIT 5–3

Database maintenance
  De-fragment table spaces
  Clean up temporary (unused) space
  Archive unused data
  Back up system

11. License
SoftHuge Industries provides the license to use its software products and copies of executable files. SoftHuge Industries retains all ownership rights to the software.
   SoftHuge does not transfer either the title or the intellectual property rights to MedPrac. MedPrac may neither sell, redistribute, or reproduce the Software nor decompile, reverse engineer, disassemble, or otherwise convert the Software to any other form. SoftHuge owns all trademarks and logos, and the customer may not copy or use them in any manner.

12. SoftHuge Industries Quality Assurance Program
The SoftHuge Industries Software Quality Assurance Program requires the completion of a Software Quality Assurance Plan for each project. The plan describes the methodology SoftHuge uses to produce the software and related documentation. The plan for SoftApps includes a Software Verification and Validation Plan and a Software Verification and Validation Report.
   The Software Verification and Validation Report ensures that the software meets the requirements in the Software Requirement Specification and the design in the Software Design Description. The report also ensures compatibility between the software and the user documentation. The three quality assurance documents are placed in storage for five years.

13. Service Support
SoftHuge employs a corrective action system to accept and act on customer complaints and process-related problems. This software support program includes telephone support, software and documentation updates released during the support period, and notice of any critical software problems. Service support is included for the first year of operation following the site test. The customer may purchase support for subsequent years.

14. Training
SoftHuge Industries maintains a training department that will conduct two training courses for up to 10 students each at the customer's facility. The courses will be SSO-1234 [SoftApps System Operation] and SDA-5678 [SoftApps Database Administration].

15. Terms and Conditions
   15.1. Software Product Conditions
      SoftHuge Industries agrees to grant, and the customer agrees to accept, a nontransferable and nonexclusive license under the following terms and conditions:
      15.1.1. The customer shall have the right to use SoftApps software solely for internal purposes on designated computers.
      15.1.2. Title to, and ownership of, the SoftApps software shall remain with SoftHuge Industries.
      15.1.3. MedPrac agrees not to provide or make available the SoftApps software to any person other than MedPrac or SoftHuge Industries employees without the prior written approval of SoftHuge Industries.

In the event that MedPrac neglects or fails to perform or observe any of its obligations under this agreement, all licenses granted to MedPrac shall terminate immediately. Within two (2) weeks after any such termination, MedPrac shall return the SoftApps software and all documentation to SoftHuge Industries and shall cease using the SoftApps software.

   15.2. Cancellation or Changes
      MedPrac may cancel this order upon written notice to SoftHuge Industries and upon payment to SoftHuge Industries of the cancellation charges specified in item 15.3.

EXHIBIT 5–3   (continued)

MedPrac agrees to pay SoftHuge Industries 75% of the contract price for goods and services if the cancellation occurs 31 days or more after the order is placed.

MedPrac agrees to pay SoftHuge Industries 50% of the contract price for goods and services if the cancellation occurs 30 days or less after the order is placed. MedPrac may not cancel the order after shipment. MedPrac may not reschedule or change any order without SoftHuge Industries' prior written consent.

15.3. Price and Payment

Terms of payment are cash upon delivery as described in the attached quotation. A finance charge of $1\frac{1}{2}\%$ per month will be assessed on any amounts outstanding beyond 30-day payment terms. Prices are in U.S. currency.

15.4. Taxes

Prices are exclusive of all federal, state, or local property, license privilege, sales, use, excise, and other taxes and government charges. The customer shall be responsible for all such taxes.

15.5. Title and Risk of Loss

Title to, and risk of loss for, Domestic U.S. shipments shall pass to the customer at the customer's shipping address.

15.6. Limitation of Liability

Under no circumstances, including negligence, shall SoftHuge be liable for any special or consequential damages that result from the use of, or the inability to use, SoftApps materials. In no event shall SoftHuge's total liability from all damages, losses, and causes exceed the amount paid to SoftHuge on this contract.

The seller and its subcontractor's liability for damages arising out of or connected with the sales contract shall not exceed the purchase price of such goods and services.

15.7. Right to Use Software

Software supplied by SoftHuge Industries may be used only on the computer system specified. It shall not be made available to any other person or entity without prior approval of SoftHuge Industries.

15.8. Delays

SoftHuge Industries shall not be liable for delays in performing or failure to perform its obligations under the sales agreement resulting directly or indirectly from acts of God; customer actions; governmental priorities; fires; strikes or other labor disputes; accidents; floods; war; riot; terrorism; delays in obtaining or inability to obtain materials, components, labor, fuel, or supplies; or any other circumstances beyond SoftHuge Industries' control. In the event of any such failure or delay, the time for SoftHuge Industries' performance shall be extended by a period equal to the time lost due to such failure or delay. SoftHuge Industries shall notify the customer promptly of any material delay.

15.9. Patents

SoftHuge Industries owns all patents associated with developments made under this sales contract.

15.10. Ownership of SoftHuge Industries Data, Etc.

Any drawings, manufacturing data, documentation, or other information delivered to MedPrac by SoftHuge Industries are the property of SoftHuge Industries, may not be reproduced or copied, and shall not be used except in connection with the goods and services described in this agreement.

15.11. Warranty

15.11.1. Basic Warranty

Equipment manufactured and software developed by SoftHuge Industries is warrantied against defects in materials and workmanship for a period of 12 months

EXHIBIT 5–3

from the date of shipment, provided that the equipment or software has been used properly. Equipment and software provided by SoftHuge Industries from other manufacturers carry the warranties provided by those manufacturers.

During the warranty period, MedPrac will return the equipment to the factory for repair or replacement. The transportation cost to and from SoftHuge Industries, including insurance, will be paid by SoftHuge Industries.

15.11.2. Warranty Exclusions

Warranty service is contingent upon the proper use of all equipment and does not cover equipment that has been modified without SoftHuge Industries' written approval, or that has been subjected to unusual physical or electrical stress, as determined by SoftHuge Industries Service personnel. SoftHuge Industries shall be under no obligation to furnish warranty service (1) if adjustment, repair, or parts replacement is required because of accident, neglect, misuse, or causes other than ordinary use; (2) if the equipment is maintained or repaired by other than SoftHuge Industries personnel without the prior approval of SoftHuge Industries; or (3) if the SoftApps software has been modified or a software application has been added to SoftApps by the customer's personnel.

software does not require maintenance. A month or two after a database application is installed, customers may complain to the supplier that the package runs too slowly. Failure to maintain the system will result in poor performance. Sellers protect the organization by warning the customer that the system requires maintenance. Such notification minimizes misunderstandings and informs the customer that it should budget funds for this effort in the future.

In one old joke, an insect asks, "How do you eat an elephant?" A second insect replies, "One bite at a time"—a gruesome story perhaps, but it serves to make the point that completing a huge project requires dividing the job into a large number of bite-sized pieces to which adequate resources are applied. Viewing a

TABLE 5–1

Work-Breakdown Structure Hierarchy

WBS No.	Project Task	WBS Level
1.	Project	1
1.1.	Task #1	2
1.1.1.	Subtask	3
1.1.1.1.	Work Package	4
1.2.	Task #2	2
1.2.1.	Subtask	3
1.2.1.1.	Work Package	4

job as an entire entity seems overwhelming; what is needed is a process that breaks the project into manageable steps. The WBS accomplishes this task. Although frequently not explicitly identified, a WBS is an integral part of the SOW. The WBS consists of a grouping of tasks that organizes and defines the total scope of the project. The WBS is prepared in outline form, so that each descending level represents an increasingly detailed definition of the project (Table 5–1). The lowest level or highest number of the WBS defines a work package—an assignment performed by a team member. The tasks may involve labor, or purchases of products or services. The WBS becomes the basis for the performance schedule.

Sometimes a buyer provides a contractual work-breakdown structure (CWBS), which generally includes less detail than the WBS used by the seller to manage the project. The customer uses the CWBS to define the level of reporting that it wants the seller to provide.

Think about a WBS as a list all of the tasks required to complete a job. In a similar vein, an organizer planning a wedding would begin by listing the activities associated with the bride, groom, bride's parents, groom's parents, catering hall, caterer, musicians, invitations, and church, synagogue, or mosque facilities. To obtain specific information about each activity, the organizer would request information from the leaders of the various activities—details of the menu from the caterer; songs and dances from the musicians; requirements for chairs, tables, linen, cutlery, and glassware from the catering hall, etc. By involving the people who will take responsibility for the tasks, the organizer obtains a detailed list of activities that must be completed to conduct a wedding successfully.

The project manager performs the same effort for a project as the wedding organizer does for a wedding. First, the project manager outlines all the known activities of the project. The project manager might base this list on experience or on historical records of other, similar projects. To obtain further details, the project manager goes to the functional managers, who thoroughly understand the specialized activities, and requests that they identify their tasks. The project manager adds the inputs from the functional managers to the previously created outline.

The completed WBS represents the basis for assigning tasks and devising a schedule. A typical WBS used for an electromechanical or light construction development project is shown in Exhibit 5–4. The final price represents a

EXHIBIT 5–4

Sample Work Breakdown Structure (WBS)

Project Widget

Project Number: 1175

WBS No.   Tasks or Work Packages

1. System
    1.1.   Define the system performance requirements
        1.1.1.   Distribute specification
        1.1.2.   Distribute statement of work
    1.2.   System architecture definition
        1.2.1.   Major Trade-off Studies: Review of alternative approaches
    1.3.   Define major electrical/mechanical assemblies
    1.4.   Cable definition
    1.5.   Unique algorithm development
    1.6.   Define software/firmware functions and architecture
    1.7.   Technical analyses
2. Design assembly #1
    2.1.   Hardware
        2.1.1.   Define hardware/software interfaces
        2.1.2.   Electrical/electronic design
            2.1.2.1. Define subassemblies/modules/functions
            2.1.2.2. Module/function specification
            2.1.2.3. Make/buy/subcontract trade studies
            2.1.2.4. Design
                2.1.2.4.1. Electrical schematic or wiring drawing
                2.1.2.4.2. Harness and connector definition
            2.1.2.5. Fabricate subassemblies
            2.1.2.6. Assemble units
            2.1.2.7. Software integration
            2.1.2.8. Calibrate and test
        2.1.3.   Mechanical
            2.1.3.1. Define assemblies/subassemblies
            2.1.3.2. Assembly/subassembly specifications
            2.1.3.3. Make/buy/subcontract trade studies
            2.1.3.4. Design
            2.1.3.5. Fabricate components and subassemblies
            2.1.3.6. Assemble subassemblies
            2.1.3.7. Integrate components and subassemblies
    2.2.   Software
        2.2.1.   Define hardware/software interfaces
        2.2.2.   Define software modules in a software quality assurance plan (SQAP)
        2.2.3.   Prepare a software requirements specification (SRS)
        2.2.4.   Make/buy/subcontract trade-off studies
        2.2.5.   Prepare a software design document (SDD)
        2.2.6.   Integrate software with hardware
        2.2.7.   Prepare software verification and validation plan (SVVP)
        2.2.8.   Perform verification and validation tests and prepare a report
        2.2.9.   Provide source code to software library and distribute software
3. Design assembly #2: WBS tasks for subsequent assemblies
4. Project Management
    4.1.   Interdepartmental coordination

EXHIBIT 5–4   (continued)

4.2. Work authorization preparation
4.3. Cost management
4.4. Technical management
    4.4.1. Establish specifications
    4.4.2. Engineering task definition and partitioning
    4.4.3. Parts coordination
    4.4.4. Internal specification review
    4.4.5. Engineering document release
    4.4.6. Engineering support to production
    4.4.7. Assembly fabrication and rework
    4.4.8. Coordinate resolution of vendor problems
4.5. Schedule management
4.6. Material procurement
4.7. Prepare and coordinate subcontracts
4.8. Internal hardware/software design reviews
4.9. Customer reviews and technical interchange meetings
    4.9.1. System requirements review (SRR)
    4.9.2. Preliminary design review (PDR)
    4.9.3. Critical design review (CDR)
    4.9.4. Interim technical interchange meetings (TIMs)
4.10. International, federal, state, and local code issues

5. Engineering equipment
  5.1. Identify equipment needed for system design or testing (e.g., CAE or CAD software, test equipment, other application software, software platform)
  5.2. Equipment acquisition plan (buy, borrow, lease, in-house)

6. Support equipment
  6.1. Identify equipment needed to support/maintain system in field
  6.2. Equipment acquisition plan for fielded system.

7. Site construction
  7.1. Plan development
    7.1.1. Architect's plans
  7.2. Identify zoning issues
    7.2.1. Obtain permits
  7.3. Prepare bidfor subcontractors
  7.4. Bid process to select construction subcontractors
  7.5. Construction
    7.5.1. Roads
    7.5.2. Earthmoving
    7.5.3. Facility
        7.5.3.1. Foundation and structure
        7.5.3.2. Electrical
        7.5.3.3. Plumbing
        7.5.3.4. Heating, ventilation, and air-conditioning (HVAC)
    7.5.4. Beautification: trees, shrubs, lawns

8. System integration and testing
  8.1. Prepare factory acceptance test
  8.2. Prepare site acceptance test
  8.3. Collect and assemble component items
  8.4. Interconnect all assemblies
  8.5. Install special hardware
  8.6. Perform software–hardware integration
  8.7. Verify quality assurance documentation
  8.8. Calibrate system

EXHIBIT 5–4

8.9.   Perform temperature tests
8.10.   Perform shock and vibration tests
8.11.   Perform reliability tests
8.12.   Perform factory acceptance test
8.13.   Crate and ship deliverables and support equipment
9. Site Installation and Testing
9.1.   Special site training [e.g., hazardous material (HAZMAT)]
9.2.   Confirm resolution of labor issues
9.3.   Unpack system
9.4.   Interconnect all assemblies
9.5.   Calibrate system
9.6.   Perform site acceptance test
10. Data
10.1.   Technical publications
10.2.   User's manual
10.3.   Training manual
10.4.   Engineering data
10.5.   Electrical schematics
10.6.   Printed circuit board artwork drawings
10.7.   Mechanical assembly drawings
10.8.   Software requirements specification
10.9.   Software design document
10.10. Software verification and validation plan/report
10.11. Software source code
10.12. Environmental test reports
10.13. Factory acceptance test report
10.14. Site acceptance test report
10.15. Management data
10.16. Labor hours data
10.17. Material cost data
10.18. Schedule
10.19. Engineering analyses and support data
10.20. Quality plan/report
10.21. Reliability plan/report
10.22. Maintainability plan/report
10.23. Failure mode and effects analysis
10.24. User guide
10.25. Training manual
10.26. Repair manual
10.27. Data/software repository
11. Operational and site activation
11.1.   Site construction/conversion
11.2.   Vehicle purchase and conversion
11.3.   Site equipment rental/purchase
12. Services and training
12.1.   Software/hardware field installation
12.2.   Warranty
12.3.   Hardware
12.4.   Software
12.5.   Maintenance
12.6.   Training
        12.6.1. Identify and obtain required training equipment
        12.6.2. Make/buy training decision

EXHIBIT 5–4   (continued)

12.6.3. Design and develop training material in-house
12.6.4. Subcontract training material
12.6.5. Conduct training
13. Industrial facilities
13.1. Factory construction/conversion/expansion
13.2. Manufacturing equipment acquisition/modernization
13.3. Factory maintenance
14. Spares and repair parts

summation of the costs for each task listed in the WBS. The project manager creates a schedule by assigning a time span for each task listed in the WBS, following consultation with the functional managers. Usually, the project manager assigns responsibility for each task assignment and deliverable item to a person or a department as part of the schedule. (Chapter 6 focuses on preparing a schedule.) The WBS facilitates tracking of the project's activities by permitting the project manager to track the time, cost, and performance of each task in the plan.

The WBS is a planning tool that enables the project manager to gain the commitment of various personnel to the project. Each task has a name or department associated with it, thus clarifying stakeholder responsibilities and minimizing the likelihood of omitting deliverable items. Including a task in the WBS permits that task to be tracked and ensures that it will have some level of visibility.

A well-written SOW minimizes interpretation on the part of stakeholders. Imprecise language such as "nearly," "approximately," and "almost" should be avoided. Expectations should be quantified and alternatives and consequences stated clearly. The customer should review and approve all specifications, documentation, schematics, tests, etc. Requiring a limited number of customer review and approval cycles prevents the customer from employing delaying tactics. Wherever questions may arise, responsibilities should be delineated.

The conclusion of the SOW specifies the seller's terms and conditions. Section 15 of Exhibit 5–3 lists typical terms and conditions. Paragraphs in this section set forth the seller's standard business policies regarding hardware and software warranties, return policy, and liability limitations in the event that things do not go as planned. Suppose, for example, that the software package is not installed as smoothly as predicted. Perhaps a development problem or a supplier labor issue caused a 30-day delay before the project was completed. The consequences of the late installation to the buyer can result in a significant loss due to missed business opportunities. If, for instance, the buyer was a nuclear power plant whose revenues exceeded $1 million per day and the seller failed to deliver a software or hardware product essential to the timely operation of the plant, the plant would stand to lose a significant sum of money, possibly resulting in a demand for damages to be paid by the seller. Usually, a clause in the terms and conditions set out in the SOW limits the seller's liability to the purchase price of the system.

Other clauses of the terms and conditions define ownership of the product, documentation, and patent rights. Many people are unaware that purchasing software only gives them a license to *use* it; the purchaser does not own the software and cannot make copies for sale. Frequently, the license only gives the purchaser permission to install the software on a single computer. Information to that effect lies within the terms and conditions of the SOW. Most often, the seller's organization has a "boilerplate," or standard, set of terms and conditions, and the project manager need only insert them at the end of the proposal.

Department Tasks and Budgets.   Many internal departments and external suppliers contribute to performing the tasks listed in the WBS. After consulting with functional managers, the project manager assigns a budget in labor hours or dollars to each department performing work on a task. Each employee recognizes that he or she has a limited time to complete an assigned task and that the task's progress will be monitored. Toward that end, every person that works on a task records the time he or she spends working on that task. The employee enters the amount of time worked on a time card, which a time-recording system ultimately places into a computer database. A typical time card may look like Figure 5–2. Each project and each task within the project have assigned numbers. Administrators assign numbers to identify projects because numbers are shorter and less confusing than names. All employees insert the numbers of the project and task on which they worked during the week. On a daily basis, they enter the number of hours worked on the task.

At the end of the week, the project manager examines the collective number of hours worked on each task associated with the project. This bookkeeping procedure represents the basis for fiscal control. If people assigned to a specific project task do not work on it, then the project manager must find out why. If people charge time to the job, but have not accomplished the expected work, the project manager again must find out why. Are employees mischarging their time, or is the task more difficult than anticipated? Certainly, if the customer is charged for each hour worked on the job, the organization has a responsibility to make certain that the billing statement is accurate.

Project planning is essential. The first two elements of the plan—the specification and the SOW—serve as the basis for a proposal submitted to the customer. The third element—the task budgets—provides the basis for the price stated in the proposal. After a customer awards a contract to an organization, these three elements of the plan become the basis for assigning resources to the project, monitoring its progress, and controlling spending on it.

The project manager's job is to deliver a product or service requested by a customer on time, within budget, and in a technically satisfactory manner. Only a well-thought-out plan enables the project manager to execute Fayol's other management responsibilities: organizing, commanding, coordinating, and controlling.

FIGURE 5–2

Typical employee time card

Blank Card

Employee name: _____   Employee ID No.: _____
Department No.: _____   Week ending date: _____

Project No.						Total
Task No.						Hours
Sunday						
Monday						
Tuesday						
Wednesday						
Thursday						
Friday						
Saturday						
Total						
Overtime Hours						

Completed Card

Employee name: John Sanchez   Employee ID No.: 451880
Department No.: 814   Week ending date: October 2

Project No.	3705	7829	3712			Total
Task No.	12	43	2			Hours
Sunday						
Monday	4	2	2			8
Tuesday			8			8
Wednesday	3	4.5	.5			8
Thursday	2	5	1			8
Friday	1	6	1			8
Saturday						
Total Hours	10	17.5	12.5			40
Overtime Hours						

REVIEW QUESTIONS

1. Define organizational planning.
2. Define scope management.
3. What are the essentials of a project plan?
4. Why is project planning so important?

5. Why is managing the scope of a project important?
6. What is the difference between an RFP and an RFQ? Which is easier to assemble and why?
7. Why does a customer distribute an RFP?
8. What should a response to an RFP contain?
9. Describe the circumstances under which an organization decides to respond to an RFP or RFQ.
10. Explain why it is necessary to involve many departments and functional managers in the preparation of a labor estimate and a schedule.
11. Describe the use of a project charter.
12. What should a project charter contain?
13. The ABC organization has received a contract from the XYZ organization to develop a widfram. Must the project manager develop a project charter? Explain your answer.
14. A technical person at the Zeta Corporation has an idea for an improvement to a product manufactured by the organization. She would like to prepare a prototype unit. Describe the information that she should present to the vice president to seek approval for funding for the project.
15. What is a milestone?
16. List five benefits of a project plan.
17. Identify the three documents required for a project plan.
18. What is the fundamental purpose of an SOW?
19. Identify 10 items included in an SOW, and describe their importance.
20. Identify the paragraphs that describe the customer's responsibilities in the sample SOW of Exhibit 5–3.
21. Describe the document that a project manager must have before preparing a schedule for a project.
22. Professionals frequently complete a time card describing their daily activities. Why is that important?
23. Describe the importance of a work-breakdown structure.
24. Prepare a list of tasks required to make a breakfast for six people. Breakfast consists of hot oatmeal, eggs, bread, fresh orange juice, a fruit cup, coffee, and cake. It must be served within two weeks. Identify the tasks that can be completed together. Organize the list into a work-breakdown structure, and assign personnel to each task. Estimate the time required to complete each task, and sketch a schedule for preparing the breakfast.
25. Describe the contents of a project specification.
26. Discuss the value of a project specification.
27. What environmental characteristics may be considered in a product or system specification?

(*Note*: In this chapter, Widget, widfram, and Zeta are fictitious products and companies created for illustrative purposes.)

CHAPTER 6

PROJECT TIME MANAGEMENT

Out of clutter, find simplicity
From discord, find harmony
In the middle of difficulty lies opportunity.
Albert Einstein, Three Rules of Work

OBJECTIVES

After studying this chapter, you should be able to

- Understand the relationship between the project schedule and the work-breakdown structure
- Understand the need for a project schedule
- Read and interpret a project schedule
- Analyze a project schedule to determine task priorities
- Identify and find the critical path of a project
- Prepare a project schedule

INTRODUCTION

Project time management includes the processes required to ensure timely completion of a project.[1] The schedule is the fundamental tool used by a project manager to plan and then control activities. At a minimum, it consists of the following:

1. a list of tasks required to complete the project
2. the time required to complete each task
3. the dependencies among tasks

Frequently, the schedule includes the departments and personnel responsible for the completion of each task. Sometimes, the project manager creates a responsibility assignment matrix (RAM) that lists the people or the department responsible for each element in the work-breakdown structure (WBS). These tools represent ways of communicating information about the project with the project team members.

The time management process begins with the creation of the WBS. (See Chapter 5.) The project manager and the functional managers identify the specific activities needed to produce and deliver the project deliverables. The project team determines the duration of each activity defined and the temporal relationships among all the project's activities. To accomplish this with the highest confidence in its accuracy, the project manager requests assistance from the functional managers, who estimate the length of time required for each task and recommend the appropriate temporal relationship. That is, the functional

---

[1] Project Management Institute Standards Committee, *A Guide to the Project Management Body of Knowledge* (Upper Darby, PA: Project Management Institute, 1996).

managers identify the task or tasks that should precede or follow any given task. The project team uses its collective expertise to estimate the duration of each activity. Some organizations keep a history of past project experiences to aid them in estimating.

Requesting assistance from the functional managers and using their recommendations promotes harmony and encourages ownership of the project among the stakeholders. If the project manager assigns durations to the tasks without consulting the functional managers, their response will be "Well, you assigned the dates, so you meet them!" Therefore, it is imperative that discussions take place, issues be raised, and disagreements be voiced and resolved before the project begins. The result will be a schedule with which stakeholders can live.

The schedule establishes a basis for communication among stakeholders. It provides the "big picture" for all participants to view and promotes an understanding of the relationships among the project's activities. The schedule permits the project's critical path to be determined. The *critical path* represents those activities that together will take the shortest time for the project to be completed. Extending the length of time for any of the activities on the critical path increases the overall duration of the project. Knowing which tasks lie on the critical path enables project managers to establish task priorities. Stakeholders understand the need to assign resources (money, labor, facilities, tools, and equipment) to activities that are on the critical path. Employees can anticipate that both project and functional managers will pay close attention to personnel working on tasks that are on the critical path. If problems arise, they want to know about them so that they can resolve the problems using the appropriate resources. Understanding the schedule clarifies and highlights the short-term objectives of the project. When the schedule is understood, so will the project's needs be.

RUDIMENTS OF DEVELOPING A SCHEDULE

Developing a schedule involves defining the activities to be accomplished, assigning responsibility for completing activities to stakeholders, identifying sequences of activities, establishing dependencies among activities by identifying successor and predecessor tasks, and designating the durations of the various activities. Managers may use a Gantt or bar chart that lists all tasks on the left. A horizontal bar is associated with each task and illustrates its duration. An example of a Gantt chart prepared with Microsoft Project is shown in Figure 6–1.

Figure 6–2 illustrates a schedule consisting solely of milestones, again prepared with Microsoft Project. Each diamond signifies a milestone. The milestone chart affords an overview of the entire project and lists only the expected beginning or ending dates of significant activities. The solid rectangular line in the figure indicates the duration of all of the activities falling under it.

Traditional Gantt charts use a horizontal rectangle to denote the duration of a task. The length of the rectangle indicates the length of time the task takes;

FIGURE 6–1

Gantt chart

Gantt Chart Wizard
icon

Gantt Chart
option

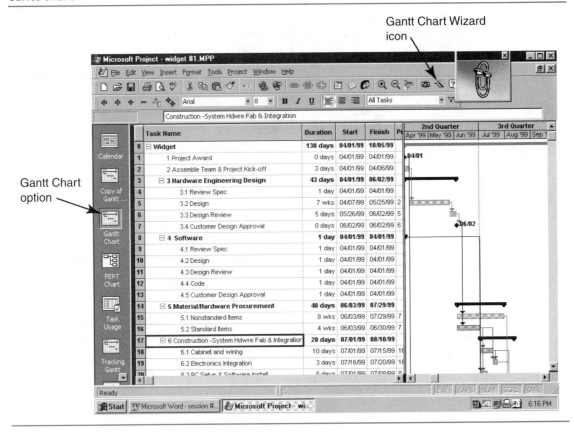

however, the user must observe the units on the time scale to assess the actual time. The horizontal axis in the figure denotes time, separated into quarters or three-month intervals. The user has the ability to make these intervals finer or coarser to suit his or her needs.

A rectangle partially filled with a solid bar illustrates that work has begun on the associated task. If the bar extends across the entire task, then work on the activity is complete.

Usually, the start of a task depends on the completion of a previous activity. This common finish-to-start relationship appears as follows:

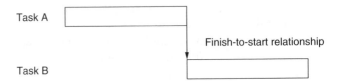

Task A

Finish-to-start relationship

Task B

FIGURE 6–2

Schedule of milestones

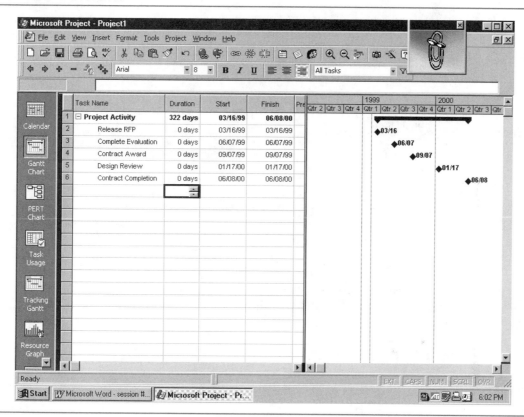

The arrow extending from Task A to Task B signifies that Task B begins after Task A finishes. The arrow identifies the dependency of Task B on Task A. Note that Task B need not follow *immediately* after the conclusion of Task A. The Gantt chart concept permits a delay before the next task begins as the following diagram shows:

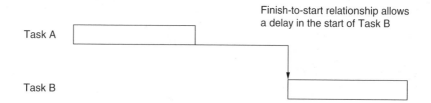

As an example of a finish-to-start relationship, when baking bread, the baker must mix the ingredients before kneading the dough. As another example, the baker places the dough in the oven only after the dough has risen. To ensure a successful product, the baker cannot deviate from the sequence of tasks. The following schedule illustrates the bread-baking sequence:

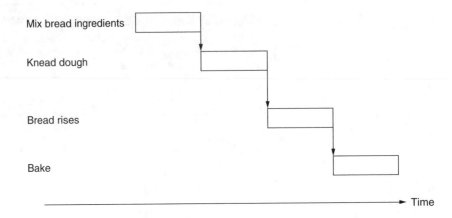

Note that all of the relationships follow a finish-to-start sequence and time always appears on the schedule's horizontal axis. For a project of very short duration, the user can adjust the time axis to read hours or even minutes.

Other relationships also exist between tasks, such as a start-to-start relationship. In the following diagram, Task D begins only if Task C begins:

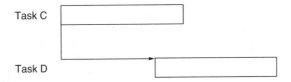

An example of a start-to-start operation involves laying tar on the surface of a road. Workers place asphalt on the road and then distribute it evenly in an interactive manner. Smoothing the asphalt and tar begins immediately following the placement of the material on the road and continues concurrently until the task is completed.

The finish-to-finish relationship demands that linked tasks finish together, as do Tasks E and F in the following diagram:

Finish-to-finish tasks frequently involve inspections or testing. For instance, the task of electrical wiring in the fabrication of a new house cannot be considered complete until the town or city inspects it. Only then can the contractor feel confident about releasing the electricians from their obligations. An example in the software development industry involves programming. Writing code and preparing documentation are two out of many processes in a large software project. The successful execution of the software verification and validation plan enables quality assurance personnel to confirm that the software operates correctly. Only at that point will the software design manager acknowledge that the software design process is completed.

Some tasks have no predecessors and can proceed at the same time (i.e., in parallel) with other tasks. These activities begin at the discretion of the project planner. Linking tasks enables the planner to shift the schedule easily if the team decides to insert an additional task into the plan. Schedule planners regard some task dependencies as mandatory, because the processes that they describe force the relationship. Project teams use their experience and judgment to establish task linkages.

CREATING A SCHEDULE

The remainder of this chapter requires the reader to use Microsoft Project. The nontechnical example that follows illustrates how schedules are developed with the use of that software. Suppose a local charity decides to conduct a fund-raising event that will feature a motivational speaker. The charity seeks to use neighborhood facilities and wishes to hold the event in four months. Committees will decide the food service and the price of tickets.

An executive committee of the charity meets to identify the tasks required to conduct the event. The members engage in a brainstorming session and create lists of tasks in a random fashion. Afterward, they organize the activities into logical groupings. Next, the committee selects a person who agrees to take responsibility for leading the effort and designates that person the project manager. The project manager then integrates the lists of activities and resolves the organization's competing needs for common resources into a viable plan. The project manager presents the draft schedule and submits it to organization members (functional managers, committee members, and other stakeholders) for comments and corrections. After incorporating the stakeholders' responses, the project manager presents a baseline operational schedule to the team.

The baseline WBS shown in Exhibit 6–1 was prepared by the project manager. The WBS also includes the stakeholders' estimate of the labor hours required for the project. Note that 0d in Microsoft Project designates a milestone. Higher level tasks consisting of lower level tasks do not have associated labor hours. Microsoft Project will automatically compute the time required for the higher level tasks from the entries associated with lower level tasks. For example, WBS numbers 8.4.1, 8.4.2, and 8.4.3 determine the hours in 8.4. The next section gives directions for entering the data into Microsoft Project.

EXHIBIT 6–1

Work-Breakdown Structure (WBS) for a Charity Organization's Speaking Event

Line no.	WBS no.	Task name or description	Labor hours	Predecessor line
1	1.	Executive group agrees to hold charity speaking event	0d	
2	2.	Executive group organizes committees and prepares draft schedule	60h	1
3	3.	Activity and committee budgets		
4	3.1.	Prepare budgets	10h	2
5	3.2.	Budget acceptable—go/no-go decision	0d	4
6	3.3.	Distribute budgets to committees	24h	5
7	4.	Agree on event date: 12/4/04	0d	6
8	5.	Site selection committee		
9	5.1.	Contact neighborhood fraternal association hall for availability	40h	7
10	5.2.	Confirm date of event	8h	9
11	5.3.	Site status decision	0d	9, 10
12	6.	Speaker selection committee		
13	6.1.	Evaluate potential speakers	80h	6
14	6.2.	Select speaker	24h	13
15	6.3.	Make offer to speaker	24h	14, 16
16	6.4.	Confirm availability of speaker	8h	14
17	6.5.	Decision on speaker	7d	15
18	7.	Critical review meeting		
19	7.1.	Organizational meeting		
20	7.1.1.	Status: budget, event date, site, speaker agreement, committees in place	8h	6, 11, 17
21	7.1.2.	Final go/no-go decision	0d	20
22	8.	Publicity committee		
23	8.1.	Prepare information flyer	40h	6, 21
24	8.2.	Mail flyer to organization members	24h	23
25	8.3.	Distribute flyer to community stores	40h	23
26	8.4.	Advertise event		
27	8.4.1.	Prepare advertisements	80h	6, 21
28	8.4.2.	Place ad in newspaper	8h	27
29	8.4.3.	Place ad on radio and TV	8h	27
30	9.	Ticket committee		
31	9.1.	Print tickets to event	80h	6, 21
32	9.2.	Distribute tickets	160h	31
33	10.	Food and refreshment committee		
34	10.1.	Decide on food and refreshments	2h	21, 6
35	10.2.	Purchases		
36	10.2.1.	Food	3h	34, 44SS-3d
37	10.2.2.	Wine and liquor	1d	34, 44SS-3d
38	10.2.3.	Refreshments		
39	10.2.3.1.	Snacks, cake, soda, coffee, tea	1.5h	34, 44SS-3d
40	10.2.4.	Supplies		
41	10.2.4.1.	Paper plates, cups, napkins, and utensils	0.5h	34, 44SS-3d
42	10.2.4.2.	Trash bags	0.5h	34, 44SS-3d

Line no.	WBS no.	Task name or description	Labor hours	Predecessor line
43	11.	Event-day activities		
44	11.1.	Day of event kickoff status meeting	30m	30, 22, 21
45	11.2.	Day of event preparations: set up committees		
46	11.2.1.	Set up tables	45m	44
47	11.2.2.	Set up chairs	45m	46
48	11.2.3.	Set up table place settings	1h	47
49	11.2.4.	Set up cocktail hour area	1h	44
50	11.2.5.	Audio system		
51	11.2.5.1.	Install	2h	44
52	11.2.5.2.	Test	30m	51
53	11.3.	Food and refreshment committee		
54	11.3.1.	Obtain pots, pans, and serving dishes	30m	44
55	11.3.2.	Prepare and cook food	4h	54
56	11.3.3.	Set up food and refreshment tables	3h	44
57	11.3.4.	Distribute food and refreshments	3h	55, 56
58	12.	Event activities		
59	12.1.	Ticket collection	3h	44
60	12.2.	Cocktail hour	1h	49
61	12.3.	Speaker meets reception committee	0.5h	60
62	12.4.	Introduction of speaker to audience	0.2h	61
63	12.5.	Speaker's talk	1h	62
64	12.6.	Thank speaker	0.1h	63
65	13.	Clean up committee		
66	13.1.	Obtain trash bags	0.2h	64
67	13.2.	Clean hall	2h	66
68	13.3.	Teams collapse and rest	1h	67

Microsoft Project

Load Microsoft Project on your computer, and select the Gantt chart option. (See Figure 6–1.) The Gantt chart icon appears in the column on the left side of the screen. Click on Project—Project Information, and enter the project start date, August 1, 2004. Select the schedule from: Project Start Date. This last statement references all activities to the project's starting date.

Task Entry

Enter each activity listed in Exhibit 6–1 under the column called Task Name. For the moment, disregard the WBS number. Do not skip lines between tasks. Figure 6–3 illustrates the entry of some of the activities into column Task Name. If you need to insert or delete lines, use the INS key and the DEL key, respectively. Save your data every 10 minutes to avoid losing information. Use the save without a baseline option. Call the file Charity Event.

FIGURE 6–3

Data entry in column task name of project

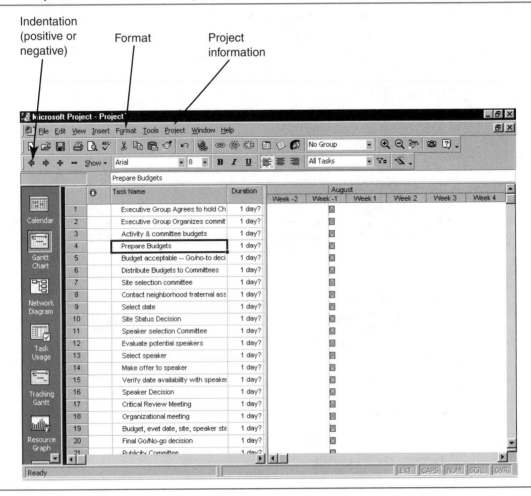

Working Time

Microsoft Project defaults to an eight-hour workday (8:00 A.M. to 12:00 noon and 1:00 P.M. to 5:00 P.M.). Other than defining Saturday and Sunday as nonworking days, the program makes no assumptions regarding weekdays. To modify nonworking days (e.g., to accommodate vacations, holidays, organization events, or a six- or seven-day workweek) or the number of hours in a working day, click on Tools—Change Working Time, and make changes as required. Use the pop-up window buttons or type the correct working time. Press OK to save your preferences.

The project organization's schedule planner controls the horizontal length of the chart by choosing to view the chart in days, weeks, months, or quarters. Microsoft Project offers a variety of options that enables the planner to use two

FIGURE 6–4

Microsoft project timescale selection

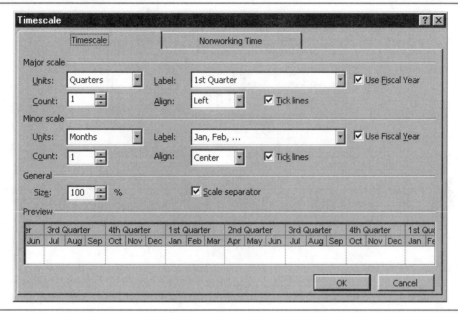

timescales simultaneously (Major and Minor Scale) and to choose the scales' units. Simply select Format—timescale. For this exercise, make the selections shown in Figure 6–4.

WBS Number

Designate a column to the left of the task name for the WBS number. To do this, highlight the task column by clicking once on the word "Task Name." Select Insert—column. Under the Column Definition window (Figure 6–5), use the drop-down menu listed under Field name, and select WBS. Click OK.

After entering the entire list of project activities and inserting the column for the WBS number, assign a WBS level number to the tasks in Exhibit 6–1. As an example, highlight the task *Prepare Budgets* on line 4. Move the cursor and click on the right arrow indent shown in Figure 6–6. The task entitled Prepare Budgets moves to the right, and the WBS number on line 4 changes to 3.1. Repeat the process for all second-through-fifth-level tasks shown in Exhibit 6–1. A level-3 task, such as 6.1.2, requires two clicks on the right arrow. If you inadvertently click too many times, use the left arrow to reduce the WBS level.

Task Duration

Duration on the Microsoft Project Gantt chart denotes the number of labor hours required to complete an activity. A job that takes one person six hours to complete will take two people three hours to complete. A word of caution is in

FIGURE 6–5

Creation of WBS column using the drop-down menu

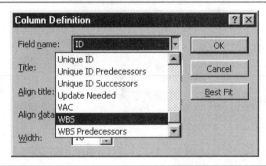

order, however: In its default mode, Microsoft Project halves the time it takes one person to complete a task if two people are assigned to the task. Life, however, does not always work in that linear fashion: Although, frequently, placing additional people on a job will save time, the relationship will not be inverse-

FIGURE 6–6

Task names with completed WBS column entry

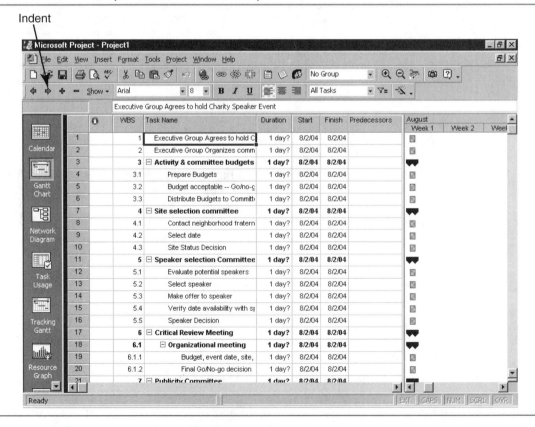

ly proportional. Indeed, in one situation, no time at all is saved: A woman requires nine months to deliver a baby, but placing two women "on the job" will not reduce the time one iota.

The standard Microsoft Project day lasts eight hours. Consequently, unless the user changes the day's length, the application automatically distributes a task requiring more than eight hours over multiple days (after taking into consideration the applied resources). Exhibit 6–1 offers recommendations for the duration of the charity event activities. Enter duration data only for the nonboldface tasks; as previously stated, Microsoft Project automatically calculates durations for tasks in bold print. Planners refer to these bold-print tasks as *rollup activities*; they correspond to summations of the lower level WBS elements that make up the higher level task.

As you enter the durations, use the abbreviations w, d, h, and m, standing for weeks, days, hours, and minutes, respectively. (Thus, 1w stands for 1 week, 3d denotes 3 days, 2h designates 2 hours, and 20 m signifies 20 minutes.) Durations may be changed if desired. Do not enter any dates in the start or finish columns. Figure 6–7 illustrates the entry of duration data into the Gantt chart.

FIGURE 6–7

Task duration data entered into the Gantt chart

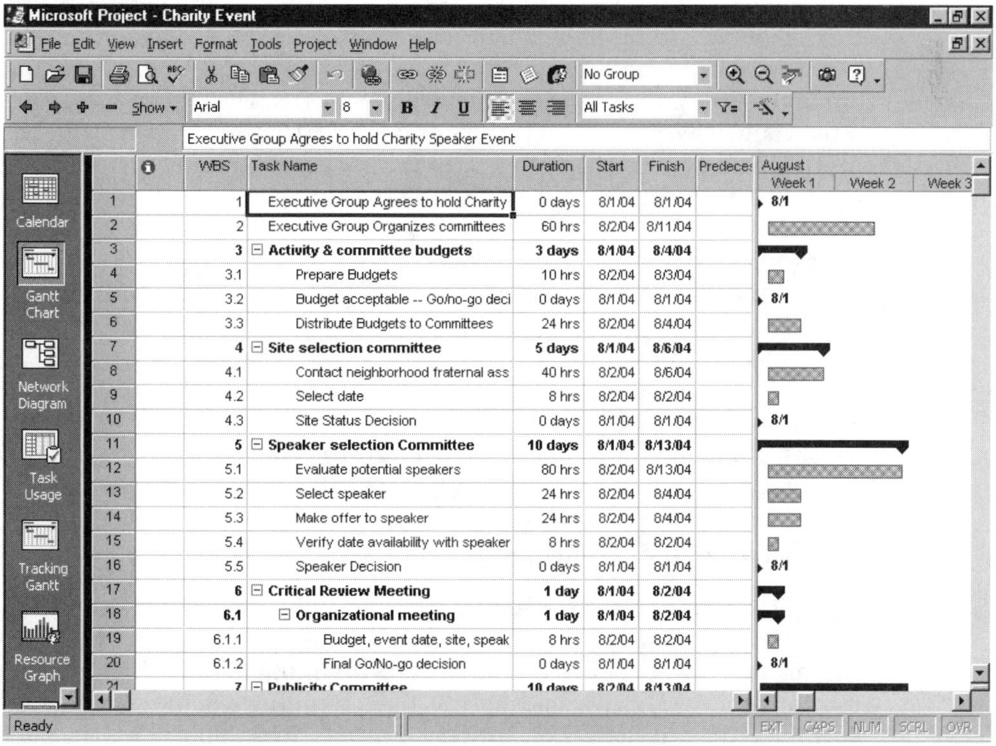

	WBS	Task Name	Duration	Start	Finish
1	1	Executive Group Agrees to hold Charity	0 days	8/1/04	8/1/04
2	2	Executive Group Organizes committees	60 hrs	8/2/04	8/11/04
3	**3**	**Activity & committee budgets**	**3 days**	**8/1/04**	**8/4/04**
4	3.1	Prepare Budgets	10 hrs	8/2/04	8/3/04
5	3.2	Budget acceptable -- Go/no-go deci	0 days	8/1/04	8/1/04
6	3.3	Distribute Budgets to Committees	24 hrs	8/2/04	8/4/04
7	**4**	**Site selection committee**	**5 days**	**8/1/04**	**8/6/04**
8	4.1	Contact neighborhood fraternal ass	40 hrs	8/2/04	8/6/04
9	4.2	Select date	8 hrs	8/2/04	8/2/04
10	4.3	Site Status Decision	0 days	8/1/04	8/1/04
11	**5**	**Speaker selection Committee**	**10 days**	**8/1/04**	**8/13/04**
12	5.1	Evaluate potential speakers	80 hrs	8/2/04	8/13/04
13	5.2	Select speaker	24 hrs	8/2/04	8/4/04
14	5.3	Make offer to speaker	24 hrs	8/2/04	8/4/04
15	5.4	Verify date availability with speaker	8 hrs	8/2/04	8/2/04
16	5.5	Speaker Decision	0 days	8/1/04	8/1/04
17	**6**	**Critical Review Meeting**	**1 day**	**8/1/04**	**8/2/04**
18	**6.1**	**Organizational meeting**	**1 day**	**8/1/04**	**8/2/04**
19	6.1.1	Budget, event date, site, speak	8 hrs	8/2/04	8/2/04
20	6.1.2	Final Go/No-go decision	0 days	8/1/04	8/1/04
21	**7**	**Publicity Committee**	**10 days**	**8/2/04**	**8/13/04**

Task Dependencies

The next step in the development of a schedule involves establishing task dependencies. The planner must identify the tasks that precede or follow other activities. As in estimating labor time, this step depends on the planner's opinions, perceptions, and preferences. The Microsoft Project Gantt chart includes a Predecessor column, which the planner completes.

The predecessor column in Exhibit 6–1 identifies tasks that precede a given line. As an example, WBS no. 8.1 on line 23 (Prepare information flyer) can begin only following the completion of the tasks on lines 6 and 21. If, during the actual project, either of those activities incurs a delay, then WBS 8.1 will not begin on time. It must await the completion of the tasks *distribute budgets to committees* and *final go/no-go decision*. The project manager then must inquire into the nature of the delay and decide how to get the job back on schedule. As the planner inserts the predecessor line numbers into the schedule, a light line drops from the predecessor task to the successor task. Figure 6–8 illustrates the insertion of the predecessor tasks into the Charity Event schedule.

Most of the dependency information you enter into the chart should be relatively straightforward. Creating a schedule that makes extensive use of dependencies permits an easily modifiable chart. For example, suppose the planner desires to insert a particular task. If he or she has previously linked all the tasks, then they automatically shift to accommodate the added task and the changed dependencies.

Sometimes the plan includes a firm date, such as the date of the charity event in our example. The executive committee scheduled December 4 for the gala event. We cannot change this date: It's "cast in concrete." Consequently, during the preparation of the schedule, we inserted December 4 as a hard date in the Gantt chart for line 44 (WBS number 11.1). The Microsoft Project indicator column [the column headed by the encircled (i) in the figure] signifies a schedule constraint on line 44 of Exhibit 6–1.

The Food and Refreshment Committee decided to purchase the food for the event three days before the actual day of the event. The predecessor constraint includes the type of food decision (line 34, WBS number 10.1) and the day of the event minus 3. That is, the food purchases precede or lead the event day, as determined by line 44, by three days. SS-3 means that the food purchases start three days before the start of the event-day activities. Therefore, the purchases on line numbers 36, 37, 39, 41, and 42 read 34, 44SS-3.

There may be times for which a successor task must *lag* the predecessor task by three days. To delay a successor task, the entry would read 44SS+3.

Responsibility Assignment Matrix (RAM)

Frequently, project planners prepare a responsibility assignment matrix (RAM), as shown in Exhibit 6–2. This is an ideal tool for assigning people to tasks and making them aware of due dates. The creator of the matrix distributes it to all team members. This avoids any misunderstandings. Some planners use the schedule to record the various responsibilities. To do this, place the cursor on

FIGURE 6–8

Charity event schedule includes predecessor information

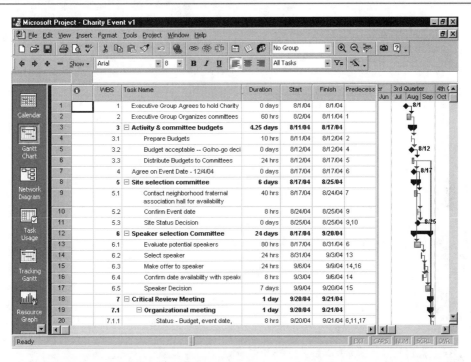

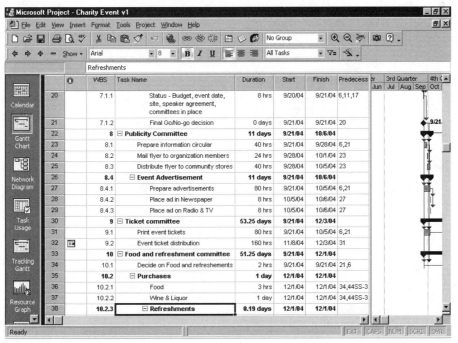

FIGURE 6–8 (continued)

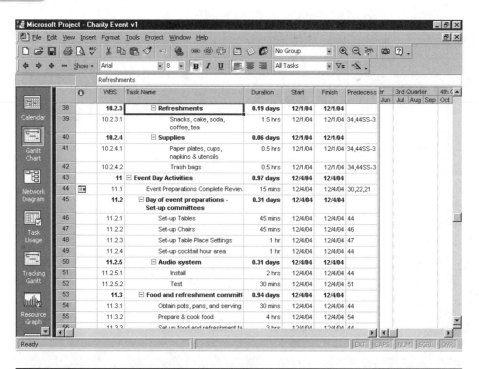

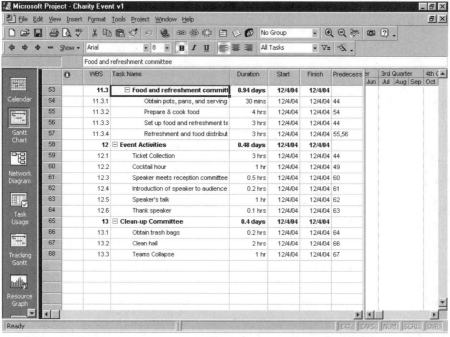

EXHIBIT 6–2

Responsibility Assignment Matrix (RAM)

WBS no.	Task name or description	Task responsibility
1.	Executive group agrees to hold charity speaking event	Executive Committee
2.	Executive group organizes committees and prepares draft schedule	Executive Committee
3.	Activity and committee budgets	
3.1.	Prepare budgets	Project manager
3.2.	Budget acceptable–go/no-go decision	
3.3.	Distribute budgets to committees	
4.	Agree on event date: 12/4/04	Executive Committee
5.	Site selection committee	Site Selection Committee
5.1.	Contact neighborhood fraternal association hall for availability	
5.2.	Confirm date of event	
5.3.	Site status decision	
6.	Speaker selection committee	Speaker Selection Committee
6.1.	Evaluate potential speakers	
6.2.	Select speaker	
6.3.	Make offer to speaker	
6.4.	Confirm availability of speaker	
6.5.	Decision on speaker	

a task and double-click on the task name. Select the Resource tab in the Task Information window. In the Resource Name line, enter the name of the group, department, or person who will assume responsibility for performing the task (Figure 6–9). The number 100% signifies that the resource will work on the job 100% of its time. If, instead, the resource spends 50% of its time on the task, the 60-hour calendar time doubles and the schedule stretches. Experiment with this feature.

Critical Path

The critical path holds those tasks that cannot be delayed without affecting the project's completion date. Microsoft Project permits the determination of this path. Click the Gantt chart wizard icon (Figure 6–1) and follow the directions that appear. Microsoft highlights the resulting critical path in red. The project manager usually informs the managers and other personnel working on the tasks in the critical path of the importance of their start and completion dates to the success of the project.

Progress and the Schedule

After the project manager develops the baseline schedule and the stakeholders agree on its value, the project manager uses it to track the progress of work on

FIGURE 6–9

Task information window

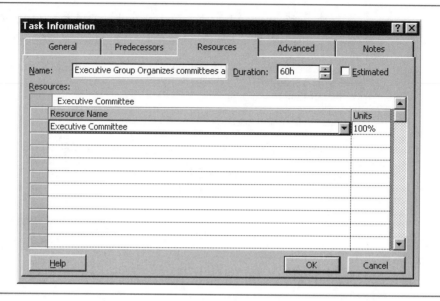

the project. Microsoft Project permits the user to enter the percentage of work completed for each task on the chart. Double-clicking the task once again brings up the Task Information window. On the General tab, the Percent complete entry area permits the project manager to enter any value between 0 and 100% (Figure 6–10). In the horizontal task bar, a solid line appears that corresponds to the amount of work completed.

Different philosophies exist among project managers with regard to filling in the Percent complete entry area. Some permit the functional manager or other person responsible for the task to select any numerical estimate that approximates the percentage of the task completed. While this approach offers the functional manager great flexibility in selecting the progress of work on the task it is highly subjective: Can the manager, for example, really distinguish between 17% and 19% of the task completed? Therefore, some project managers restrict the values that may be selected to only five: 0, 25, 50, 75, and 100%. Others believe in assigning only three numbers: 0, 50, and 100%. In this case, if the functional department has not yet begun the task, then the schedule reflects the completion of 0% of the task. The project manager assigns 50% completion as soon as the functional department begins the task. Only after the task is completed does the project manager assign 100%. This approach attempts to simplify matters, but if a scheduled task lasts for more than four weeks, the project manager may not have an accurate indication of its progress for most of that time. Then, at the end of a long working period, the project manager could face an unpleasant surprise!

While he or she is preparing the schedule, the project manager requests functional managers to examine efforts of long duration and separate them into

FIGURE 6–10

Task Information window used to enter percentage of a task completed

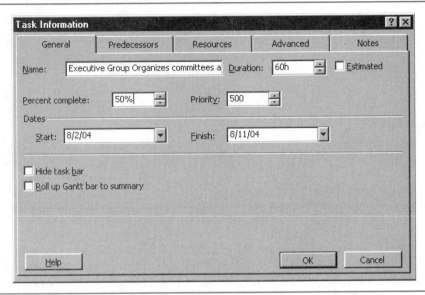

subtasks. One- or two-week durations are best, and no subtask should last longer than four weeks. The project manager asks functional managers to arrange matters such that each activity has an easily measured and well-defined output. This gives the project manager maximum insight into how the project is progressing. A major contributor to the project's success is the stakeholders' expectations, so clarifying everyone's roles and the work expected of each stakeholder is paramount.

Printing Niceties

The planner can tidy up the completed schedule by adding the project name to the head of each printed sheet, the date the planner prepared the schedule, and the planner's name to the printed output. To enter this information, click Page Setup on the File menu. After clicking the Header, Footer, or Legend tab and selecting the Left, Center, or Right tab, add the information in the text box.

SIDEBAR: THE EIGHT-HOUR DAY

Most planners use an eight-hour day in preparing the schedule. However, does one really work on the job for eight hours? If a worker's official hours are from 8 A.M. to 5 P.M. with an hour for lunch, then the worker is "on the job" for eight hours. Over 52 weeks, eight hours a day, five days a week, results in 2,080 labor hours during a year. But what about vacations and holidays? The benefit packages in most organizations include two weeks, or 80 hours, of vacation time and 10 paid holidays during the year. Further, think about all the nonproductive

TABLE 6–1

A Worker's Approximate Annual Labor Hours

Task	Daily	Weekly	Annually
Department meeting		1	50
Vacation			80
Designated holidays			80
Personal and sick time			30
Training			30
Coffee break	$\frac{2}{3}$ (40 minutes)	3	150
Total nonworking time			420
Baseline employment hours		40	2,080
Baseline work hours			1,660

1,660 labor hours per year averages 6.5 hours per day.

time a worker engages in during the workday—time spent at department meetings, on coffee breaks, in office chitchat, and in conversations with colleagues about the latest political scandal or the baseball scores. And how about sick days and personal days? Table 6–1 indicates that, when nonproductive work activities are taken into account, workers average less than seven hours of productive work per day. Accordingly, Microsoft Project can adjust the schedules by changing the work hours from eight to seven per day. A schedule that uses a seven-hour day will extend the time for completion of a project by 12%, compared with a schedule based on eight work hours per day. However, few executives will accept such a change or the reasons just advanced in support of it. Rather, they will argue that (1) the organization compensates workers for eight-hour days and expects eight hours of work, (2) the planner should adjust the schedule for holidays and vacations, and (3) sick and personal time should not be planned for in advance because employees may then take it as a matter of course.

SUMMARY

The Gantt chart or bar chart assists project managers in organizing jobs. The schedule forms the basis for all project planning and predicting. Project managers should never unilaterally assign labor hours or durations to activities during the preparation of the schedule: Functional managers must contribute to the schedule's development as well. Participation in the estimation process forces "ownership" and requires functional managers to take responsibility for their decisions. The project manager leads the team in identifying the work activities, assigning priorities, and developing task dependencies and durations. The project manager uses the schedule as a communication tool: Team members gain an understanding of their roles and responsibilities on a project by reading the specification and the developing estimates. During the project, monitoring the schedule on a daily basis informs all participants of potential trouble spots.

The project manager and the project team benefit from the use of scheduling tools. The schedule enables management to plan for the best possible use of resources in order to achieve a given objective within time, cost, and resource limitations. The schedule facilitates "what if" exercises. With an understanding of the critical activities of a project, slack time, uncertainties, and the crucial task elements, the project manager and the functional managers can experiment with the schedule by applying a variety of resources at different times to determine their overall impact on the project.

Planning the schedule takes place during the proposal phase of the (potential) project and consists of the following steps:

1. The project manager highlights the deliverables and distributes the specification to the functional managers.
2. The starting and ending dates of the project are established.
3. A responsibility assignment matrix (RAM) identifies the participants role in the proposal.
4. A kickoff meeting is held to review the task assignments.
5. The required capital equipment is identified.
6. The functional managers submit the names and titles of departmental personnel they recommend for each task in the project.
7. The functional managers submit their estimates of the duration of each task.
8. The project manager establishes task dependencies:
   - Which tasks can be done in parallel?
   - Which tasks require the completion of other tasks before they can start?
9. The project manager prepares a draft WBS.
10. The functional managers review a draft of the schedule.

REVIEW QUESTIONS

1. Identify whether the following statements are true or false:
   a) The vertical axis on the Gantt chart matrix lists all the tasks to be performed.
   b) Each row in a Gantt chart contains a single task that must be completed during the work effort.
   c) Each row in a Gantt chart contains a WBS number.
   d) The horizontal axis on the Gantt chart has columns indicating the estimated duration of a task and, sometimes, the name of the person or department assigned to the task.
   e) A solid bar on the horizontal axis indicates that a task that is underway is progressing.

2. Select the best answer: A critical path
   a) contains the maximum slack time in the schedule.
   b) involves a set of unrelated tasks.
   c) consists of a set of dependent tasks that together take the longest time to complete.
   d) consists of all the tasks performed by a single department or person.
3. Tasks falling on the critical path
   a) should receive special attention by both the project manager and the personnel assigned to them.
   b) require minimal attention.
   c) will be performed by an external organization.
   d) will be performed by the project manager's department.
4. Developing a schedule involves
   a) defining the activities to be accomplished.
   b) assigning responsibility for completing activities to stakeholders.
   c) identifying logical sequences of activities.
   d) establishing dependencies among activities by identifying successor and predecessor tasks.
   e) designating the duration of each task.
   f) all of the above.
5. The accompanying list represents typical tasks involved in remodeling a bathroom. Use the list to prepare a schedule by doing the following:
   a) Establish a starting date for this project.
   b) After reviewing the tasks shown, identify the milestones.
   c) Assign a duration for each task.
   d) Assign responsibility for each task.
   e) Assign task interdependencies.
   f) Prepare a schedule by entering the data from parts a) through e) using Microsoft Project.
   g) Determine the project's critical path.

Bathroom remodeling task list

Task no.	Task description	Duration	Dependency
1	Decision to redesign bathroom		
2	Design concept and layout		
3	Obtain construction permit		
4	Select components		
5	Plumbing fixtures		
6	Electrical fixtures		
7	Wall and floor cabinets		
8	Tile		
9	Windows		
10	Shower closure		
11	Seek design input from contractors		
12	Receive contractor bids		
13	Plumber		
14	Electrician		
15	Tile layer		

16	Carpenter
17	Painter
18	Award Contract(s)
19	Payment 1
20	Procure material
21	Bath and faucets
22	Shower and faucets
23	Toilet
24	Sink and faucets
25	Tile
26	Floor cabinet
27	Medicine cabinet
28	Towel rack
29	Toilet paper holder
30	Soap dish
31	Tooth brush holder
32	Window
33	Shower door
34	Payment 2
35	Order and receive trash container
36	Remove existing walls and floor
37	Remove old fixtures
38	Plumbing
39	Electrical
40	Delivery of equipment
41	Rough installation
42	Carpentry
43	Window
44	Install plumbing pipes
45	Install electrical wiring, switches, fixtures
46	Install wallboard
47	Install wall and floor tile
48	Install accessories
49	Install plumbing fixtures
50	Test and evaluate
51	Pick up trash
52	Paint
53	Town inspection
54	Final payment

6. Plan for installing a computer network

The following list represents typical tasks involved in installing a computer network. Use the list and prepare a schedule by doing the following:

a) Establish a starting date for this project.

b) After reviewing the tasks shown, identify the milestones.

c) Assign a duration for each task.

d) Assign responsibility for each task.

e) Assign task interdependencies.

f) Prepare a schedule by entering the data from parts a) through e) using Microsoft Project.

g) Determine the project's critical path.

Computer network installation task list

Site survey
    Air-conditioning
    Electric capacity
    Placement of electric outlets
    Available rooms
Plans
    Define number and location of users
    Air-conditioning plan
    Electric power distribution and placement of outlets
    Equipment location
    Network architecture plan
        Cabling type (fiber optic, wire, RJ-45, 10baseT, category 5, etc.)
        Wide area network (WAN)
        Local area network (LAN)
            Server protocol
                Ethernet
                Token ring
                TCP/IP
                Novell
            Routers
            Bridges
    Software and software tools
        Firewall
        Security
        Virus detection
        E-mail
        World Wide Web
        File transfer protocol
    Internet service provider trade study
    Internet connectivity option trade study
        Dial-up access
        Leased line
    Infrastructure planning
        Room construction
        Furniture (desks, chairs, etc.)
        Cabling
        Internet connections
        Client workstation connections
        Identify central wiring area
    Impact of local construction code
    Required licenses and permits
    Preparation of implementation plan
Computer specification
    Server
    Workstation
    Hubs, bridges, and routers
Design review
Initial and ongoing support
    Assemble and train staff
    Select network management and system administration tools
    Develop a user address plan
    Develop help-desk procedures
    Develop end-user technical support policies

Purchases
- Computers
- Furniture
- Cable and connectors
- Hubs, bridges, and routers
- Wire trays
- Dropped ceiling equipment
- Miscellaneous cabling equipment and tools

Construction
- Obtain local permits and licenses
- Rooms
- Heating and air-conditioning equipment
- Install cabling trays and cabling
- Electric power connections
- Internet connections
- LAN connections

Install furniture

Install computer
- Unpack
- Install software
- Place and connect computers in approved locations
- Assign and install user addresses

Site test
- Prepare a system test procedure
- Perform test

User training

CHAPTER 7

PROJECT ESTIMATION AND COST

*Always bear in mind that your own resolution
to succeed is more important than any other one thing.*
Abraham Lincoln

OBJECTIVES

After studying this chapter, you should be able to

- Understand the difference between bottom-up and top-down estimating
- Understand the elements that enter into a project's cost
- Understand the meaning of direct and indirect costs
- Identify indirect cost components
- Understand the difference between cost and price
- Read and interpret a project's financial statements
- Participate in a project cost estimate effort

INTRODUCTION

Together with the project cost-estimating team, the project manager establishes a budget before the project begins. Every employee action on the project has cost implications. Typically, the cost-estimating team consists of the project manager, functional managers, and selected commercial partners and subcontractors. The team has the objective of approximating the costs of the resources needed to complete the project. During the planning stage of the project, the team must predict the cost of the work packages. Following the awarding of the contract, the project manager monitors carefully both the progress of the work and the funds expended. At the job's conclusion, financial analysts compare the predicted costs with the actual costs to determine the accuracy of the estimate and the amount of profit the organization earned on the project. The profit may determine the project manager's next job—sometimes a harsh reality.

DIRECT AND INDIRECT COSTS

A project's costs consist of a wide assortment of expenditures, some obvious and some not. Perhaps the most obvious expense is the employee's base salary. However, labor costs represent only a portion of the cost associated with a project. Employees receive fringe benefits and require office furniture and computers. They share tools, offices, furniture, conference rooms, coffee machines, and water coolers. Basic operating costs such as rent and utility bills have to enter the equation. Accountants separate all costs into direct and indirect costs.

Direct costs identify with a single product, project, or contract. Employee salaries associated with designing, building, testing, and installing a product or providing a service represent one of the largest direct costs. Other direct costs include the cost of project-related supplies and material and subcontracted costs. The next three subsections examine several significant direct costs pertaining to projects.

Material and Material-Handling Costs

All materials and supplies required for a job represent a direct project cost. In addition to purchases, this category includes the lease or rental of special hardware or software tools and equipment. Also, organizations usually add a handling charge to the material and equipment purchased for a specific job for which they expect the customer to pay. Material-handling costs cover a host of expenses that include the costs of storage, inspection to verify receipt of the correct material, breakage, theft, restocking fees, and borrowing money to obtain the material. Many organizations charge customers an additional 10 to 25% of the material cost to offset these expenditures.

Travel and Living Expenses

Travel, living, and entertainment expenses include the costs associated with a business trip or hosting customers to lunch or dinner. Charges associated with a business trip include air, bus, train, and taxi fares; reasonable costs for breakfast, lunch, and dinner; car-rental expenses; hotel charges; and parking fees. Travel and living costs can be direct or indirect. Charges applied to support a specific contract or project are direct costs. Travel and living costs in support of a proposal effort are indirect. Many organizations add a percentage of travel and living expenses to cover the costs of making and sometimes rescheduling reservations and penalty charges for changing reservations.

Other Direct Costs (ODC)

Other direct costs (ODC) include the cost of labor supplied by people and organizations not directly affiliated with the organization that received the contract. A typical example of ODC includes the fee charged for engaging a consultant to assist the staff. Frequently, because organizations either lack the requisite number of personnel to complete a task or do not have in-house expertise in a certain technology, they bolster their technical expertise in a discipline by employing independent consultants. Sometimes an organization may request the consultant to provide an independent assessment and review of the work completed to date. Often, organizations *outsource* work—that is, subcontract a portion of the project's work to external organizations. Other ODC items include the rental or purchase of equipment, such as copy machines, telephones, and FAX units, dedicated to the project. Postage or overnight mail deliveries related to the project also fall into the ODC category. If the contract requires attendance at a conference, then typical charges to the ODC account also include conference registration fees and the cost of special courses.

Sales Commission

As with many of the accounting and conventions discussed in this section, organizations have options with regard to categorizing sales commissions. Some organizations combine them with general management and administration costs. Other organizations place sales commissions into their own separate category.

Profit

Profit is the lifeblood of business. Among the causes of a business not making a profit are poor estimating, inept management, or sudden market changes, all of which may result in unintentional losses. Or, if an organization desires to venture into a new area, it may choose to entice customers with lower prices than are customary or perhaps even offer to perform a project at cost.

In general, although organizations may permit some projects not to make a profit, they cannot continue to lose money, or they will go belly up.

Industry executives managing publicly traded companies feel pressure to produce short-term profits to satisfy Wall Street analysts and stockholders' demands. In return for ongoing short-term profits, the financial community expects immediate increases in the value of the company's stock. So a commercial profit-making organization must make a profit to remain viable. Many dot-com businesses created in the early 2000s failed because they did not make a profit. How much profit does the financial community expect of businesses? General Electric, one of the best-operated businesses in the world, earned a profit (net income before taxes, divided by gross revenues) of 13–15% from 1998 to 2000. During the last few years, the Walt Disney Company's operating profit hovered around 10%. Organizations doing business with the US government earn about a 12% profit. At the other extreme, during 1999 and 2000 Microsoft's profits reached 40%.

INDIRECT COSTS

Indirect costs include all costs that are not direct. Indirect costs apply to two or more products, projects, or services provided or performed by the organization, including support costs incurred for common or joint objectives. The indirect costs associated with a particular project cannot be readily or specifically identified.

Operational costs are the sum of all the direct and indirect costs associated with a department, a business unit, or an organization.

Overhead Costs and General and Administrative Costs

Often, indirect costs are divided into two subcategories: overhead costs and general administrative (G&A) costs. Overhead costs are indirect costs that support a specific part or function of the company. For example, manufacturing organizations distribute factory maintenance costs among the various manufacturing jobs performed in the factory, and administrators integrate engineering library costs into the engineering department overhead and not with material handling or the accounting department. In addition to the cost of purchasing, leasing, or renting buildings and equipment in which some of the activities of a project take place, other basic overhead costs include the costs of licenses and certifications to do business; facility heating; lighting; malpractice, liability, fire, and theft insurance; and building, equipment and property maintenance, as well as costs associated with staffing; supporting libraries; advertising; indirect labor, such as plant security, clerical, and administrative support personnel; social security, unemployment, and worker's compensation insurance; and fringe benefits, such as vacations, medical coverage, dental and disability insurance, and pensions.

In contrast to overhead costs, G&A costs are required to support the business as a whole and are not associated with any particular department, project, or program. Common examples of G&A costs are the salaries of the chief executive officer and his or her staff, legal and accounting costs, marketing expenses, research and development costs, and bid and proposal (B&P) costs.

The classification of direct versus indirect costs has to do with the relationship of cost to a final cost objective. Overhead and G&A costs are indirect because they benefit more than one cost objective. The classification of the cost of an activity or a position into direct or indirect is not a reflection of the importance of or need for the activity or position. The activity of factory equipment maintenance, for example, usually an indirect cost, is just as necessary as the position of machine operator, yet the cost of the one usually is classified as an indirect cost, whereas the cost of the other is a direct cost.

The organization's accounting system collects cost information. As projects incur costs through the purchase of labor, material, and equipment, as well as other expenditures, the accounting system assigns and distributes these costs to departments and projects. Accounting systems create an indirect expense rate, which project managers must add to the individual's labor rate to determine the true cost of employing that person. The project manager quotes a price to the customer for the use of an employee that includes the employee's salary, indirect costs, sales commission, and profit. The formula for calculating this price is

$$\text{customer price for employee labor} = \text{employee base salary} + \text{overhead costs}$$
$$+ \text{ G\&A costs} + \text{sales commission} + \text{profit.}$$

This formula represents the fully burdened labor price that the customer pays to use an organization's employee. Most often, organizations relate overhead costs to a department and calculate the overhead as a percentage of the employee's base salary. The Villa-Tech example later in the chapter illustrates this approach.

Some organizations follow an accounting policy of not applying overhead and G&A to ODC activities, because a lower sales price results if the organization wraps a profit around a consultant's charges, but not overhead and G&A charges. In this case, reselling a consultant's efforts enables the organization to make a profit without using its own resources, and that's always a winner. Organizations do charge the customer a sales commission and profit on ODC items.

BOTTOM-UP ESTIMATING

Bottom-up estimates begin with a detailed WBS that the project manager develops together with the functional managers. The project manager requests support from each functional manager to estimate the cost of each work package assigned to his or her department. The estimate accounts for all of the resources needed to support the design and development, testing, and installation of any

TABLE 7–1

Project Cost Summary

Task no.	WBS no.	Tasks or Work Packages	Electrical Engineering	Mechanical Engineering	Software Engineering	Network Engineering
10000	1.	System				
11000	1.1.	Define the system Performance requirements				
11100	1.1.1.	Review specification				
11120	1.1.2.	Review statement of work				
12000	1.2.	System architecture definition				
12100	1.2.1.	Major trade-off studies				
13000	1.3.	Define major assemblies				
13020	1.3.1.	Electrical assemblies				
13050	1.3.2.	Mechanical assemblies				
13100	1.3.3.	Cable definition				
14000	1.4.	Unique algorithm development				
15000	1.5.	Define software/firmware functions and architecture				
16000	1.6.	Technical analyses				
20000	2.	Assembly #1				
21000	2.1.	Hardware				
21100	2.1.1.	Define hardware/software interfaces				
21200	2.1.2.	Electrical				
21210	2.1.2.1.	Define subassemblies /modules/functions				
21220	2.1.2.2.	⋮				
21230	2.1.2.3.					
		Subtotal				

software or equipment, as well as the resources required for training and any customer hand-holding. The project manager receives the estimates for each project element and sums them into a total for the project. Table 7–1 illustrates the format for collecting data, using a partial WBS. Provided that the organization has a good understanding of the job, bottom-up estimating should result in an accurate estimate; however, the process is labor intensive and time consuming.

A large electromechanical system may involve an enormous number of technical specialties, departments, and people, including many of the following:

- Electrical/electronics engineering
- Mechanical engineering
- Software engineering
- Networking engineering

Department Labor Hours

Tech	Field service	Publi-cations	Training	Purchases of Materials ($)	Travel and Living ($)	ODC ($)	Line-item Cost ($)

- Systems engineering
- Model shop
- Engineering assistants
- Hardware test technicians
- Software test technicians
- Factory technicians
- Field service support
- Purchasing
- Publications
- Training
- Configuration management

- Quality assurance
- Reliability and maintainability engineering
- Specialty engineering, such as hazardous-material control, environmental testing, and nuclear engineering
- Project management
- Incoming inspection
- Administrative support (secretarial and financial)
- Shipping
- Heating, ventilation, and air-conditioning (HVAC)
- Legal
- Marketing
- Technical library

For the majority of these entries, the job function is either intuitive or self-explanatory. The engineering departments design products and equipment or provide services within their disciplines. The model shop builds limited numbers of products, in contradistinction to the factory, which fabricates larger quantities. The model shop generally works closely with engineers and technologists during a project's construction phase and requires less instruction than the factory. The software- and hardware-testing groups test products to verify that they meet the customer's requirements. The purchasing department receives approved orders for goods and services and attempts to obtain the best price for them. The publications department accepts the documentation prepared by the engineering organization and formats it to meet the organization's standards so that the finished document has the same look and feel as other documents released for publication. The department sometimes reviews and corrects grammar and spelling, as well as preparing artwork for the documents. The incoming-inspection department examines packages to verify that their contents agree with what is written on the packing slip. The department then passes the packing slip to accounts payable for payment to the supplier. The quality group addresses issues involving quality assurance, quality control, process improvement, standards, audits, and national or international quality certifications. Configuration management monitors the project's deliverables—documentation, hardware, software, and services such as training, maintenance, and product repair. Sometimes a product has several variations, and configuration management keeps track of the product's versions and releases so that the customer receives the correct order. Discrepancies between the customer's order and the product or service delivered are discussed with, and resolved by, the project manager. The sales department works on identifying a prospective customer, receiving an RFP or RFQ, or taking an order. The marketing department leads the process of identifying future markets for the organization to enter, selecting future products, and preparing advertisement campaigns.

The project manager obtains estimates from each of the foregoing departments. On the basis of their understanding of the job, the functional managers estimate department labor hours, purchases of material, the business travel (number of trips and length of stay) required for the job, and the need for consultants. Most project managers list the data in a spreadsheet similar to Table 7–1.

Labor hours include time required to gain familiarity with the documentation required for the job; time spent in special training required to learn to use a new tool; time spent preparing for and attending design reviews and other technical interchange meetings; travel time to visit and evaluate prospective suppliers; and design, development, and testing time.

EXAMPLE: VILLA-TECH BID

To illustrate the concepts associated with developing a bid for a project, we shall examine a fictitious company called Villa-Tech. Normally, the organization's accountants calculate the salary rates, overhead rates, and G&A rates and distribute this information to the project managers; however, in what follows, we perform the computations to enhance the student's understanding of the technique.

Villa-Tech intends to bid on a job. The project manager has distributed the customer's data and a draft WBS and schedule to the functional managers. The functional managers then prepare and submit the following to the project manager: a technical response at the level of the contributor's expertise, the relevant section of the WBS and schedule, and the associated cost. The project manager places the data into a spreadsheet in order to calculate the customer's price.

Villa-Tech accountants have decided on the following financial ground rules:

- Material-handling costs: Add 10% to all purchases, rentals, and leases
- Travel and living fees: Add 15% to all travel, entertainment, and living costs
- Profit: 15%
- Sales commission: 6%
- Do not apply overhead and G&A to any material purchased
- Apply the organization's standard sales commission and profit to all purchased material
- Do not apply overhead, G&A, sales commission, and profit to travel costs

Overhead rates

The accounting department determines that the wages paid to the engineering staff at the Villa-Tech Company go to electrical, mechanical, software, and networking personnel. The annual Villa-Tech company engineering salaries total $1,711,000 (shown in Table 7–2) and represent the engineering department's direct labor costs. However, $1,711,000 does not represent Villa-Tech's *total* cost for these employees. Accountants at Villa-Tech aggregate all the indirect costs that support the 20-person engineering staff into an engineering overhead pool, as shown in Table 7–3. Although there are generally accepted accounting practices, organizations use different rules for assigning overhead and for distinguishing

TABLE 7–2

Villa-Tech Engineering Payroll

Engineering Department or Discipline	Number of Personnel	Total Engineering Direct Labor
Electrical	4	$340,000
Mechanical	3	$261,000
Software	9	$810,000
Networking	4	$300,000
Total	20	$1,711,000

overhead from G&A costs. The approach used here is representative of the overhead calculation of many firms.

Engineering staff salaries aside, the table lists the expenses required to operate the company's engineering departments. In addition to the $1,711,000 direct labor charges, Villa-Tech spends $781,220 to support its engineering organization. Accountants define the engineering overhead rate as the ratio, in percent, of the annual engineering indirect expenses to the annual engineering direct labor costs, or

$$\text{engineering department overhead rate} = \frac{\text{annual engineering indirect expense}}{\text{annual engineering direct labor costs}} \times 100\%.$$

TABLE 7–3

Villa-Tech Engineering Overhead Expenses

Expense	Description	Annual Cost Allocated
Indirect labor	Administrative, clerical, and secretarial	$75,000
Federal, state, or local mandated costs	Social security (FICA), unemployment, and worker's compensation insurance	$214,320
Fringe benefits	Vacation; medical, dental, and disability insurance; retirement pension costs	$267,900
Training	Nonproject or contract-related training and educational expenses	$80,000
Indirect operating expenses	Share of rent and utilities (e.g., oil, gas, electricity, and telephone), share of organization's liability insurance, leasing of copy machine, office supplies, postage, depreciation of computers and associated equipment, professional and business organization memberships	$132,000
Maintenance and repair	Copy machine and other equipment repair contracts, share of facility maintenance and repair	$12,000
Total indirect expenses		$781,220

The Villa-Tech engineering department overhead rate is

$$\text{engineering department overhead rate} = \frac{\$781,220}{\$1,711,000} \times 100\% = 45.6\%.$$

This means that almost $.46 of indirect charge is added to every $1 of direct labor charged to the contract or project. While the overhead rate continually changes, organizations tend to keep the overhead rate constant for the year.

General and Administrative Costs

Villa-Tech has a small executive management team. The general and administrative costs pertaining to the team total $2,640,000, as shown in Table 7–4.

Villa-Tech accountants have determined that the company's annual payroll is $11,200,000. An organization's G&A rate, in percent, is the ratio of the annual G&A expenses to the annual direct labor costs; that is,

$$\text{organization's G\&A rate} = \frac{\text{annual G\&A expenses}}{\text{annual organization direct labor costs}} \times 100\%.$$

In this case, Villa-Tech's G&A rate is

$$\text{organization's G\&A rate} = \frac{\$2,640,000}{\$11,200,000} \times 100\% = 23.5\%.$$

This means that $.23\frac{1}{2}$ of G&A charge is added to every $1 of direct labor assigned to the project or contract.

Burdened Wage

Table 7–5 illustrates the method of arriving at a worker's fully burdened hourly wage for several disciplines and departments. To determine the dollar amount to charge a customer, accountants start with the department's average salary and add overhead, G&A costs, sales commission, and profit. Examining the table

TABLE 7–4

Villa-Tech General and Administrative Expenses

Engineering Department or Discipline	G&A Expenses
President/CEO & staff	$350,000
Vice president	$155,000
Marketing department	$290,000
Corporate accounting	$280,000
Annual research-and-development budget	$775,000
Bid and proposal budget	$540,000
Legal staff	$250,000
Total	$2,640,000

TABLE 7-5

Villa-Tech Employee's Burdened Hourly Wage

Category	Department or Discipline							
	Electrical Engineering	Mechanical Engineering	Software Engineering	Network Engineering	Technician	Field Service	Configuration Management	Training
Average department hourly labor costs	$38.60	$37.50	$41.00	$36.50	$22.00	$29.75	$15.45	$31.00
Overhead, 45.6%	$18	$17	$19	$17	$10	$14	$7	$14
General and administrative, 23.5%	$9	$9	$10	$9	$5	$7	$4	$7
Sales commission, 6%	$4	$4	$4	$4	$2	$3	$2	$3
Profit, 15%	$10	$10	$11	$10	$6	$8	$4	$8
Burdened hourly wage	$80	$77	$85	$75	$45	$61	$32	$64

reveals that a customer will pay Villa-Tech slightly more than double an employee's hourly salary for the use of that employee's services. A company cannot charge less than the burdened hourly labor wage and remain in business for long. Unless the company reduces overhead or G&A expenses, the only significant flexibility it has surrounds the profit or sales commission the company chooses to apply. By its nature, overhead is difficult to change in the short run, but profit and sales commission are easy to modify.

Functional Manager Estimates

After due deliberation, the Villa-Tech functional departments submit estimates to the project manager, such as those shown in Table 7–6. The functional managers may have based their estimates on their professional judgment, historical data, a parametric approach, a wild guess, or any other means. We shall see shortly how the project manager uses these estimates.

Risk Analysis

A project's risk is discussed in depth in Chapter 10. Here, we identify a method for including risk funding in the cost estimate. Every work activity has some measure of risk and uncertainty associated with it. Adding the costs for each work package making up the WBS should yield a bid that is accurate to within $\pm 10\%$ of the actual costs, which is an acceptable risk. Some individual estimates may turn out high and others low, but at the project's conclusion, these variations average out.

The functional managers identify a limited number of tasks with an uncertainty in duration or cost ranging from 20% to 75%. The cost of labor and materials for very risky tasks (i.e., those that harbor a risk that is more than 75%

TABLE 7–6

Functional Department Estimates

Functional Department	Labor Hours	Purchases, Leases, and Rentals of Materials	Travel, Living, and Entertainment	ODC
Electrical engineering	1,675	$45,000	$800	$2,400
Mechanical engineering	495	$31,000	$500	$2,100
Software engineering	2,237	$37,000	$1,000	$3,700
Network engineering	234	$29,000		
Technician	348	$3,000	$500	
Field service	150	$4,500	$2,500	
Configuration management	45			
Training	110	$4,500	$4,200	
Total	5,294	$154,000	$9,500	$8,200

TABLE 7–7

Including the Project's Financial Risk in the Cost

Risk Item no.	Calculation	Task no.	WBS no.	Tasks or Work Packages	Electrical Engineering
1	WBS item				
1a	Maximum risk in hours or $				
1b	Probability of risk				
1c	Weighted risk, hours or $ (= line 1b multiplied by line 1a)				
2	WBS item				
2a	Maximum risk in hours or $				
2b	Probability of risk				
2c	Weighted risk, hours or $				
	Risk impact Total (1c + 2c + ...)				

likely to happen) should be considered a certainty and the entire effort placed in the baseline estimate. Certainly, there should be fewer than 10 activities involving more than a 20% risk; otherwise, executive management might seriously question the logic of pursuing the job at all. The cost estimator identifies these activities in a separate chart (Table 7–7). The estimator then enters the tasks' nominal labor hours, cost of materials, travel and living funds, and ODC into the chart. The risk is then quantified in hours or dollars. For each task, the estimator assigns a probability of risk ranging from 0.25 to 0.75. The weighted risk is the product of the probability of risk and the maximum risk in hours or dollars. The weighted risk is calculated for each risk item. The last line in the chart sums the weighted risk hours and dollars for all of the risk items. The project manager transfers these results to Table 7–8.

Department Labor Hours									
Mechanical Engineering	Software Engineering	Network Engineering	Tech	Field Service	Publications	Training	Purchases of Materials ($)	Travel and Living ($)	ODC ($)

Villa-Tech Project Cost Summary

Table 7–8 is a summary of the results of the bottom-up project estimate started in Table 7–1 for the Villa-Tech project. To generate Table 7–8, the project manager inserted estimates into the spreadsheet of Table 7–1 for which functional managers provided labor, material, travel, and ODC costs. After due consideration, the Villa-Tech project manager, together with the functional managers, deemed the risk to complete the project's activities to be within $\pm 10\%$ of the cost and therefore added no risk funding to the price. Summing the individual columns in Table 7–8 yields a price of $640,704 to the customer. Villa-Tech executives consider this price in the light of the organization's desire and need for the job. After due diligence, they submit a bid to the customer.

TABLE 7–8

Villa-Tech Project Cost Summary

Category	Electrical Engineering	Mechanical Engineering	Software Engineering	Network Engineering
Project subtotal, hours	1675	495	2237	234
Nonlabor project subtotal, $				
Risk impact Subtotal 1, includes risk				
Department hourly labor costs	$38.60	$37.50	$41.00	$36.50
Department labor costs, $	$64,655	$18,563	$91,717	$8,541
Material-handling charges, 10%				
Travel and living overhead charges, 15%				
Overhead, 41%	$29,483	$8,465	$41,823	$3,895
General and administrative, 23.5%	$15,194	$4,362	$21,553	$2,007
Subtotal 2	$109,332	$31,389	$155,093	$14,443
Sales commission, 6%	$6,560	$1,883	$9,306	$867
Subtotal 3	$115,892	$33,273	$164,399	$15,309
Profit,15%	$17,384	$4,991	$24,660	$2,296
Total Price, $	$133,275	$38,263	$189,059	$17,606

Total price for project: $640,704

PROJECT SPENDING PROFILE

The project life cycle discussed in Chapter 3 and reproduced in Figure 7–1 provides an approximate illustration of spending on the project at any point in the cycle for a large project. Integrating or summing up the costs with respect to time yields the cumulative project spending profile, or "S" curve, shown in Figure 7–2. Projects usually start spending money slowly. The initial activities require planning. The project manager develops work packages to make certain that the team members perform productively. The packages, which contain brief descriptions of specific work activities, schedules, and

Technician	Field Service	Configuration management	Training	Purchases of Materials	Travel and Living	ODC
348	150	45	110			
				$154,000	$9,500	$8,200
$22.00	$29.75	$15.45	$31.00			
$7,656	$4,463	$695	$3,410			
				$15,400		
					$1,425	
$3,491	$2,035	$317	$1,555			
$1,799	$1,049	$163	$801			
$12,946	$7,546	$1,176	$5,766	$169,400	$10,925	$8,200
$777	$453	$71	$346	$10,164		$492
$13,723	$7,999	$1,246	$6,112	$179,564	$10,925	$8,692
$2,058	$1,200	$187	$917	$26,935	$1,639	$1,304
$15,782	$9,199	$1,433	$7,029	$206,499	$12,564	$9,996

associated budgets, authorize employees in the various departments to start the project. The project manager assembles a team. Employees prepare documentation for subcontracts. These initial tasks require a relatively small number of people; consequently, the spending is low. The rate of spending increases during the development effort, during which time departments make major purchases and the bulk of the money for labor is spent. As the project enters the testing and installation phases, spending tails off. The project usually concludes with the completion of the site acceptance test and training, both of which activities involve a relatively small number of the organization's personnel.

FIGURE 7–1

Project life-cycle phases

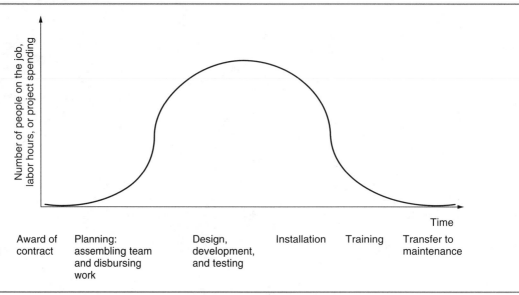

FIGURE 7–2

Time distribution of project labor or cost ($)

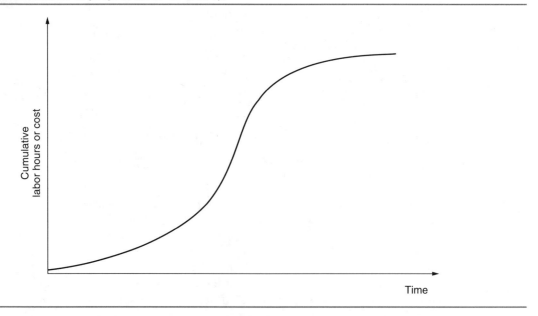

BOTTOM-UP ESTIMATE

The accuracy of the bottom-up estimate depends on the quality of the input received from the stakeholders participating in the process. The team of stakeholders examines every task in the WBS and provides expert judgment regarding the labor involved in completing the activities. The team estimates the time and materials required for the project on the basis of the members' experiences performing similar activities on other projects. By submitting an estimate, the individual estimators make a commitment to complete the job within the hours specified. Many people participate in the estimating, resulting in a highly labor intensive and expensive effort. A concern arises if team members lack expertise in new or unfamiliar technologies; then their estimates lack credibility. Still, project cost evaluators even take issue with estimators who have expertise, as individual biases may slant the estimate and some estimators fail to document their work appropriately. For this reason, organizations frequently maintain a historical record of the costs of previous jobs to support the staff's expert judgment. Cost data associated with previously completed work authorizations enable the team to develop accurate estimates for the new project under consideration. Using documented past experience, the team can arrive at a reasonable rationale for an activity's costs.

TOP-DOWN ESTIMATE

Although the bottom-up approach to project estimating is accurate, it is labor intensive and takes time for the team to complete. A top-down approach yields a project estimate in a relatively short time and uses a minimum of labor hours to support the estimate. Top-down estimates use rules of thumb, parametric models, analogies, or commercial databases. Project planners and estimators can choose to apply these techniques to the entire job or only a portion of the project.

RULE-OF-THUMB COST-ESTIMATING APPROACH

Three examples of cost-estimating relationships or rules of thumb based on historical experience are 2.5 hours of software labor time to develop a line of source code, 2 hours of labor time to write a single page of text in a technical document, and $125 per square foot for home construction. Project planners and estimators arrive at these estimates after participating in a variety of projects, whereupon the estimates, in effect, become rules of thumb. Sometimes an entire industry accepts rule-of-thumb values as a good reference point, while at other times the values are company specific.

PARAMETRIC MODELING

Parametric modeling involves the use of a project's characteristics (parameters) in a mathematical model to predict a gross estimate for the project's development costs. Once a group has achieved confidence in a parametric model, the calculation is fast and inexpensive. Practitioners find this objective approach to cost estimating consistent and repeatable. As with all estimates, the result depends on the quality of the information inserted into the system. Also, because the model requires calibration by the user, its effectiveness is limited to the use of old technology. If the technical staff decides to use new technology, the results will require some tinkering. Only after the project is completed and the actual labor results are inserted into the model will the parametric system provide a more accurate labor estimate with the use of new technology. Some organizations employ estimates obtained from parametric models as independent checks of cost estimates arrived at by other methods. Managers call this practice a "sanity check" on the calculations obtained from a bottom-up estimate.

Several commercial databases use parametric models. *Price Systems* (formerly RCA Price and GE Price) models both hardware and software. As with all parametric models, the systems require extensive training and calibration on the part of the user before being applied to actual bids.

The *PRICE-H Model* provides hardware system cost estimates based on

- quantitative parameters such as system complexity, quantity, weight, and size;
- qualitative parameters such as environmental specification, equipment function, packaging, and level of integration; and
- schedule-driving parameters such as months to the first prototype, manufacturing rate, and amount of new design.

The *PRICE-S system* calculates software development costs from system concept through operational testing and evaluation. Costs are calculated and reported for design engineering, programming, data, project management, quality assurance, and configuration management.

COCOMO, a model designed by Barry W. Boehm, gives a labor estimate for developing a software product. Boehm's team developed the first COnstructive COst MOdel after studying about 60 projects at TRW. "Basic COCOMO is good for rough order of magnitude estimates of software costs, but its accuracy is necessarily limited because of its lack of factors to account for differences in hardware constraints, personnel quality and experience, use of modern tools and techniques, and other project attributes known to have a significant influence on costs."[1] Teams at USC revised the software cost estimation model in the 1990s to reflect the changes in professional software development practices that evolved since its development. COCOMO II provides for a range of project costs and schedules. The software tool permits a

---

[1] Boehm, B. W., *Software Engineering Economics* (Englewood Cliffs, NJ: Prentice-Hall, 1981).

planner to examine the effects of adjusting requirements, resources, and staffing with respect to costs and schedules (e.g., for risk management or job-bidding purposes).

The following list of Web sites provides a starting point for those who are interested in pursuing additional information about parametric estimating techniques:

Galorath, Inc.: *www.galorath.com/tools-overvw.shtm*
Mainstay Software Corp.: *www.mainstay.com*
NASA/Air Force Cost Model: *www.jsc.nasa.gov/bu2/NAFCOM.html*
PRICE Systems: *www.pricesystems.com*
Quantitative Software Management: *www.qsm.com*
COCOMO Models: *sunset.usc.edu/research/cocomosuite/index.html*
Cost Estimating Resources: *www.jsc.nasa.gov/bu2/resources.html*
DOD Acquisition Reform: *www.acq.osd.mil/ar/ar.htm*
Software Engineering Institute (SEI): *www.sei.cmu.edu*
Software Engineering Laboratory (SEL): *sel.gsfc.nasa.gov*
Software Technology Support Center (STSC): *www.stsc.hill.af.mil*
International Society of Parametric Analysts (ISPA): *http://www.ispa-cost.org*
Defense Acquisition Deskbook: *web2.deskbook.osd.mil*

ESTIMATING BY ANALOGY

Estimating by analogy uses the actual cost of a similar previous project as the basis for estimating the cost of the current project. The approach assumes that comparable elements of the new and existing systems and subsystems cost the same. The project planner, together with other stakeholders, concludes that a prospective job opportunity is a constant percentage more or less difficult than a similar previous job. On the basis of their collective experience, they arrive at a percentage that expresses the degree of difficulty of the prospective project compared with the reference project. The estimator multiplies the cost of the reference job by this percentage to arrive at a cost for the opportunity under consideration. Managers sometimes use the technique to estimate total project costs if only a limited amount of detailed information exists about the project. Here again, people may have difficulty estimating new technologies because of the lack of an earlier reference project.

As an example of estimating by analogy, suppose a company receives an RFQ on the purchase, installation, networking, and testing of 100 computers. The estimator assigned to the project recalls that a previous network installation of 150 computers in an office building cost $750,000, including all direct and indirect costs. On the basis of the principle of estimating by analogy, the planner concludes that, since 100 computers represents two-thirds of the previous job, a reasonable estimate for the proposed project would be two-thirds of $750,000, or $500,000. This approach is fast, easy, and economical, but is heavily dependent on the accuracy of the information about previous work. It also requires the expertise of people qualified to evaluate and compare different jobs.

LEARNING CURVE

The concept of a learning curve recognizes that employee productivity improves as the person gains familiarity with the sequence of activities involved in the production process. Repeating a task results in a learning effect. ("Practice makes perfect.") Up to a point, as people gain familiarity with a process, they become more skilled, and the time taken to complete the process decreases. Musicians and athletes understand the learning curve well. As they train, their confidence grows; they increase their speed, improve their reliability, and gain accuracy. Plotting the number of wrong notes that a student learning a musical instrument plays while practicing a new piece might result in something like Table 7–9.

The table shows that the student experienced a learning effect. Initially unfamiliar with the piece, the student gained confidence and expertise after each repetition, and the number of incorrect notes decreased. The majority of the learning benefit occurred over the first few attempts, but there was continual slight improvement over time.

In a 1936 article, the concept of the learning curve concept was applied to the aircraft industry.[2] The article described a theory for obtaining cost estimates based on the repetitive production of airplane assemblies. Ever since, estimators have applied learning curves to all types of work ranging from simple to complex tasks.

According to the idea behind the learning curve, each time the quantity produced doubles, the cumulative average time to produce a unit reduces by a constant percentage of the previous cumulative time. As an example, suppose a technician performs a site acceptance test on a recently installed computer system. The functional manager estimates that the first unit will require 100 hours of testing, including the time required to prepare a written report. The functional manager believes that subsequent testing will follow an 80% learning curve. Applying the learning curve concept results in an 80-hour-per-unit average testing time for the first two units and a 64-hour-per-unit average testing time for the first four units. Table 7–10 shows the results of this 80% learning curve.

TABLE 7–9

Improvements Resulting from Practicing an Instrument

Number of Repetitions	Number of Incorrect Musical Notes
1	20
2	12
3	9
4	7
5	6
6	6
7	5
8	4

---

[2] Wright, T. P., "Factors Affecting the Cost of Airplanes," *Journal of Aeronautical Science*, vol. 3, no. 4 (1936): 122–128.

TABLE 7–10

Eighty Percent Learning Curve Applied to a Test of a Computer System

Number of Units Tested, n	Learning-Curve Factor	Average Estimated Time to Test Units (Hours/Unit)	Cumulative Estimated Time to Test n Units (Hours)
1		100	100
2	80%	80	160
4	80%	64	256
8	80%	51.2	409.6
16	80%	40.96	655.36

The first unit required 100 hours to test. Doubling the quantity of one to two units results in an average of 80 hours to test each unit, for a total of 160 hours for the two units. Doubling the two units to four reduces the average time required to test and prepare a report to 80% of 80 hours, or 64 hours, which results in a total estimated time of 256 hours. The learning curve continues as shown in the remainder of Table 7–10.

Table 7–11 illustrates the time required to perform the identical tests as in Table 7–10, but this time using a 90% learning curve. Note that the average test time increases compared with that of the 80% curve. The upper limit of 100% for the learning curve means that learning does not take place at all. Each unit then takes the same labor time as the first. (See Table 7–12.) A 50% learning

TABLE 7–11

Ninety Percent Learning Curve Applied to a Test of a Computer System

Number of Units Tested, n	Learning-Curve Factor	Average Estimated Time to Test Units (Hours/Unit)	Cumulative Estimated Time to Test n Units (Hours)
1		100	100
2	90%	90	180
4	90%	81	324
8	90%	72.9	583.2
16	90%	65.61	1,049.76

TABLE 7–12

One Hundred Percent Learning Curve Applied to a Test of a Computer System: no Learning Takes Place

Number of Units Tested, n	Learning-Curve Factor	Average Estimated Time to Test Units (Hours/Unit)	Cumulative Estimated Time to Test n Units (Hours)
1		100	100
2	100%	100	200
4	100%	100	400
8	100%	100	800
16	100%	100	1,600

TABLE 7–13

Fifty Percent Learning Curve Applied to a Test of a Computer System

Number of Units Tested, n	Learning-Curve Factor	Average Estimated Time to Test Units (Hours/Unit)	Cumulative Estimated Time to Test n Units (Hours)
1		100	100
2	50%	50	100
4	50%	25	100
8	50%	12.5	100
16	50%	6.25	100

curve results if the worker takes no additional time to test the next doubled number of systems (Table 7–13). A 50% learning curve is akin to a perpetual-motion machine; it is difficult to conceive of testing n systems for the price of one.

The estimator can use the log–log graph in Figure 7–3 to calculate the labor hours required to complete a repetitive task. Suppose that testing the first unit requires 100 hours. Then we can estimate the labor hours required to test 10 units by using the graph. For a 10-unit production run, the average number of hours required to test a unit by using a 75, 80, and 85% learning curve is approximately 39, 49, and 60 hours, respectively. The cumulative numbers of hours

FIGURE 7–3

Parametric graph of learning curve

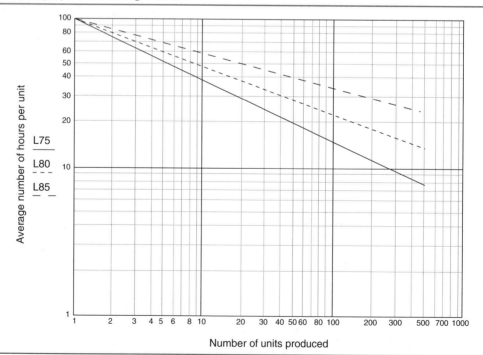

FIGURE 7–4

Use of the learning-curve parametric graph

Number of units produced	1	2	5	10

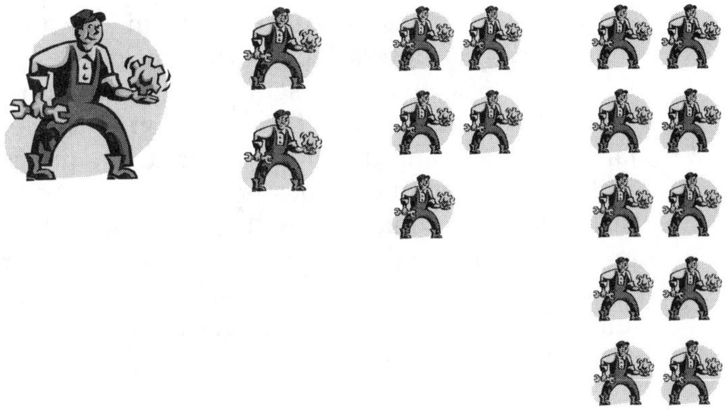

	1	2	5	10
Labor hours required for unit 1	150	150	150	150
Ratio of labor estimate for unit 1 to baseline reference (100 hours)	1.5	1.5	1.5	1.5
From Figure 7–3, average number of labor hours per unit with a 75% learning curve	100	75	52	39
Adjusted average number of labor hours with a 75% learning curve	150	113	78	59
Total labor hours with a 75% learning curve	150	126	390	590

required to test 10 units, assuming 75, 80, and 85% learning curves, are 390, 490, and 600 hours, respectively. Of course, if no learning took place, the time required to test 10 units would be 1,000 hours.

Figure 7–4 illustrates how to use the graph of the learning curve to calculate the labor hours for multiple prototype units with an initial estimate other than 100 hours. Suppose a planner uses the graph to estimate the labor hours required to build 2, 5, and 10 computer prototype units. Figure 7–3 provides data for the number of units, based on a 100-hour first unit. The estimator feels confident that testing the first unit will take 150 hours. He or she then creates an adjustment factor, which is the ratio of the labor estimate for unit 1 to the baseline reference of 100 hours (150/100) for unit 1. Figure 7–3 shows that, for a 5-prototype run, the average number of labor hours per unit with a 75%

learning curve is 52 hours. The estimator accordingly adjusts the average number of hours to compensate for the 150-hour initial effort. This is done by multiplying 52 hours by the adjustment factor 1.5, which results in an average of 78 hours per unit. The total number of hours required to produce 5 units is found by multiplying 78 hours by 5, which yields 390 hours.

Learning curves usually range from 75% to 90%. A 90% learning curve represents a cautious selection that anticipates a modest amount of learning, whereas a 75% curve represents an aggressive estimate that expects the stakeholders to learn rapidly. The selection of the learning curve can affect the labor estimate, and therefore the price of a project, dramatically. Even if the technician or engineer does not contribute to the estimate for a repetitive task, the project manager will have applied this curve to the estimate. The project manager will expect to see reductions in the labor effort as the repetitive work progresses. Any technologist performing the repetitive task should anticipate a visit from the project manager if the reduction is less than the estimate predicts.

PROJECT ESTIMATING SUMMARY

Predicting the cost of a project accurately is vital to the survival of any organization. The project manager has the responsibility for assembling and gathering estimates of

- labor required
- costs of materials
- costs of new equipment and tools
- special training costs
- the amount of business-related travel
- consultants' costs
- other required project resources
- risk

The project manager also is responsible for coordinating the bids of prospective subcontractors.

To remain competitive, organizations must bid the lowest price, yet deliver a technically superior product or service in the fastest time with the best quality, fulfilling the modern technology mantra, "Faster, cheaper, smaller, better!" This is a challenge, to be sure, and the team, led by the project manager, must meet it.

The estimating process begins with the decision to submit a bid. After reviewing the specifications and other documentation pertaining to the project, the estimator meets with the functional managers to decide on the methodology used to calculate the price (top down or bottom up) and on the learning-curve percentage. The estimator compiles and analyzes data on all costs associated with the project—costs such as the cost of materials, labor, location, and equipment. Since most organizations earn only a relatively small profit margin on many projects, it is vital to obtain an accurate estimate. Because a top-down estimate requires appropriate historical data, as well as software and training of personnel, smaller organizations that have not acquired the requisite software may decide to use a bottom-up approach (sometimes in combination with estimating by analogy) to complete the estimate. Many senior executives use their own favorite rules of thumb to test the "sanity" of the organization's final estimate.

Estimating the impact of a new technology on a project represents a challenge to almost all of the cost-estimating approaches discussed. Technical staff unfamiliar with the use of a new tool will require time to gain the required expertise. The staff also may require formal training in the use of new products or different versions of existing products. Cutting-edge efforts may even call for the use of tools or equipment with "bugs"—usage problems not yet worked out. Manufacturers sometimes offer "beta" software packages, products not yet formally released for sale because minor technical issues remain concerning their use. The use of unproven software will slow down a project. Teams must make allowances for new tools, equipment, and technologies. Aggressive labor estimates in these cases will likely come back to haunt the organization. Clearly, project cost estimating is as much an art as a skill and improves with experience.

If time permits, multiple estimating techniques can be used to bolster the technologist's expert judgment. Executives will examine the resulting estimate from a broad perspective, paying particular attention to the final price and comparing it with what the organization knows about the competition and the customer's expectations. Management will also take a close look at the anticipated percent profit and exposure to risk. Having quantified the risk, the project manager should be prepared to discuss the following issues:

- technical and performance concerns
- challenges to the schedule
- the availability of labor in the organization
- the cost and availability of equipment and tools
- the cost and availability of other required resources
- required training for personnel
- problems with suppliers
- competitive situations
- other cost drivers

After reviewing and digesting this information, management will decide either to go with the estimating team's recommendation, to adjust the team's recommended price, or, less often, not to bid on the job.

COST MANAGEMENT

The organization that wins the contract may congratulate itself, but there is no time for celebrating: Now the organization must perform. Although not the only concern, making a profit is high on the list. As mentioned earlier, most corporate profits are in the 10–15% region. The project manager must protect against excessive spending, and that requires careful cost control procedures. Cost control requires cooperation from every stakeholder and, at a minimum, includes the following factors:

- organizational support
- preparation and distribution of budgets, together with work authorizations based on the WBS
- monitoring the schedule, technical performance, and the budget
- gathering and reporting data
- cost and schedule variance analyses
- baseline maintenance and control (i.e., manage the customer)

Financial and Schedule Analysis

Project cost management begins with a set of expectations that includes a realistic and accurate estimate of the costs associated with the project, together with an equally realistic schedule. It certainly is not a good first step if suppliers and functional managers gasp and throw up their hands in horror upon initially examining the budget and schedule. By the same token, the project manager has the right to expect that stakeholders feel committed to the project by providing appropriate resources at the times designated by the schedule. The project manager must be confident that people will work on the job when they are required to, that material will arrive on time, that suppliers will deliver equipment on time, and that personnel will obtain the requisite training to use the equipment and tools on time. After the project manager creates and distributes budgets to the functional managers for each of the work packages identified in the WBS, he or she expects that stakeholders will strive to meet the schedule's demands. Unfortunately, because this doesn't frequently happen, the project manager monitors the budget and schedule carefully in order to identify problems at an early stage of the project. In support of this effort, the organization completes and submits time cards so that financial administrators can determine who is working on what job and how much time they are spending on it.

Financial analysts review data on labor, purchases of material, ODC, travel, etc., on a weekly basis. At the beginning of the project, the project manager calculated a spending profile for the budget. Each week, financial administrators compare the budgeted distribution of funds with actual expenditures. If the actual charges are too high (Figure 7–5), it could signify a technical problem (bad news!), or, on the positive side, it could mean that the schedule is farther along than initially planned. In the former case, the project manager seeks to identify the cause of the problem and then tries to secure greater expertise in order to eliminate it.

If the actual charges are lower than those budgeted (Figure 7–6) different issues exist. Perhaps the functional managers overestimated the complexity of the work, and the expected amount of work was accomplished by spending less money than anticipated. (The probability of this happening is only slightly

FIGURE 7–5

Comparison of project's budgeted funds with actual expenditures: overspending

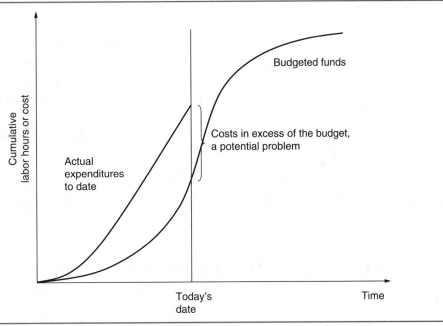

FIGURE 7–6

Comparison of project's budgeted funds with actual expenditures: underspending

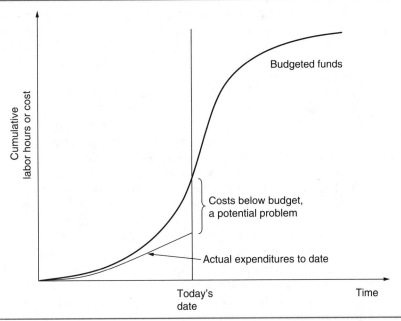

better than a used-car salesperson telling the truth.) The more likely reason for a budget underrun falls into one or more of these categories:

- Fewer people than promised have worked on the job and the project is behind schedule.
- The purchasing department has not ordered equipment or material.
- Suppliers have not shipped equipment or material.

Examining the schedule should reveal where the problem lies. To resolve it, many project managers use the earned-value method, a powerful quantitative tool for monitoring the schedule and the financial progress of the project discussed in Chapter 11. Earned value requires that the organization have extensive software and administrative capabilities, as a great deal of information must be collected and analyzed in a short time. An enterprise resource-planning (ERP) system is the ideal vehicle for collecting data. An ERP system combines all financial, human resource, manufacturing, inventory, engineering, and purchasing software packages into a single integrated system accessible by the organization's employees.

Stakeholders Requiring Special Attention

Many project managers periodically visit, or at least maintain contact with, suppliers of critical material and equipment used on a project. The project manager contacts these vendors regularly and discusses technical issues and the progress of the schedule with them in an effort to eliminate or, at the worst, minimize surprises. If technical or schedule-related issues surface, the project manager needs time to work around them. The project manager may devise alternative plans, modify schedules, reshuffle labor, or even consider withdrawing the contract from the subcontractor if the problems warrant such an action.

Engineers and technicians enjoy tinkering. They love to experiment and to "tweak" just a bit more performance from the system. While scientific curiosity may be an admirable technical trait, if left uncontrolled, it can cost time and money. The project manager must sometimes remind the technologist to provide customers with the products and services they agreed upon contractually. The customer should get what it paid for and not a bit more—if more means adding to the cost of the project or the lengthening the schedule. Conversely, if the functional manager or project manager requests some sort of a change in the work, it behooves the technologist to request an increase in the budget or schedule. After all, the technician or engineer developing the product or service will also be judged on his or her adherence to the schedule and budget.

Perhaps the most difficult aspect of cost control involves managing customers. Invariably, at some point in the project, customers discover that they require a change to the contract—perhaps some additional features, an additional piece of equipment, another report, or a newer version of some software. The changes wrought from an innocent realization that the customer missed something in the specification of the original contract may be enormous. Once the project has started and the team proceeds, tasks are completed quickly. A change to the contract would require redoing some of the work, thereby incurring additional labor charges. Items returned to a supplier may incur restocking fees. The use of a new or revised software package may bring with it unforeseen system integration issues that cost time. The project manager walks a delicate line, balancing contractual agreements with the desire to "delight the customer." The project manager wishes to satisfy the customer in hopes of obtaining repeat business, yet also wishes to make a profit on the project. Frequently, the project manager's annual review or financial bonus depends on the success of the project: It must turn a profit.

A common approach to resolving issues involves good old "horse trading." The project manager exchanges an existing contractual element for the change that the customer desires. The project manager should attempt to exchange items of similar cost. For example, suppose a customer desires to replace an old, but reliable, software package with a recently released version. Suppose also that the functional manager would love to use the new package because it contains several features that customer's have requested. In that case, a "win–win" situation emerges. Management may view the customer's request as an opportunity to invest a small amount of money to update the organization's product. Perhaps the new software incorporates features that the organization would like to develop as part of the project. Then using the new software might save money. Sometimes an organization will agree to a customer's demand in exchange for relieving a difficult contractual specification.

One of the project manager's rules of thumb should be not to change the SOW without a corresponding increase in contract funding. Some government contractors have used this idea to their advantage. Recognizing that the vast majority of contracts involve changes after the contract is awarded, they bid the job with figures that reflect little or no profit. After they win the contract, they charge significant sums for the changes that invariably ensue.

REVIEW QUESTIONS

1. "A project manager has responsibility for the technical content, cost, and schedule pertaining to a project." Explain this statement.
2. What quantitative measures can a project manager use to determine that a project's activities are progressing satisfactorily?
   a) Examine the budget.
   b) Compare the budget for labor and materials with actual expenditures.
   c) Compare the schedule with actual progress on the project.
   d) Ask the functional managers to provide figures.
   e) Ask the company's vice president to provide figures.
3. Explain the difference between bottom-up and top-down estimating.
4. True or false? A project manager uses a learning curve to estimate the labor time required to perform repetitive activities.
5. The time required for a person to perform an activity a second time will usually take (<u>more</u>, <u>less</u>) time than is required to perform the activity the first time. Explain.
6. Describe the difference between direct and indirect costs.
7. Explain the purpose of a material-handling fee. Do you think such a fee is justified? Explain.

8. Give examples of other direct costs (ODC) that may be charged to a project.
9. Describe the difference between overhead and G&A costs.
10. Your boss has developed the following rules of thumb pertaining to the time taken to prepare a document:

    Each PowerPoint slide requires 45 minutes per page, including research time.

    Each text page requires six hours.

    Each graphic (picture, drawing, etc.) requires two hours.

    The contract requires the preparation of a training manual. On the basis of similar previous jobs, the trainers estimate that a manual will contain 25 pages of text and 12 graphics. They estimate that they will require 37 slides to teach the course associated with the product. Estimate the time (in hours) that will be required to complete the training manual and to present the training class.
11. Why does the use of a new hardware or software tool entail some measure of risk? How should the project manager or functional managers minimize this risk?
12. A small service business wishes to determine the amount of money to charge its customers. The service manager calculates that the average salary the company pays its technicians is $32 per hour. The company's accountant informs the service manager that the overhead expense and G&A rates are 50 and 25%, respectively. The company president informs the service manager that a 20% profit is expected. What should the service manager charge the company's customers for labor on an hourly basis?
13. Explain the difference between the price a customer pays for a product or service and the developer's cost for the product or service.
14. As the project manager for a medium-sized company, you have collected the following data from the organization's functional department managers during an effort to prepare a proposal:

Functional Department	Average Salary ($)	Labor Hours	Department Overhead Rate (%)	Purchases, Leases, and Rentals of Materials ($)	Travel, Living, and Entertainment Costs ($)	Fees for Consultants ($)
Electrical engineering	$45.50	1,775	55	$45,000	$800	$4,400
Mechanical engineering	$42.75	225	55	$31,000	$500	$5,100
Software engineering	$48.10	2,400	45	$37,000	$1,000	$6,200
Network engineering	$53.00	160	48	$29,000		
Technician	$31.60	310	35	$1,000	$500	
Field service	$29.30	145	40	$1,500	$2,500	
Training	$28.75	90	30	$570	$4,200	

The company's accountant informs you that the organization's G&A rate is 33%. The software department indicates that it has a 10% risk associated with the development process. No other department has identified any significant risk. The company's vice president expects to earn a 15% profit and has asked you to prepare a chart that summarizes the project's costs and the price to the customer. She would like to discuss the project with you tomorrow afternoon.

a) What information will you bring to the meeting with the vice president?

b) Will you request support personnel to accompany you to the meeting? If so, whom will you bring and why?

c) Prepare the financial material that you will show to the vice president that leads to the suggested customer price. Keep in mind that the material must be clear—indeed, almost self-explanatory. Minimize written material and try to organize the material into charts.

15. The following problem simulates a small-business activity: Create a three-member team corresponding to the three owners of CompRep, a small company that performs system maintenance and repair. The principals represent three different perspectives. Gayle provided the majority of risk funding to start the business and becomes involved in major business decisions. She invested $100,000 in the business at its founding. As the major investor, she is interested in protecting her investment and expects to see at least a 10% annual return on her money. Keisha provides the technical expertise. She is thoroughly familiar with the construction, maintenance, repair, and networking software associated with computers. She has passed the A+, N+, Project+, MCP, MCSE, CNA, and CCNA certification examinations. Her motto is "Never fear, Keisha is here." She receives a salary of $45,000 per year. Tamir is in charge of sales. During the past three years, maintenance and repair contract sales have grown consistently from $200,000 in the first year to last year's $450,000 total. Tamir works on a 6% commission of the gross sales price. He wants to offer customers a low contract price to get their business. After all, no sale means no commission and no salary for Tamir.

The CompRep owners have decided to bid on a two-year computer maintenance and repair project for a local school district. The district has 780 computers located in two buildings that are 10 miles apart. The schools are open for operation 180 days per year. On average, 1% of the computers fail each week of operation. The following chart illustrates the historic component failure rate for the school district's computers:

Component	Distribution of Component and Module Failures (%)	Annual Average Cost of Materials ($)	Average Labor Hours Spent in Diagnosis and Repair
Power supply	45	75	1.2
Memory chip	15	68	0.6
Floppy disk	8	27	1.5
Hard drive	5	179	2.5
Sound card	3	79	0.8
Video card	3	119	0.8
Motherboard	5	375	2.5
Network interface card	6	65	0.9
Other interface cards	9	55	1.0
Cables and connectors	1	30	1.0

The CompRep facility lies midway between the two schools. The contract demands a 24-hour turnaround time for repairs. Service personnel may gain access to the school from Monday to Friday between the hours of hours of 8:00 A.M. and 4:00 P.M. Distributors guarantee to deliver replacement components within 48 hours of placing an order. The existing business presently grosses $450,000 annually. The owners wish to expand the business, and winning this contract represents a significant step in that direction.

As the owners of the company, the team you have created must calculate a competitive price to submit to the school district. In addition to Keisha and Tamir, CompRep employs another computer technician and a receptionist, for a total of four full-time employees. A bookkeeper and a computer technician make up the company's half-time employees. As your team goes through the bidding process, questions will arise that require the principles to make certain assumptions. Note these questions and the assumptions reached about CompRep and its business. Use the following chart to answer the questions that follow:

Item	Quantity	Annual Expense ($)	Comment
Salaries of full-time employees	4		
Salaries of part-time employees	2		
Legal expenses		$1,500	On retainer to review documents
Advertising expenses		$7,500	
Rent		$30,000	
Utilities		$8,000	
Liability insurance		$4,000	
Office supplies			
Membership in professional and local organizations			
Maintenance and repair of facilities		$1,000	
Office equipment costs			FAX, copy machine, cell phone, office phone

a) Complete the annual costs omitted in the chart.
b) Calculate CompRep's annual payroll.
c) Calculate the overhead and G&A expenses. Assume that FICA and Medicaid taxes total 10% of the employees' annual salaries.
d) Decide whether you need to stock certain hardware components. If you do, identify which components and the quantity to purchase.
e) What profit should CompRep seek?
f) What was the increase in the cost of living last year? How would you find this out?
g) Because the term of the contract is two years, separate the costs into year 1 and year 2 to take into account the likelihood of increases in labor and materials due to inflation.
h) Based on the data provided, how many trips to each school are required during the year? What is the annual transportation cost? Use a travel expense of $.33 per mile in your calculations.
i) How much labor time is required to fulfill the requirements of the contract?
j) What price will CompRep submit to the customer for the two-year computer maintenance-and-repair contract? Support your team's decision with the appropriate spreadsheet calculations.

CHAPTER 8

PROJECT COMMUNICATION

> *There is a* w *and an* e, *but no* i, *in teamwork.*

OBJECTIVES

After studying this chapter, you should be able to

- Understand the role of communications in projects
- Prepare crisp, informative, and to-the-point memos
- Conduct a worthwhile meeting
- Understand how to follow up on actions decided upon at meetings

INTRODUCTION

Communication is a process whereby people exchange information. Organizations use a variety of means to inform and influence others, including the following:

- Written messages, such as memos and reports
- Discussions that use verbal and nonverbal exchanges of information
- Telephone conversations
- Audio and video conferencing
- Meetings
- Lectures
- Graphics (charts, illustrations, photographs, clip art, and graphs)

Project communication deals with the processes required to ensure the timely and appropriate generation, collection, dissemination, storage, and ultimate disposition of information.[1] Project managers spend a large portion of their day receiving or distributing information. The delivery of this information frequently demands that the project manager have excellent social as well as technical skills. Knowing *how* and *when* to say and present information is just as important as knowing *what* to say.

COMMUNICATION MANAGEMENT

During the early phases of a project, project managers promote the exchange of technical requirements, data, interface descriptions, information about assignments, schedules, work authorizations, and contractual documents among stakeholders. Throughout the project, the project manager prepares and reports information about the status or performance of some aspect of the project after receiving data from the stakeholders. Members of the organization submit interim reports to management, regulatory agencies, suppliers, and the customer. All stakeholders need to be quickly informed about significant issues that arise during the project. The project manager controls and coordinates this flow of information. The end of the job brings with it a flurry of documentation preparation that includes test reports, descriptions of the final product or service, training and maintenance manuals, and financial analyses. Delivery and installation of the newly developed product requires a good deal of interaction between project and customer personnel. Finally, just before closing out the project, the staff prepares a list of "lessons learned" and shares the information with colleagues. In this way, everyone benefits from one another's experience.

Table 8–1 illustrates the various kinds of information exchanged by technologists during the project. Depending on the recipient, technologists prepare

---

[1] Project Management Institute Standards Committee, *A Guide to the Project Management Body of Knowledge* (Upper Darby, PA: Project Management Institute, 1996).

TABLE 8-1

Information Transfer Considerations

Feature	Examples
Target audience	Colleagues, manufacturing department, customers, technicians, management, government regulators, suppliers
Type of material	Data sheets, specifications, documents, drawings, graphics, reports, proposals, letters, orders, statements, invoices, schematics, manuals, contracts, samples, memos, technical information, directions, standard forms
Transfer time	Overnight, immediate, future
Transfer method	E-mail, U.S. mail, overnight delivery, courier service, telephone conference, voice mail, video, meetings, lectures
Electronic format	ASCII files, rtf, Word files, Macintosh or PC, voice, video, other application-specific software
Electronic images	Gif, jpeg, bmp, tif
Media	Paper, vellum, electronic (e.g., zip drive, floppy disk, CD, magnetic tape), computer display, overhead transparencies, 35-mm slides

material in different ways. Personnel frequently submit monthly reports and descriptions of problems and issues by e-mail. Many use overhead transparencies or give a PowerPoint presentation for larger audiences. Unbelievably, governmental agencies and some large organizations still insist on using typewriters to complete some standard forms.

Communication Pathways

A project usually requires decisions and actions to be taken in a large number of areas. Most information exchange takes place in a lateral direction: among colleagues in functional groups. Figure 8–1 illustrates the usual communication pathways followed by project stakeholders. For example, only the project manager should speak with the customer; in effect, the project manager is the customer's point of contact with the organization. Responsibility for the organization's commitment to perform a task or agree to a change normally rests with the project manager. If the project manager is discussing a topic with the customer that involves details with which the project manager does not feel comfortable, then he or she frequently requests a technical person to participate in the discussions. The project manager also leads management briefings. Functional groups, the manufacturing department, and suppliers support the effort as required. If permanent or temporary workers are to be hired, then each of the internal stakeholders works directly with the human resource department.

FIGURE 8–1

Communication pathways

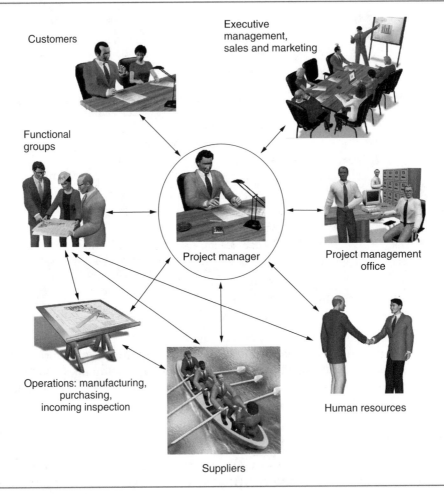

Customers

Executive management, sales and marketing

Functional groups

Project manager

Project management office

Operations: manufacturing, purchasing, incoming inspection

Human resources

Suppliers

Communication Protocols

In their zeal to impress all people in the organization with their unbounded knowledge, new employees sometimes let the ease with which names may be added to the e-mail list overcome their good judgment. Employees should always inform their immediate supervisor first about anything and everything. Problems, issues, customer compliments or complaints, late deliveries, system failures, machine breakdowns—everything—should be reported to the supervisor. Novice technicians love to announce to anyone who will listen that they have discovered the "next best thing since sliced bread." They have solved problems that have troubled the organization since its inception. Trouble arises when their boss's boss is among those listening. Informing him or her before informing the boss violates courtesy as well as an unwritten organizational cardinal rule. Weber's organizational hierarchy still applies: Workers should follow the chain of command and give their supervisors the courtesy of assessing their findings. Then the supervisor should suggest the time and place at which the information should be announced and the people to whom to announce it.

Organization's personnel have an assortment of political agendas. Upsetting a supervisor may impede a worker's advancement; making the boss look good may bring choice job opportunities and a better chance for a salary increase. Remember, the functional manager assigns work and recommends people for promotion and salary adjustments. The worker should develop his or her supervisor into an ally, treading lightly and sharing the glory until the worker has learned to operate in the political organizational jungle.

COMMUNICATION PROCESS

The project manager has the responsibility for the flow of information. He or she makes needed information available to project stakeholders in a timely manner.[2] The project manager decides on the content of a message, to whom to send the message, its tone, and the degree of technical complexity it possesses. Highly technical information sometimes needs to be translated into language that all can understand. Politically sensitive or damaging messages require that words be selected so as to minimize the organization's discomfort. Project managers use communication to build consensus.

Words are interpreted in different ways, depending on one's background. Sociology teaches that people from different cultures have different expectations and perceptions, and the same holds in different organizational environments. Consider, for example, the following e-mail messages:

Message 1	COME SEE ME!
	BOB
Message 2	See me at your earliest convenience.
	Bill

Upon reading the first message, one is likely to think, "Uh oh, what have I done now?" The tone of the second message is not quite as threatening. Many people familiar with e-mail interpret a message in all capitals as shouting. It may be, though, that Bob is not an experienced typist and does not want to bother with lowercase letters.

Figure 8–2 illustrates a message interpreted differently by two people. Maria comments that she would like to eat strawberries for lunch, and Tom interprets the message as a request for strawberry pie. This is a minor misunderstanding, but it is not unusual. On the one hand, one should be specific in conveying information to others in order to minimize misinterpretation. On the other hand, one has to respect the sensitivities of different cultures. Some

---

[2] *Ibid.*

FIGURE 8–2

The communication encoder–decoder environment

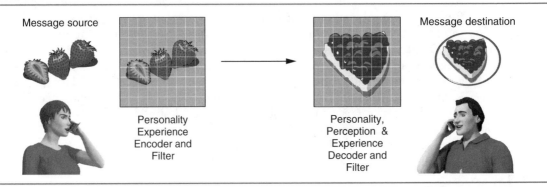

Message source

Personality
Experience
Encoder and
Filter

Personality,
Perception &
Experience
Decoder and
Filter

Message destination

cultures prefer a forthright and frank presentation; others find that approach offensive. Everyone brings a unique personality and background experience to the workplace, which may color their interpretation of the information.

CONDUCTING EFFECTIVE MEETINGS

Project managers spend a lot of time in meetings, chiefly because meetings are a cost-effective way to convey information to a group of people. It is certainly less time consuming to meet collectively than individually. At a meeting, the participants discuss the information presented and begin to clarify issues. Frequently, issues arise that require further information. At the conclusion of the meeting, the chair reviews the activities discussed and assigns various responsibilities. That is, the chair selects people and asks them to obtain answers to questions that arose during the meeting.

An effective meeting requires preparation (Figure 8–3). Before calling the meeting, the project manager thinks through what he or she expects to accomplish. An agenda is prepared to clarify the purpose of the meeting. The agenda should reflect the meeting's priorities. After the project manager allocates time to each topic on the agenda, he or she sends the prospective attendees a notice of the meeting. Included in the notice are the agenda and information on the starting time, the place, and the anticipated length of the meeting. The last item acknowledges the fact that people have busy schedules and represents a courtesy to enable them to plan the remainder of their day. The project manager should start the meeting on time; if people are late, the meeting should be conducted without them. If a project manager habitually begins meetings late, people will come to them late.

Data, documents, and special information are distributed in advance of the meeting, especially if the group will review or make decisions regarding the material presented. All participants should be permitted to comment on the

FIGURE 8–3

Procedure for conducting effective meetings

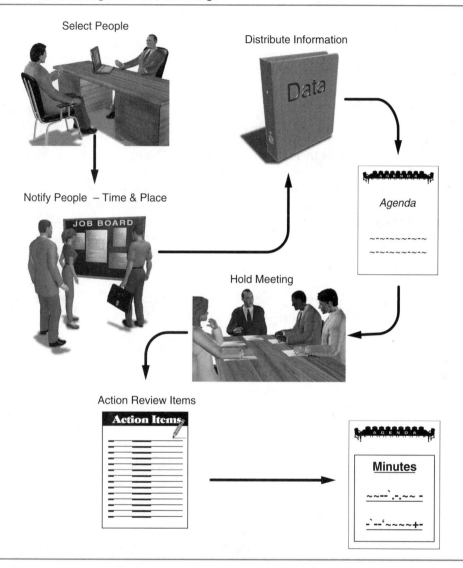

Select People

Distribute Information

Notify People – Time & Place

Agenda

Hold Meeting

Action Review Items

Action Items

Minutes

material, but no one must dominate the discussion. At the start of the meeting, the project manager assigns a person to take minutes. Copies of the minutes are sent to the participants within a reasonable time following the meeting.

No meeting is complete without assigning action items. During the course of most meetings, participants raise issues requiring examination and resolution. The chair assigns the responsibility for resolving these issues to appropriate people and expects the issues to be resolved by an agreed-upon date, usually determined by the person assigned the responsibility, unless the work demands a specific, independent deadline date. Often, the participants decide to hold another meeting to review their progress on, or completion of, the tasks for which they are responsible.

MEMOS

Memos represent the grease for the communication machinery that makes things happen in medium-sized to large organizations. A memo is a no-nonsense communication document that is designed to quickly inform or ask something from people within an organization or work group. Employees use memos to tell their supervisors that they have accomplished a specific task or have confronted a problem in attempting to do so. Many project managers keep a memo record of the activities performed on a project. They create a paper trail recording the actions and agreements among the project's stakeholders. While most memos are brief, they should follow good technical-writing principles, using clear and accurate language. Memos reflect on the organization and the person that wrote it. Stakeholders jump to the conclusion that the writer of a sloppily written and unclear memo is unfocused.

E-mail messages are now by far the most common form of memo. In fact, every memo should follow e-mail format, which is as follows:

Date:
To:
From:
cc:
Subject:
      Body of memo

The term "cc" comes from carbon copy paper. While the technology is obsolete, the term persists. People placed on the cc list receive a copy of the memo. In "cc'ing," the chain of command should be observed. Memos distributed to the proper personnel will gain the trust and respect of management.

Memos should be short and to the point, no more than one page. The purpose is stated clearly in the first paragraph, preferably in the first sentence. Supporting and clarifying information appears in subsequent paragraphs. The journalist's questions—who, what, when, where, and why—are answered. Bulleted lists get the idea across succinctly. With bullets, the receiver of the memo can immediately get an idea of its importance and decide whether to read the additional information. Jargon should not be used, unless one is certain that the reader will understand it. To be on the safe side, unusual expressions and acronyms should be defined. Information that is quantitative, such as performance information, status reports, measures of progress, forecasts, and other numerically based reports, may be cast into charts with appropriate column headings. Copies of the memo should be sent only to those people who have a need for the information.

A memo should be both polite and upbeat. Unless its purpose is simply to inform, the memo should conclude with specific recommendations for actions, to be taken on specific dates. Managers value the professional who identifies a problem and provides recommendations for solving it.

Finally, the memo is proofread. In addition, its tone is examined. Criticism is softened, and harsh comments are deleted. English usage should be checked, as should spelling, preferably with a word processor's spell checker. Finally, the memo should be proofread again: A spell checker will not catch correctly spelled words used incorrectly. Obvious grammatical errors and misspellings reflect badly on the writer of the memo.

LISTENING

Perhaps the most difficult aspect of communication is listening. Everyone loves to talk and have his or her views heard, so it is questionable just how much people listen to others.

The single most important step one can take to improve his or her listening skills is to stop talking and pay attention to people. Listen to their verbal statements and watch their nonverbal gestures. Make eye contact with the speaker. The eyes pick up the nonverbal signals that people send out when they are speaking. Be patient and let the talker get his or her idea across. Go easy with arguments and criticisms. Ask questions, listen to the answers, and repeat the speaker's words. Remain open to new ideas.

People feel strongly about issues and want to be taken seriously. Even in cases where one disagrees with a person's argument, listening to it helps to build a rapport with that person. In a group setting, one should state one's points firmly, but in a friendly manner. Opinions should be supported with facts, and points made by other members of the group should be acknowledged.

During the project life cycle, there is constant **negotiation**—the process through which two people or groups with differing wishes or views strive to reach a satisfactory agreement. The parties may not be mutually satisfied with a negotiated outcome, but they can accommodate the decision.

Negotiations cannot begin until both parties listen to each other. Only after groups begin to understand one another can they work toward a resolution of their disagreement. Listen and ask for your colleague's opinions. Negotiation is a two-way street: The parties present and build on each other's ideas. The structure of a compromise solution frequently evolves when the parties borrow ideas and meld them together.

Listening is just one of the "people skills" that project managers develop. A project manager gets things done through people by respecting them and fostering their trust. The best project manager is one who lets people "do their thing" and lets them know how they are doing. Micromanaging is the key to failure. Good project managers offer their praise freely, because praise does not cost anything and can sometimes make employees who feel undervalued more cooperative. An open and active communications policy should be established early in the project.

VERBAL COMMUNICATION

Telephone Protocol

Telephone conversations consume project managers for much of the day. The project manager speaks with suppliers, aids technicians in obtaining technical information, requests a status report from a software functional manager, asks FedEx about its delivery schedule, requests travel information, reassures a customer regarding its order, discusses a personnel issue with a member of the human resource department, requests financial information from an administrative assistant, and talks with other internal and external stakeholders about a myriad of issues. The project manager follows correct protocols during these telephone conversations. At the beginning of a phone call, the person called identifies him- or herself. A typical greeting might be "This is Jane Dawkins speaking. May I help you?" The caller immediately states something like "Good morning, this is José Padua. I am a project manager from Villa-Tech, and I am inquiring about _____."

Courtesy and tact are mandatory, even when the customer has just finished complaining about an instrument that was omitted from the last shipment, causing a week's slippage in the schedule. The recipient of the complaint should remain calm and courteous during the customer's tirade, all the while explaining that the omission was inadvertent and will never happen again. After the call, one should continue to remain calm and proceed with business as usual, in order to avoid jeopardizing relationships with other customers.

It helps to take notes during a telephone conversation. Then, at the end of the call, one has a record to go back to to refresh one's memory regarding what the call was about. The exchange may warrant a summary e-mail sent to the caller, with copies to a colleague or supervisor. Sometimes, one sends the summary e-mail only to oneself as a permanent record of the conversation. E-mail affords an excellent opportunity to maintain a historic record of communications relating to a project.

Face-to-Face Meetings

Speaking in front of both large and small groups is a fact of organizational life. The project manager does it every day. Such talks should inform, persuade, and involve the participants. Conversations with one or two people should be conducted in a businesslike manner, sticking to technical or business matters. Small talk and non-business-related conversations should be minimized, and discussions about politics, religion, race, ethnicity, gender, sex, and personal or family matters should be avoided altogether. People hold strong opinions especially about politics and religion, and some may find even seemingly innocent conversation on these subjects offensive. Talk about any of the topics just mentioned risks creating enemies out of coworkers and stakeholders.

Discussions about sex will likely offend someone, and one risks disciplinary charges, charges of sexual harassment, and even dismissal. Talking about personal or family problems makes people uncomfortable. Chances are that they have similar problems of their own and do not want to be reminded of them. Neutral topics include sports, hobbies, computers, software, a noncontroversial book, food, cooking, and travel.

Research shows that many people dread public speaking. An ideal way to overcome stage fright involves the use of visuals such as overhead transparencies and PowerPoint presentations to support one's talk. Visual aids enable the speaker to plan and control the talk. The following tips help make a presentation go more smoothly:

- State the purpose of the presentation.
- Speak loudly, using variation in voice tone and volume to emphasize key points. Also, speak naturally—neither too fast nor too slowly.
- Make eye contact with individuals in the audience. Look at a person, and speak directly to him or her. After a minute, pick someone else and do the same. This enhances communication with the audience.
- Liven up the presentation by using graphics (pictures, graphs, charts, etc.) to make a point.
- Smile.
- Show enthusiasm.
- Do not wander. Stick to the topic as outlined in the visuals.
- Summarize the main points of the talk at the end.
- Ask for something. A researcher presenting the results of a study to top management might request funds to pursue an avenue of research. A salesperson might ask a group of prospects for an order. A project manager might request a customer to accept a delayed delivery in exchange for a longer product warranty.
- Offer a question-and-answer period.
- Distribute handouts describing the talk.

REVIEW QUESTIONS

1. What type of communication techniques do organizations use?
2. Identify the steps to follow in conducting a meeting.
3. Define action items. Give three examples.
4. Politeness and saying "please" and "thank you" when speaking with stakeholders
   a) is not necessary.
   b) is appropriate protocol in all situations.
   c) is far too formal for today's times.

5. If a customer is abusive on the phone, the appropriate reaction(s) is (are) to
   a) hang up.
   b) say that it is not your job to handle complaints.
   c) grin and bear it.
   d) transfer the call to your supervisor.
   e) yell at the customer because you will not accept abuse from anyone.

6. When speaking on the phone with stakeholders,
   a) take notes.
   b) identify yourself early in the discussion.
   c) summarize the action items at the end of the discussion.
   d) send an e-mail summarizing the discussion.
   e) all of the above.

7. The first paragraph in an e-mail should
   a) describe the purpose of the memo.
   b) ask how the family and kids are doing.
   c) set the stage: Describe the historical background surrounding the issue.

8. Describe five suggestions for a presentation to a group.

9. You are taking a customer out to lunch. Identify five nonbusiness topics to discuss during the meal.

10. Suppose you are an evangelical Christian. You have recently discovered that your work associate is an atheist. This view is abhorrent to your thinking. You are considering raising the issue during lunch, with the idea of converting the person to your religious views. Identify three reasons describing why you should and should not hold this conversation.

11. Which of the following are good presentation tips? (Select all that apply.)
    a) Speak softly and fast so that the group will pay attention.
    b) Do not offend anyone by looking directly at him or her.
    c) Do not inject any humor into the discussion when dealing with serious subjects.
    d) Liven up your presentation by using graphics to make a point.
    e) Smile.
    f) Show enthusiasm.
    g) Do not wander. Stick to the topic as outlined in the visuals.
    h) Summarize your main points at the end.

CHAPTER 9

QUALITY

> *Show me someone who has done something worthwhile,*
> *and I'll show you someone who has overcome adversity.*
> Lou Holtz

OBJECTIVES

After studying this chapter, you should be able to

- Define quality
- Understand the role of quality assurance in managing projects
- Identify the major contributors to the field of quality
- Understand the role of quality policies, planning, assurance, and control in organizations
- Compare and contrast quality planning, assurance, and control in organizations
- Understand the meaning and importance of ISO, CMM, and other quality plans
- Support ISO, CMM, and other quality efforts in your organization
- Contribute to the software quality assurance effort in your organization

INTRODUCTION

How does one define quality? If some are right, "There is very little agreement on what constitutes quality. In its broadest sense, quality is anything that can be improved."[1] Still, an authoritative source defines quality management as the processes required to ensure that the project will satisfy the needs for which it was undertaken.[2] Quality applies to products and services. A software process is a set of activities, methods, and practices used to develop and maintain software. Quality involves procedures, techniques, and tools used to ensure that a product meets or exceeds an agreed-upon specification. Quality also involves uniformity and repeatability in products and services.[3] The commuter expects the train to arrive at the station at 7:27 A.M. Arriving significantly earlier or later leads to disappointment and dissatisfaction with the service. Software that consistently performs as advertised satisfies the consumer and gives the impression of a quality product. Organizations must adjust to their customers' dynamically shifting expectations.[4] Indeed, the focus of quality has shifted from zero *defects* in products to zero *defections* of customers.[5] Some offer a view of quality that integrates the ideas of conformance to requirements and adaptability and innovation on the part of the organization.[6] Simply put, quality is a process aimed at retaining existing customers, winning back lost customers, and winning new customers.[7]

Intuitively, we can understand that the poor quality increases the cost of a product or service and decreases the organization's profits. Traditional costs of poor quality are attributable to the cost of scrap material, reworking of products, extensive inspection, rejections of products, and customers' use of warranties due to failures or faulty operation of products. Less obvious costs of poor quality stem from engineering changes, long development times, more manufacturing setups than planned, extra labor required to expedite the purchase of materials, excessive testing time to validate a product or service's operation, lost customer loyalty due to late delivery or not meeting the customer's expectations, and excess inventory due to overordering of materials. *Quality* is a broad term that encompasses a myriad of issues; every employee contributes to a product or service's quality or lack thereof.

---

[1] Imai, M., Kaizen: "The Key to Japan's Competitive Success" (New York: Random House, 1986), p. xxiii.

[2] Project Management Institute Standards Committee, **A Guide to the Project Management Body of Knowledge** (Upper Darby, PA: Project Management Institute, 1996), p. 6.

[3] Deming, W. E., **Out of the Crisis** (Cambridge, MA: MIT Center for Advanced Engineering, 1986).

[4] Pralahad, C. K., and M. H. Krishnan, "The New Meaning of Quality in the Information Age," **Harvard Business Review** (September/October 1999): 109–118.

[5] Reicheld, F. F., and W. E. Sasser, "Zero Defections: Quality Comes to Service," **Harvard Business Review** (September/October 1990). Reprint 519X:2.

[6] Pralahad and Krishnan, **op. cit.**

[7] Kerzner, H., **Project Management: A Systems Approach to Planning, Scheduling, and Controlling**, 7th ed. (Berea, OH: John Wiley & Sons, 2000).

THE QUALITY "GURUS"

Today's quality movement traces its roots back to the 1920s, with contributions to the field by Walter A. Shewhart and Joseph Juran at Western Electric. Shewhart, the father of modern quality control, pioneered the use of statistical techniques in control processes aimed at minimizing defective output. He combined elements of statistics, engineering, and economics in his work. W. Edwards Deming (Figure 9–1), who also worked briefly at Western Electric, based much of his work on Shewhart's teachings. Following World War II, Deming introduced statistical quality control concepts and the idea of total quality management to Japan. He advocated the use of a process first proposed by Shewhart as a systematic approach to problem solving. Proponents called the approach the *Deming–Shewhart cycle*, or simply the *Plan–Do–Check–Act* cycle, which Deming took to be the essence of continuous quality improvement. He stressed that management has an obligation to constantly improve the system of production and service. The Plan–Do–Check–Act cycle (Figure 9–2) permits management to install a process that promotes ongoing quality improvement. The process presupposes that inspecting the product or service at the end of the job is too late and too costly. Plan–Do–Check–Act shifts the paradigm from *detection of defects* to *continuous examination of the process*, thereby proactively attempting to prevent problems.

Although Deming began to discuss these concepts in the 1930s and 1940s, American industry did not accept his ideas until the 1980s. In 1986, Deming presented 14 points (see chapter 4) that he believed applied to small or large organizations and to service as well as manufacturing organizations.[8] The points are controversial and at times contradict industry practices and the approaches described by other "gurus." Table 9–1 examines some of these differences.

The Union of Japanese Scientists and Engineers (JUSE) sponsored Deming's lectures to Japanese industry during the early 1950s. The material so influenced Japanese industry that it named a quality award after him. The Deming award

FIGURE 9–1

W. Edwards Deming (quality management philosophy and continuous quality improvement)
Photo courtesy of the MIT press

---

[8] Deming, *op. cit.*

FIGURE 9–2

The Deming–Shewhart Plan–Do–Check–Act cycle.

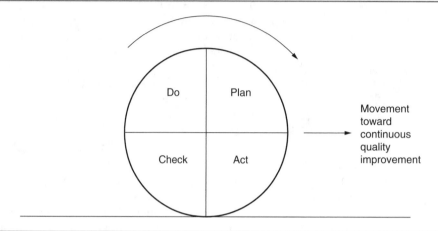

is given annually to organizations worldwide that meet demanding quality standards. In 1960, Deming received Japan's Second Order of the Sacred Treasure award for his contribution to that country's reindustrialization.

Joseph M. Juran followed Deming to Japan in 1954. Like Deming, Juran had received training in statistics. His lectures, also sponsored by the JUSE, added to Japan's focus on quality improvement. Juran, too, received the Second Order of the Sacred Treasure award for his contribution to Japanese industry. He developed the idea of a *quality trilogy*: quality planning, quality improvement, and quality control:

Quality Planning
- Determine the customer's needs.
- Develop a product or service that responds to those needs.
- Optimize the features of the product or service so that it meets both the organization's and the customer's needs.

Quality Improvement
- Develop a process that produces the product or service.
- Optimize the process.

Quality Control
- Prove that the process can produce the product under operating conditions.
- Transfer the process to a manufacturing process.
- Optimize the manufacturing process.

TABLE 9–1

Dissenting or Alternative Views Regarding Some of Deming's 14 Points

Point no.	Deming's Text	Dissenting or Alternative View
4	End the practice of awarding business on the basis of its price tag. Instead, minimize total cost. Move toward a single supplier for any one item, on the basis of a long-term relationship of loyalty and trust.	Most organizations, including the U.S. government, require a minimum of three bids before awarding a contract. Many purchasing departments would look with suspicion upon a department that awarded a contract to another organization without a bidding process.
5	Improve the system of production and service constantly and forever, to improve quality and productivity and thus continually decrease costs.	The effort to improve the system constantly and forever requires meetings of employees at all levels in the organization and may not show immediate results. Managers may resent a subordinate making suggestions to improve a process while the subordinates are in a meeting with their superiors.
6	Institute training on the job.	Many organizations offer minimal training and expect employees to train themselves on their own time.
8	Drive out fear, so that everyone may work effectively for the company.	Coercion is commonly exercised by many managers. Some managers and supervisors continue to use stated or implied threats, such as "Four hours of free overtime per week is expected of all employees" or "Do this task, or I will assign you to second shift."
10	Eliminate slogans, exhortations, and targets that ask the workforce to produce zero defects and rise to new levels of productivity. Such exhortations only create adversarial relationships, as the bulk of the causes of low quality and low productivity belong to the system and thus lie beyond the power of the workforce.	For many years, slogans such as "Zero Defects!" (recommended by Philip Crosby) and "Quality Is Job One" were used by industry to motivate workers.
11	(b) Eliminate management by objective. Eliminate management by numbers and numerical goals.Substitute leadership.	Most production and sales organizations use numerical goals to motivate their employees.
12	(b) Remove barriers that rob people in management and in engineering of their right to pride of workmanship. In particular, abolish the annual merit rating and management by objective.	American business and industry regards the annual employee review too "holy" to tamper with.
13	Institute a vigorous program of education and self-improvement.	Many organizations offer fewer than 40 hours per year of staff development.

Central to Juran's message is the belief that quality requires planning. To achieve success, the organization should integrate improvements in quality into its corporate plan. Organizationwide plans should include identifying customers' needs, establishing optimal quality goals, creating metrics to facilitate measurement, and developing processes capable of meeting quality goals under actual operating conditions. Quality requires teamwork and problem solving. Ultimately, Juran declared, quality is *the fitness of a product to a purpose*.

Japanese industry's adoption of the quality concepts advocated by Deming and Juran played a large role in turning around a country that had been decimated by war into a quality powerhouse within a decade. During the 1950s, Japan exported a variety of merchandise to the United States, ranging from trinkets for sale in five-and-dime stores to automobiles. This inexpensive merchandise would break apart and fail in a short time. Japanese vehicles had a reputation of turning into a "rust bucket" after a few years of use. Japanese automakers failed to sell their cars in the U.S. market because of their poor quality and performance. By the late 1960s, after quality concepts were well diffused throughout the country's production system, Japanese cars became competitive with U.S. products. Although it took some time, Japanese industry turned around its reputation for producing poor-quality merchandise. After a series of domestic oil crises caused by the Arab–Israeli war in 1973 and the Iranian revolution of 1979, U.S. consumers were willingly paying a premium for a fuel-efficient Japanese-built automobile that met their needs and provided reliable service.

Armand Feigenbaum advocated the concept of *total quality control*. The idea was to involve all business functions, including design, engineering, administration, marketing, purchasing, manufacturing, production, inspection, packaging, delivery, installation, and service, in the pursuit of quality. *Everyone* had responsibility for quality—not just the quality professionals. Feigenbaum stressed the fact that quality does not mean "best" in any absolute sense; rather, it means "best for the customer's use and selling price."

Philip Crosby advocated satisfying customers' needs and expectations by implementing the following four absolutes of quality management:

- "Quality" means "conformance to requirements."
- The system by means of which quality is achieved is prevention.
- The performance standard is zero defects.
- The measurement of quality is the price of nonconformance.

Crosby championed the slogans "Do It Right the First Time!" and "Zero Defects!" which many organizations adopted. The U.S. military placed posters around its facilities reminding civilian and military personnel about these twin aims of quality. Crosby's writings emphasized that poor-quality products could prove disastrous for an organization. He believed that quality paid for itself in the end.

Karou Ishikawa developed a tool to assist in the analysis of process quality. The "Ishikawa" or "cause-and-effect" diagram uses statistical data to classify the causes of inadequate quality into the following categories:

- materials
- processes or work methods
- equipment
- measurement

For example, materials may differ when sources of supply or size requirements vary. Equipment or machines also function differently, depending on variations in their parts—variations that affect a product's quality. Ishikawa's work led Japanese firms to focus their attention on improvements in these four areas.

QUALITY AND THE PROJECT MANAGER

Quality is paramount in the eyes of the project manager. It leads to a satisfied customer, which makes the job easier. Producing quality products and services has an impact on a project's schedule and cost. To some managers, quality costs additional money. They believe that the price of goods and services will surge astronomically if the organization follows Crosby's goal of zero defects. Other quality practitioners argue that quality ultimately leads to a reduction in cost, and the practices that ensure quality should be a way of doing business. Creating a quality product or service involves a variety of organizationwide practices that the project manager must be aware of. Two well-known methods used by organizations to improve quality are inspection and constant improvement in processes and products.[9] Both affect a project's cost, schedule and usage of resources. Both require planning to incorporate the processes into the schedule.

The costs of quality involve evaluating products and services for conformance to a set of standards. Many organizations rely on inspecting the product at various stages in its production or development. In some production operations, inspectors merely remove units that are out of tolerance or faulty from the line without considering the underlying reasons for the failures. By contrast, modern approaches to quality focus on prevention; that is, personnel continually examine the product, service, or process with the aim of improving it. Continuous quality improvement brings with it the expectation that higher productivity, lower costs, higher profits, and higher quality all result from the effort. The Japanese use a quality control method called *kaizen*, which means "continuous improvement in personal life, home life, social life, and working life as a whole." With respect to the workplace, "kaizen" denotes continuing improvement involving managers and workers, and customers and suppliers

---

[9] Aguayo, R., "Dr. Deming: The American Who Taught the Japanese about Quality" (New York: Fireside Books, 1991).

alike. Implementing kaizen processes leads to more competitive products and services. Management concepts such as total quality management (TQM) and quality circles involve employees at all levels within the organization meeting to examine or create processes and procedures that lead to improvements in products or services. Those who practice kaizen believe that a great number of small improvements over time will create substantial improvement in an organization's performance.[10] Kaizen ideas encourage people to continually question current practices and seek a better way of doing something. Kaizen does not demand perfection—only continual movement towards the ideal—as well as contributions from the cross-functional team.

QUALITY POLICY

An organization starts its quest for quality by establishing a *quality policy*, which is a statement setting forth principles of operational practice. The quality policy promotes uniformity and consistency in the processes and procedures used by the organization. The policy identifies specific guidelines for performing work. Functional experts prepare the section of the quality policy manual pertaining to their jobs. After reviewing the document, the organization's executive management approves and supports the policy. This commitment on management's part is crucial to the success of the quest for quality. It means that managers will not dispense with quality just to meet a deadline and ship a product. Managers' commitment to quality receives the real test when the end of the fiscal quarter approaches and they have not reached their sales goal. Will management support the organization's efforts to maintain a product or service of which the company can feel proud, or will management buckle under to the sales or production department's drive to meet monthly quotas? Will employees adhere to and implement the policies under stressful conditions? Imagine the pressure: The customer calls hourly, demanding delivery. Bonuses for shipping on time are at stake for the vice presidents on down to the sales department personnel. Perhaps a follow-up contract hinges on the successful delivery of the product. All this places a huge psychological and perhaps physical burden on the purchasing, manufacturing, engineering, and training departments to follow the purchasing, fabrication, installation, testing, and documentation procedures they have established. However, if the organization's reputation for delivering a reliable, robust, easy-to-use, unbreakable, technically superior product is to be upheld, personnel must adhere to the quality policies.

It is common for customers to request a review of an organization's quality policy before placing an order. They may wish to determine whether the organization performs operations in conformity with accepted industry practices. The quality policy quickly helps outsiders understand the organization's

---

[10] For example, visit *http://www.kaizen-institute.com* on the World Wide Web.

procedures. Many customers are leery of placing business with a firm that has little depth and has not trained its staff to follow standard operating procedures. If a cadre of employees follows unwritten and undocumented procedures to accomplish the tasks, the customer becomes uneasy. The customer becomes concerned that the job will not be completed satisfactorily and within the allotted time if one of those crucial people leaves and the remainder of the organization chooses not to follow the undocumented task procedures. Therefore, the organization counters this anxiety by developing a methodology that enables others to complete the task.

The organization's quality policy manual frequently includes statements related to the topics shown in Table 9–2—typical topics that each department or function deals with. The project manager need not be intimately familiar with the policies, but he or she must be aware that they exist and must know whom to contact if additional information is required. If a policy exists, then the project manager must implement it in the overall project plan. That translates into allocating the time, budget, and resources needed to complete the quality policy requirements.

QUALITY PLANNING, ASSURANCE, AND CONTROL

As an organization matures, it experiences a greater and greater need for quality processes and the associated documentation. Frequently, the motivation for instituting such processes arises from a desire to do business with customers that demand a well-defined quality policy. For example, many European companies demand ISO 9000 compliance, and electric power companies, such as the Tennessee Valley Authority, demand that an organization have a quality policy in place and that employees use it. After they establish broad policies, many organizations institute three quality management processes:

- *Planning.* Selecting quality standards
- *Assurance.* A process that ensures that members of an organization implement the written plans and policies and selected standards of the organization
- *Control.* Quality control centers on a monitoring activity that measures and evaluates data. On an assembly line, it includes inspections that focus on testing the product and rejecting faulty items. In a service environment, control is used to objectively compare an organization's performance with preestablished criteria. The quality control group then analyzes and interprets the information obtained with an eye toward improving the product or service.

Figure 9–3 depicts the need for organizations to build a quality structure on well-rooted and -supported quality policies. Quality planning, assurance, and control follow from these policies. Ultimately, the combination will blossom into satisfied customers.

TABLE 9–2

Typical Quality Policy Topics in an Organization

Department or Function	Typical Policy Topics
Executive management	Mission; vision; values; organization chart; strategy; tactics
Human resources	Personnel policy manual; job descriptions; recruitment; hiring process, including psychological testing and scheduling of interviews; orientation for new employees; phone list; discipline; employee reviews; salary guidelines; employee training; compliance with regulations and requirements of U.S. Departments of Labor and Justice
Engineering	Documentation requirements; design guidelines; design reviews; testing; selection of components; preferred standards; selection of software; preparation of proposals, formats, and reviews
Project management	Documentation and activities required to begin, manage, and terminate a project (for example, requirements list, project charter, SOW, schedule, WBS, periodic monitoring of actual versus expected costs, etc.)
Quality	General guidelines; ISO requirements; internal quality audits; preparation of quality records; control of quality records
Other functional department guidelines	Training and personnel qualifications; ongoing training; customer-supplied products and equipment; identification and control of customer items
Manufacturing	Training in usage of equipment; safety training; fabrication techniques; processing of purchased materials; clothing
Sales and marketing	Distribution of territory; warranty; introduction and development of new products; pricing
Information technology (IT)	Policies on desktop and portable computers; networking; Internet access; firewall; external and internal access to E-mail; organization Web page; computing system maintenance and upgrade; data backup; business records and information storage.
Accounting	Accounting practices
Legal	Contract acceptance review; standardized terms and conditions; government regulatory issues
Documentation and publishing	Preferred publishing software; format guidelines
Purchasing	Selection of suppliers; preferred vendors; vendor negotiations; multiple bid requirement
Incoming inspection	Control of nonconforming material and equipment
Instrument maintenance and repair	Calibration and control of test equipment; instrument maintenance frequency
Field service	Corrective and preventive actions; customer servicing; clothing; speed of response to customer request
Training	Developing and preparing customer courses and seminars
Safety and environmental	Handling of hazardous materials; protection of workers from hazardous material; worker safety policies
Handling, storage, packaging, and delivery	Material and equipment handling; static sensitive-device handling; ambient storage conditions (e.g., temperature and humidity); shipping and delivery
Security	Employee access to the facility
Facility maintenance	Equipment replacement schedule; equipment maintenance schedule; building maintenance; compliance with U.S. Department of Labor Occupational Safety & Health Administration (OSHA) requirements; compliance with U.S. Department of Justice Americans with Disabilities Act (ADA) requirements

FIGURE 9–3

The quality tree of organization life

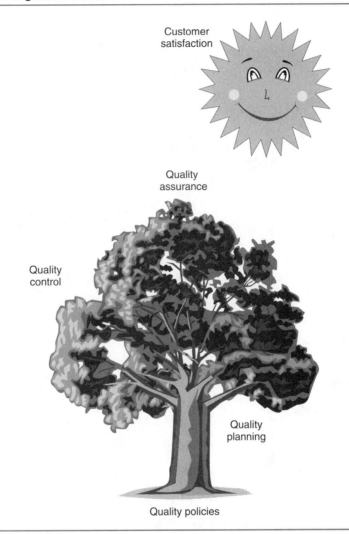

The continuous quality improvement cycle shown in Figure 9–4 follows from the "gurus'" work. As discussed by Deming, Juran, and others, quality is a never-ending sequence involving all employees. During the planning process, departments and functional disciplines identify standards that they agree to meet. To ensure a quality product, the staff develops standard operating procedures that personnel follow. After personnel receive training in the organization's procedures, the quality assurance staff audits them to verify that they are aware of and use the procedures. Data are collected, analyzed, and compared

FIGURE 9–4

Continuous quality improvement cycle

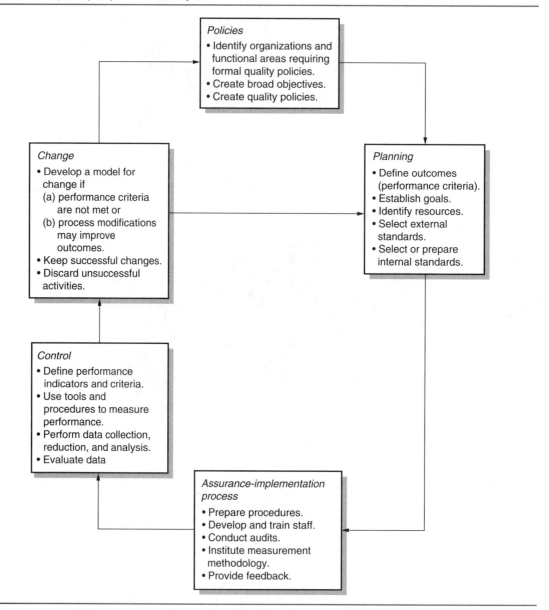

with a reference database. As part of the evaluation process, the organization encourages staff members to suggest improvements to processes. After discussing potential improvements, the staff develops procedural changes. The staff tests the recommended change while continuing to collect and analyze data. Changes that make the product easier to produce, cheaper, better, simpler, smaller, and faster become permanent, whereas those that fail to show improvement are discarded. As a consequence of operational changes, organizations periodically review and update outmoded policies and procedures.

Quality Planning

Quality planning involves identifying and selecting quality standards relevant to the project and determining how to satisfy them. The standards include both internally and externally driven requirements. Internal standards comply with each department's methodology for performing work. Such standards may have evolved from product testing, safety considerations, and experience or past successful practice. Following are some examples of internal standards:

- Physical or educational criteria required to perform a job
- Minimum test scores required to perform a job
- Checklist used to verify a hardware or software development effort during a design review
- Software or hardware installation procedures
- Usage of standard software, tools, system components, or equipment
- Inspection of items purchased
- Handling of hazardous materials

External standards may include requirements derived from professional or international organizations, as well as local, state, and federal government guidelines and regulations. Contracts may require that products delivered meet generally accepted industry standards prepared by organizations such as those shown in Table 9–3. At times, a customer may impose its own internal standard on a contractor.

The organization's quality plans clarify stakeholders' expectations regarding the design, development, fabrication, and installation processes. Employees understand the nature and complexity of the design review(s) at the outset of the project. Software and hardware developers recognize that at some point in the process, the design freezes. That is, the design can change only for good reason and must pass through an approval cycle. Supporting documentation, such as an engineering change notice, must accompany the proposed change. These precautions exist because of the high likelihood that a design change following the "official design release" will affect another department's work. The approval process forces other departments to become aware of the modification by requesting functional managers to sign off on the paperwork. A change in the design of a product may trigger a variety of reactions. Depending on the nature of the change, the purchasing department may have to order a different part, the installation or maintenance procedure may need to be changed, or the new version of the software may introduce compatibility problems. A formalized notification process informs all departments of the impending change and permits them to take appropriate action.

TABLE 9–3

Typical External Standards

Standard	Purpose
Software Engineering Institute (SEI)	Software standards for product design, development, testing, and documentation
European Software Institute	Software standards for product design, development, testing, and documentation—used primarily in Europe.
Institute of Electrical and Electronic Engineers (IEEE)	The IEEE standards cover the fields of electrical engineering, electronics; the allied branches of engineering; and the related arts and sciences. Design, development, testing, and installation of electronic hardware, computer software, and computer networking standards.
American Society for Quality (ASQ)	Standards in the field of quality management, environmental management, dependability, and statistics
American National Standards Institute (ANSI)	ANSI registers and distributes standards from accredited developers.
International Organization for Standardization (ISO) (e.g., ISO-9001: 2000, ISO/IEC JTC 1)	Covers international standardization in the field of information technology, which includes the specification, design, and development of systems and tools dealing with the capture, representation, processing, security, transfer, interchange, presentation, management, organization, storage, and retrieval of information.
U.S. Department of Defense Military Standards	Military standards covering everything from the selection of components to welds and from the preparation of specifications to the testing of products. Design, development, testing, and installation of electronic hardware, computer software, and computer networking used for military purposes
Malcolm Baldrige Award	Group that establishes quality standards for business, academic, and health organizations. Recipients of awards are outstanding contributors in these areas.
U.S. Department of Labor Occupational Safety and Health Administration (OSHA)	Occupational safety, health, and ergonomic standards to protect workers in organizations

Policy plans spell out the organization's philosophy of managing software and hardware documentation such as requirements' statements, schematics, drawings, manuals, specifications, test plans, and test results after stakeholders have accepted the changes. The documentation policy establishes a paper trail or product history that frequently assists the organization in identifying the reasons for problems that arise in the midst of change.

Typically, after a product is tested, material that is purchased cannot change without approval from the engineering development team. Frequently, engineers transfer the tests used to verify the operation of the development system to the manufacturing organization. Technicians do not change these tests arbitrarily. Even the equipment used to test the developed system "freezes." The project manager requests the technicians to record the test equipment manufacturers' model numbers and software versions so that the test can be repeated accurately in the future. This type of control ensures an accurate baseline system configuration.

Among the many external organizations that provide outlines for establishing a quality plan are the Institute of Electrical and Electronic Engineers (IEEE), the Software Engineering Institute (SEI), the European Software Institute (ESI), the International Organization for Standardization (ISO), and the Malcolm Baldrige Award organization. All these organizations have their place and are important. The six-sigma concept (discussed later in this chapter) does not have an organization that promotes it, but many companies have adopted that approach to quality. For the most part, the various programs that are outlined do not conflict with one another and, indeed, are mutually supportive. Each program affects the project manager's process and documentation responsibilities. The project manager does not have to perform the work that is mentioned, but he or she must understand the *process*, so that the project gets done on time and within budget. Usually, the customer accepts the quality program that is already in place at the organization; however, some customers demand that the contractor use one or more external standards. We next briefly examine several quality plans that organizations commonly use.

IEEE Software Quality Plans.   The software project plan documents the work necessary to conduct, track, and report on the progress of a project. The plan contains a full description of how the technical staff will perform the work. The Institute of Electrical and Electronic Engineers (IEEE) developed a set of software life-cycle standards representing its view of the best commercial practices. Table 9–4 lists some of these standards. Some software development organizations follow a combination of the specifications, using, for example, the following five plans:

> Software Quality Assurance Plan (SQAP): IEEE 730.1
> Software Requirements Specification (SRS): IEEE 830
> Software Design Description (SDD): IEEE1016
> Software Verification and Validation Plan (SVVP): IEEE1012
> Software Verification and Validation Report (SVVR)

The SQAP serves as a contract between the project team and the software quality assurance department. The SQAP identifies the specific tasks the department must perform in support of the team. Among these activities are the following:

- Reviewing project plans
- Identifying software standards, practices, and conventions to be used on the project
- Specifying a method of verifying compliance with the selected standards, practices, and conventions
- Describing the configuration management activity to ensure that documents associated with the project (such as the project management plan, the SQAP, the test plan, and deliverable documentation) are maintained under change control

TABLE 9–4

IEEE Software Quality Standards

IEEE Quality Standard	IEEE Standard Number
Software Quality Assurance Plans	730–1998
Guide for Software Quality Assurance Planning	730.1–1995
Software Configuration Management Plans	828–1998
Software Test Documentation	829–1983
Guide for Software Requirements Specifications	830–1984
Software Unit Testing	1008–1987
Software Verification and Validation Plans	1012–1998
Recommended Practice for Software Design Descriptions	1016–1987
Software Reviews and Audits	1028–1988
Guide to Software Configuration Management	1042–1987
Software Productivity Metrics	1045–1992
Software Project Management Plans	1058–1998
Guide for Software Verification and Validation Plans	1059–1993
Software Quality Metrics Methodology	1061–1992
Software User Documentation	1063–1987
Developing Software Life Cycle Processes	1074–1991
Software Maintenance	1219–1998
Guide to the Project Management Body of Knowledge	1490–1998

- Auditing software personnel to verify that they follow the software plans
- Coordinating software review meetings
- Participating in the risk management program
- Monitoring the software test program

The SRS collects and formalizes the customer's requirements in a systematic and comprehensive manner. The document's goal is to define the system in order to meet the user's needs. Some contracts demand that the software developer submit the SRS to the customer for review and approval. This requirement assures the customer that the developer has correctly interpreted the customer's requests and discussed all of them in the document. The customer and contractor must negotiate and resolve all discrepancies before work can proceed.

The SDD represents a detailed version of the SRS, examining the system's functions and subfunctions before coding begins. In addition to providing a detailed description of the internal design details of each function, the SDD defines naming and coding standards, specifies the software architecture, includes appropriate design analyses, and describes interdependencies among the software functions and system interfaces. The SRS may specify interfaces such as operator, computer, and input/output devices (e.g., a bar code reader, terminal, or printer). These interfaces frequently consist of linkages between third-party software and a report writer. The descriptions in the SDD can take the form of narratives, flowcharts, or any other medium on which the team agrees. The information becomes the basis for coding and software testing.

Following the completion of the SDD, the programmers write code, using the agreed-upon software tools. The software verification and validation plan

(SVVP) uses the SDD as the basis for functional testing. *Verification* involves reviewing, inspecting, testing, and checking a product, procedure, or function in order to ascertain that processes, services, or documents conform to specific requirements. *Validation* requires the software developer to evaluate software throughout the development process, to ensure that the software complies with the *user's* requirements. Programmers devise a plan that tests every aspect of the software and its interfaces. The test cases and procedures call for quality assurance technicians to evaluate the software's operation. Software developers prepare documentation that contains detailed instructions and templates for every aspect of the software-testing process. The tests, performed by software quality assurance technicians, ensure that the developers have implemented the customer's requirements as expected. The technicians record the results of test cases and then, after testing has concluded, prepare a software verification and validation report (SVVR) that describes the status of the software package to stakeholders. In addition to verifying that the software program has correctly implemented all of the customer's requirements, the software test technicians determine the robustness of the package. That is, they intentionally make mistakes while using the application, they combine unusual key combinations, and they pursue unintended pathways in the software package. The object of this effort is to determine the software's sensitivity to human error. If the technicians find that the software locks up the computer or breaks down in some fashion, they indicate that further work is required of the developers. After the SVVR is approved, the quality assurance department releases the software for manufacture and distribution.

Capability Maturity Model® (SW-CMM®) for Software. The Software Engineering Institute (SEI) is a federally funded research-and-development center sponsored by the U.S. Department of Defense (DOD) and operated by Carnegie Mellon University in Pittsburgh. In the 1970s and 1980s, military and commercial software projects consistently fell behind schedule, exceeded budgets, and did not meet customers' operational requirements. Typically, organizations completed commercial software projects a year late and overran budgets by 100%![11] In a review of one DOD software organization's 17 major projects, auditors discovered that software developers missed the average 28-month schedule by an average of 20 months. In one case, a planned four-year project took seven years to complete, and nothing associated with the project was ever delivered on time! Clearly, there was a problem. The U.S. Department of Defense engaged Carnegie Mellon University to participate in the development of a methodology to bring the management of software projects under control. Subsequently, SEI created a model to establish a coherent software design process that organizations could follow. The Software Capability Maturity Model (CMM or SW-CMM) assists managers in judging the maturity of an organization's software processes. The model does this by categorizing the processes (Table 9–5) used by the organization on a scale from poor to outstanding—or, as SEI terms it, from ad hoc, chaotic processes to mature, disciplined processes. As described

---

[11] Paulk, M. C., "The Rational Planning of (Software) Projects," *Proceedings of the First World Congress for Software Quality*, San Francisco, CA, June 20–22, 1995.

TABLE 9–5

Software Capability Maturity Model (CMM)

CMM Level	CMM Level Descriptor	CMM Level Characteristics	Key Process Areas	Organization Focus
5	Optimizing	Processes are continually improved by quantitative feedback and through testing innovative ideas and technologies.	Defect prevention, technology change management, and process change management	Implement continual, measurable improvement in the software process
4	Managed	Detailed measures of the software process and the quality of the product are collected. The process and product are quantitatively understood and controlled.	Quantitative process management and software quality management	Establish a quantitative understanding of both the software process and the software products built
3	Defined	The software process for both management and engineering activities is documented, standardized, and integrated into the organization. All projects use an approved, tailored version of the organization's standard process for developing and maintaining software.	Organization process focus, organization process definition, training program, integrated software management, software product engineering, intergroup coordination, and peer reviews	Establish an infrastructure that institutionalizes effective software engineering and management processes across all projects
2	Repeatable	Basic project management processes are established to track cost, schedule, and functionality. The necessary discipline is in place to repeat earlier successes on projects with similar applications.	Requirements management, software project planning, software project tracking and oversight, software subcontract management, software quality assurance, and software configuration management	Establish an understanding between the customer and the software developer; establish basic project management controls
1	Initial	The software process is characterized as ad hoc and occasionally even chaotic. Few processes are defined, and success depends on individual effort and heroics.		

Source: Software Engineering Institute (*http://www.sei.cmu.edu*).

TABLE 9–6

The Software Engineering Community's Compiled List of Published Maturity Levels (as of June 5, 2001)

CMM Level	Number of Declared Organizations	Percent Distribution
1	0	0
2	35	17
3	76	37
4	40	20
5	52	26

Source: Software Engineering Institute (*http://www.sei.cmu.edu*), July 2001.

on the SEI Web site,[12] CMM places an organization into one of five "maturity levels." Organizations that develop software with this model have as an objectively measurable predictability, customer responsiveness, and control so that managers can accurately predict software development costs and delivery times.

Each major process area defined in the CMM is described in terms of the key practices that contribute to satisfying its goals. The key practices describe the infrastructure and activities that contribute most to the effective implementation and institutionalization of the process area.

Most small organizations remain at level 1, without technical and managerial plans and schedules and unable or unwilling to monitor budgets. In addition, requirements are sometimes fuzzy, and the organization may or may not hold formal or informal design reviews. Two hundred three organizations had the courage to declare their CMM status level (Table 9–6). Approximately 37% placed themselves at level 3—which is a significant achievement.

The CMM has had a wide influence on software design processes and quality improvements. It may be the best known and most widely used model worldwide for improving software processes. As with all of the quality methodologies discussed, it demands that employees receive training in its use. By following the model, software developers learn that software development consists of more than writing code. The software CMM promotes evolutionary or incremental change as espoused by a kaizen-style or CQI approach. That is, the model supports gradual, cumulative improvement to business processes, rather than revolutionary changes. Adhering to the CMM prevents the project manager from acting so as to "Ship it now and fix it in the field." This kind of sloppy management damages the organization's reputation and credibility.

ISO Standards. The International Organization for Standardization (ISO) is a worldwide federation of national standards bodies from approximately 140 countries.[13] ISO's mission is "to promote the development of standardization and related activities in the world with a view to facilitating the international

---

[12] *http://www.sei.cmu.edu/cmm/cmm.sum.html.*
[13] See *http://www.iso.ch/iso/en/ISOOnline.frontpage.*

exchange of goods and services, and to developing cooperation in the spheres of intellectual, scientific, technological and economic activity. ISO's work results in international agreements that are published as International Standards."[14] Many of ISO's ideas link directly to the perspectives espoused by Crosby, Deming, Feigenbaum, Ishikawa, and Juran.[15] In common with the quality plans previously discussed, ISO standards strive to

- form a foundation for improving the consistency and profitability of a project
- provide stability, improved products and services, and customer satisfaction and reduce waste
- increase employee awareness of company requirements and procedures
- establish a basis for continual improvement

The standards ISO 9000, ISO 9001, ISO 9002, ISO 9003, and ISO 9001:2000 all deal with managing quality in organizations. People use the generic term "ISO 9000 certification" to denote certification with respect to ISO 9001, ISO 9002, or ISO 9003. The difference is one of scope. The ISO Web site distinguishes the three standards in the following way:

- ISO 9001 sets out the requirements for an organization whose business processes range from design and development to production, installation, and servicing.
- ISO 9002 is the appropriate standard for an organization that does not carry out design and development. The organization may be involved in producing, installing and servicing products. The 9002 designation is appropriate for a distributor or manufacturer that lacks design functions.
- ISO 9003 is the appropriate standard for an organization whose business processes do not include any of design control, process control, purchasing, and servicing. The company uses inspection and testing to ensure that final products and services meet specified requirements.

As with all quality systems, success in ISO 9000 compliance requires extensive employee training. Although the primary purpose of such compliance is to improve the quality of products and services, the marketing aspects of achieving certification should not be overlooked. Some organizations—for example, those in the automotive industry and European-based organizations—will purchase products and services only from companies that have achieved ISO 9000 certification. Often, a company's sales and marketing departments use ISO 9000 certification as a marketing tool.

The ISO is in the midst of a transition. The three levels of certification (ISO 9001, ISO 9002, or ISO 9003) have been replaced by a single certification (ISO 9001:2000). Organizations have until December 15, 2003, to move over to the

---

[14] *Ibid.*

[15] Smith, J. A., and I. I. Angelic, "The Use of Quality Function Deployment to Help Adopt a Total Quality Strategy," *Total Quality Mangement* 6, no. 1 (1995): 35–44.

new standard. ISO 9001:2000 defines eight quality management principles for improving performance:[16]

1. Focus on the customer.
2. Provide leadership.
3. Involve the organization's personnel.
4. Take a process approach to improving quality.
5. Take a system approach to management.
6. Improve products and processes continually.
7. Adopt a factual approach to decision making.
8. Foster mutually beneficial supplier relationships.

The CMM and ISO 9000 series of standards share a common concern with quality and process management. A comparison of the two systems indicates that, by following ISO 9000 procedures, an organization would satisfy most of the level-2 and many of the level-3 goals of the CMM.[17] Because some of the practices set forth in the CMM are not addressed in ISO 9000, it is possible for a CMM level-1 organization to receive ISO 9001 registration. Conversely, some areas addressed by ISO 9001 are not addressed in the CMM. Very likely, a CMM level-3 organization would have little difficulty in obtaining ISO 9001 certification, and a level-2 organization would have significant advantages in obtaining certification.[18] The two models continue to evolve and influence each other.

An organization that complies with ISO 9000 quality plans employs processes that describe and control every element of the project life cycle. As part of the ISO qualification process, an external group audits the organization to verify that it actually performs the quality routines it purports to perform. In preparation for external reviews, the internal quality department audits the organization's departments periodically to verify that all department members have familiarized themselves with the processes. The ISO recognizes that every organization uses processes that are unique to it. The question with regard to obtaining ISO certification is, Does the organization practice what it preaches? In other words, do the organization's members consistently follow the policies and procedures outlined in the quality plan? Organizations that answer these questions in the affirmative have minimal difficulties passing audit examinations.

Six Sigma.   All of the quality plans discussed in this chapter share a great many properties. All of the plans focus on customer satisfaction, emphasize data analysis, strive for improvements in products and processes, and demand the involvement of senior management. Six sigma focuses as well on customer satisfaction and continual improvement in reducing defects. Six sigma alone quantifies the defect-rate objective to 3.4 defects per million installations,

---

[16] The complete document may be found on the ISO Web site, *op. cit.*

[17] Paulk, M. C., *A Comparison of ISO 9001 and the Capability Maturity Model for Software*, Technical Report CMU/SEI-94-TR-12, ESC-TR-94-12 (Pittsburgh: Software Engineering Institute, Carnegie Mellon University, July 1994).

[18] *Ibid.*

TABLE 9–7

Typical Defect Failure Rates in Selected Industries and Professions

Industry or Profession	Defect Failure Rate	Approximate Defect Rate, Percent
IRS phone-in tax advice	(2.2σ)	25
Restaurant bills, doctors' prescriptions and payroll processing	(2.9σ)	8.5
Average company	(3.0σ)	6.7
Airline baggage handling	(3.2σ)	5
Best-in-class companies	(5.7σ)	0.002
U.S. Navy aircraft accidents	(5.7σ)	0.002
Watch that is off by 2 seconds in 31 years	(6σ)	0.00034
Airline industry fatality rate	(6.2σ)	0.00032

Source: Harrold, D., "Designing for Six Sigma Capability," Control Engineering Online, *http://www.controleng.com/archives/1999/ctl0101.99/01a103.htm.*

products manufactured, etc. The method also specifies tools designed to both identify and correct the defects.

How good is good? Motorola asks whether the following defect rates are acceptable:[19]

- 20,000 lost pieces of mail every hour
- Unsafe drinking water almost 15 minutes every day
- 5,000 incorrect surgery operations per week
- Two short or long landings at most major airports each day
- 200,000 incorrect drug prescriptions each year
- No electricity for almost seven hours each month

These numbers reflect a defect rate of about four sigma, or a bit less than one failure in every 100 units produced. Would a 1% failure rate be acceptable for a heart rate monitor or a pacemaker? Is one airplane crash in every 200 take-offs acceptable? Table 9–7 identifies defect failure rates in several industries. A test grade of 99 out of 100 may be praiseworthy, but 99% is unacceptable in many industries. A person may have second thoughts about contacting the IRS for tax advice if the agency provides the wrong answer one out of four times. Perhaps the IRS could benefit from quality training! Actually, the average company at the 3σ level could use help.

In the 1980s, Motorola decided to strive for something better and coined the term "six sigma." The plan uses a DMAIC (define, measure, analyze, improve, and control) program to effect change in business processes. Six sigma is an alternative approach to that shown in Figure 9–2, although it does not differ dramatically from it. Besides Motorola, General Electric, Allied Signal

---

[19] Harrold, D., "Designing for Six Sigma Capability," Control Engineering Online, *http://www.controleng.com/archives/1999/ctl0101.99/01a103.htm.*

(Honeywell), Sony, and Cummins Engine have used the six-sigma approach to achieve customer satisfaction.

Although six sigma's tools and methods include many of the statistical tools used in other approaches to quality, in project management they are employed in a systematic, project-oriented fashion. Six sigma requires extensive employee education. From 1996 to 2000, General Electric (GE) invested heavily in six-sigma activities, training the vast majority of its employees—almost 300,000 people. The company hired outside consultants to support the effort. Former CEO Jack Welch committed the organization to the effort because he strongly believed that it would pay for itself. (Remember, rarely does a CEO in the capitalist system embark on a project without expectations of a healthy return on investment.) Portions of the executives' bonuses were linked to the introduction of six sigma—this had to be serious business! By all accounts, the quality program has proven highly successful at GE.

The six-sigma training program borrows titles from the martial arts and creates master black belts, black belts, and green belts, all of whom have varying levels of competency. The master black belts are the teachers, black belts provide project leadership, and green belts work for a black belt and lead smaller projects. The tools that these quality practitioners use include (1) histograms that show the range and distribution of the product's variances, (2) Ishikawa diagrams, (3) checklists to verify the order and number of the tasks to perform, (4) diagrams showing the factors that contribute the most defects, (5) graphs that plot output versus time, and (6) scatter diagrams, a statistical technique that plots variations with respect to a reference data set. The quality "gurus" discussed in this chapter introduced many of these techniques. Six sigma built and expanded on the concepts that were already widely used by different businesses and industries. The approach integrated many of the concepts into a cohesive package, introduced quantitative targets, and further emphasized the value of training large numbers of employees.

Quality Assurance

The foregoing examples of quality plans involve specific actions that employees must follow to provide a product or service. The quality assurance process attempts to create a culture that centers on the use of reliable processes and systems involving checking and feedback. Quality assurance concentrates on policy and procedural mechanisms for quantifying organizational performance. The typical means of implementing quality assurance involves employee training, followed by an auditing process.

To make certain that employees follow the recommended plans and procedures, the organization that promotes quality assurance encourages departments to prepare forms and procedures (Table 9–8) that define what to do and how to do the department's work. Usage of these forms creates a paper trail that confirms that employees used approved design, fabrication, testing, and installation methods in performing their activities. In medium-sized to large organizations, the quality assurance department audits functional departments periodically to verify that employees understand and follow recommended procedures.

TABLE 9–8

Typical Quality Assurance Documentation

Organization Chart	Procedures
Proposal documentation	Firmware development procedure
Statement of work	Hardware development procedure
Specification	Document control procedure
Work-breakdown structure	Project management procedure
Schedule	System configuration procedure
Forms	Software development procedures
Project kickoff meeting assignments	(e.g., SQAP, SRS, SDD, SVVP, and SVVR)
Responsibility assignment matrix (RAM)	Product- or service-testing procedures
Engineering change notice (ECN)	Work instruction
Product or system configuration checklist	Work authorization
Project management checklist	Product assembly instructions
Guidelines	Computer setup instructions
Hardware development guidelines	Manufacturing equipment instructions
Software development guidelines	Computer backup instructions
	Test integration instructions

Total quality management (TQM) is the generic concept behind quality assurance. Continuous quality improvement is espoused in one form or another by all of the "gurus" mentioned at the beginning of this chapter. With executive management's support and blessing, all employees on a project meet on a regular basis to discuss ways of improving the products and services they offer. Everyone has the right—in fact, the responsibility—to think about the product and service and say, "I think we should do this...," "The customer believes that the product would be better if...," "We could save money if we did this...," "The competition is doing..., so why don't we do...," or "This supplier's product gives us these problems..., so we ought to consider using supplier XYZ."

At a TQM meeting, no one is shy and all viewpoints are expressed. Each member of the organization, from manager to line worker, has a unique perspective that helps to pinpoint problems and improve the product or service. An open discussion improves the odds that quality will be enhanced. At all costs, the Abilene paradox should be avoided. The paradox is a well-known tale in management literature wherein each member of a family (read, team) privately is opposed to an action, but encourages others to do it for fear of offending them or appearing negative.

Quality Control

"In quality control, you are controlling the down side. You are stipulating how many defects, how many minus numbers, are acceptable."[20] During the manufacturing process, quality control involves inspecting products, measuring vari-

---

[20] Geneen, H., and A. Moscow, *Managing* (New York: Avon Books, 1985), p. 35.

ations from norms, and collecting and then analyzing data. At selected stages of the design, fabrication, or manufacturing process, technicians test the product to verify that it performs according to expectations. Variances outside of a preset tolerance range need to be examined to determine the reason for the discrepancy. Among the reasons for a large variation are poor design, worn tools, unclear fabrication directions, tired workers, and suppliers providing defective materials. The process must be studied to determine appropriate solutions to the problem.

In a service environment, quality assurance typically makes use of focus groups, customer surveys, and other forms of customer feedback. Surveys exist to determine whether the company is doing its job of "delighting the customer." Most college students have completed course and faculty evaluation reports. These reports represent one aspect of a college's ongoing quality improvement system targeted at upgrading the content of courses and assisting faculty in improving their presentation of subjects. Restaurants place evaluation forms on tables to help them evaluate the quality of the customer's dining experience. They seek comments regarding food, service, or facilities that will help them better serve the diner or reward outstanding employees. Typical restaurant surveys ask the diner to comment on a scale from poor to excellent on items such as the following:

- the nature of the greeting they received upon entering the establishment (e.g., was it pleasant or rude?)
- speed of service
- quality of food
- value
- cleanliness of restaurant in general and restroom in particular

An airport in the United Kingdom conducts surveys to determine passengers' perceptions of its service. Travelers rate the airport from poor to excellent on their day's experiences in the following areas:

- ease of finding one's way through the airport
- flight information screens
- availability of flights to a destination
- ease of making connections with other flights
- availability of baggage carts
- courtesy and helpfulness of airport staff
- restaurant facilities
- shopping facilities
- washrooms
- passport and visa inspections
- customs inspection
- comfortable waiting at arrival areas
- cleanliness of airport terminal
- speed of baggage delivery service

- ground transportation to and from the airport
- parking facilities
- sense of security
- ambience of the airport
- overall satisfaction with the airport

A Holiday Inn hotel in downtown Vancouver requests customers to comment on their stay by responding to a survey that rates their satisfaction from very dissatisfied to very satisfied on a five-step scale. The following areas are surveyed:

- outside appearance of hotel
- condition of lobby
- service at check-in (friendly, efficient, prompt?)
- guest room
  - overall cleanliness
  - bath facilities
  - heating and air-conditioning
  - comfort of bed
  - television or radio
  - condition of furniture
  - condition of bedspread, drapes, and carpet
- service provided by hotel staff
  - responsiveness to guest's needs
  - friendliness
  - attitude and appearance
- restaurant
  - quality of food and beverage
  - cleanliness
  - quality of service
- telephone services (wake-up calls, messages, long distance and local services)
- lighting
- hotel safety and security (lighting, locks, safety deposit box)
- accuracy of billing
- service at checkout (friendly, efficient, prompt?)
- value received for price paid

Whether in preparation for a specific project or a more general purpose, organizations collect and analyze both quantitative and qualitative data. Organizations identify and select the corrective actions to pursue as they follow the Deming–Shewhart plan–do–check–act cycle. In the operations area, quality control also treats post-manufacture issues, such as the distribution, installation, servicing, and use of a product.

RESPONSIBILITY FOR QUALITY

No matter which quality approach the organization follows, the project manager has the responsibility for implementing the process selected. The project manager works with the organization's quality department, functional managers, suppliers, executive management, customers, and all other stakeholders to make certain that they follow the prescribed quality policies. In particular, the project manager works with the stakeholders to

- identify quality-related problems
- recommend solutions
- execute solutions
- stop work temporarily if the product or service does not conform to expectations
- prepare the required documentation

The costs for implementing quality measures should be included in the project's price during the preparation of the RFQ or RFP. Juran believed that quality does not happen by accident; rather, it must be planned. The project manager is responsible for making certain that the organization carries out the plan successfully.

REVIEW QUESTIONS

1. W. Edwards Deming, Joseph Juran, and Phillip Crosby were instrumental in the development of quality management thought. Go to each of the following Web sites, and compare and contrast their philosophies: W. Edwards Deming Institute *(http://www.deming.org)*, Juran Institute *(http://www.juran.com)*, and Philip Crosby *(http://www.philipcrosby.com)*.
2. Identify four quality management theorists and give a brief description of their contributions.
3. What are the three aspects of a quality program?
4. Describe four quality plans used by organizations.
5. Describe the five Software Capability Maturity Model (CMM) levels.
6. Is a quality level of 1 defect out of 100 sufficient? Explain your answer.
7. At the Juran Institute's Web site *(http://www.juran.com,)* are several of Juran's articles available for downloading. Select one article and develop a two- or three-paragraph summary of its key points.
8. Visit the Malcolm Baldrige Web site *(http://www.quality.nist.gov)* and examine the profiles and Web sites of the most recent winners. What aspects of their quality management system distinguish them?
9. A page on the Malcolm Baldrige Web site *(http://www.quality.nist.gov)* identifies the features of outstanding colleges. Compare and contrast five attributes expected of quality colleges with those of a college with which you have some familiarity.

10. Do you agree with the statement "Personal quality standards and business quality standards have little in common?" Explain your answer.

11. Do you agree with the statement "Quality relates to the process as much as to the goal?" Explain your answer.

12. "Only idealists talk about quality." Explain why you agree or disagree with this statement.

13. The organization that sponsors ISO 9000 is the International Organization for Standardization. Why, then, does it refer to itself as ISO? Why not IOS? If you need assistance, look on the ISO Web site (*http://www.iso.ch*).

14. Visit the Malcolm Baldrige Web site and determine the quality requirements advocated there. Compare them with those of any other quality plan discussed in this chapter.

15. Contact a local organization that has a quality assurance program—perhaps an engineering design, development, and manufacturing organization, a hospital, or your college. Prepare a written report to determine the employees' perceived value of the program. Interview both members of the quality assurance organization and members of functional departments affected by the program. In separate interviews, ask them the same questions. Sample discussion items and questions asked of the stakeholders include the following:

> Have the members explain the quality assurance process to you. Do the stakeholders seem to understand the program?
> Does every department in the organization have a quality plan? If not, why?
> Describe the conditions under which the organization has suspended or would suspend the quality assurance program.
> Name three benefits of the quality assurance program.
> How does the quality assurance program streamline the work process?
> Does the quality assurance process make the final product or service more consistent and reliable?
> Does the quality assurance process cost or save money? How much?
> Describe the organization's ongoing quality improvement activities if any.

> After you compile the information, compare and discuss the results.

16. Divide the class into three-person teams, each of which will select a topic for a report and class presentation. The team will perform research and write and present a report on a subject that deals with some aspect of quality. For example, consider discussing a major contributor's research in the quality field, a policy or procedure used to promote quality products and services in industry, or organization's experience before, during, or after implementing a quality program. The following partial list of topics represents a starting point:

Individual Quality Contributors	Policies and Procedures	Organizations
W. Edwards Deming	Six sigma	Motorola
Armand Feigenbaum	ISO 9000	General Electric
Genichi Taguchi	Total quality management	United Technologies
Dodge and Romig	Statistical process control	A Malcolm Baldrige award winner
Acheson Duncan	Software Capability Maturity Model (CMM)	A Deming Award winner
Walter Shewhart		Tennessee Valley Authority
Philip Crosby		
Kaoru Ishikawa		
Joseph Juran		

As part of your work, you may want to elucidate the following items:

What is quality?

What is quality assurance?

Do producers' and consumers' definitions of quality differ?

Have organizations implemented the plans described? If so, to what degree of success?

Describe the significant operational changes that resulted from the implementation of the ideas discussed. Did the organization find the changes beneficial?

How long did it take to implement the quality plan?

Identify the costs of quality.

Submit a report within two weeks of the assignment date. Base your class presentation on the report. Each presentation should take no more than 15 minutes—4 minutes for each presenter and 3 minutes for questions and answers. Do not read your written report to the class; instead, plan on a PowerPoint slide presentation.

CHAPTER TEST

Answer true or false:

1. Quality is preventing problems rather than picking up the pieces afterward.
2. Quality can always be improved.
3. The most important reason for a quality program is to have satisfied customers.
4. Constant attention to quality is unnecessary.

5. Quality involves the little things as well as the big things.
6. A quality program must have management support to be successful.
7. Quality guidelines are best communicated by word of mouth.
8. Customers pay little attention to quality.
9. A quality program must be integrated with the organization's goals and profit plans.
10. Quality means conformance to standards.
11. Quality should be operative in all parts of a business.
12. Quality requires commitment.

CHAPTER 10

PROJECT RISK

> *When one door of happiness closes, another opens;*
> *but often we look so long at the closed door*
> *that we do not see the one which has been opened for us.*
> Helen Keller

OBJECTIVES

After studying this chapter, you should be able to

- Understand the concept of risk management
- Understand the four processes and actions applied to manage risk
- Understand the risks that are present during the proposal stage of a project
- Use a template to estimate the cost of risk during the proposal pricing stage
- Gain familiarity with the risks that might occur during the project execution phase
- Recognize the role played by the selection of technology in the risk management process
- Contribute to resolving the risk management effort in your organization

INTRODUCTION

Risk deals with the uncertainty of attaining a goal or objective. *"Project risk management* includes the processes concerned with identifying, analyzing, and responding to project risk. It includes maximizing the results of positive events and minimizing the consequences of adverse events."[1] The following processes and actions may be used to manage risk:[2]

- *Risk identification.* Identifies the risks that are likely to affect the project and document the characteristics of each
- *Risk quantification.* Evaluates risks and their interactions in order to assess the range of possible project outcomes
- *Risk response development.* Defines the steps to be taken to thwart the threats posed by risks
- *Risk response control.* Identifies and implements responses to changes in risk over the course of the project.

Risk management recognizes that things can go wrong throughout the life cycle of the project and demands that project managers prepare for such an eventuality. During the project planning stage, the project manager, together with the functional managers, suppliers, and other stakeholders, reviews the customer's requirements. The team assesses the ability of the system that is under development to meet those requirements and identifies any areas of concern. If a customer's requirement or objective seems questionable, the team documents the issues (technical or otherwise) and estimates their impact on the cost, schedule, and resources available to the project. The stakeholders prepare an action plan to mitigate the risk if any of the problems identified do in fact arise. The project manager sets aside a contingency budget to fund the necessary actions. As the project progresses, the team members track and report on the various activities, all the while paying attention to the emergence of the noted risk indicators. If the anticipated problems arise, then the stakeholders implement the corrective action plans.

RISK IDENTIFICATION AT THE PROPOSAL STAGE

Contract

Most customers award a *firm, fixed-price contract.* The price includes all of the costs, overhead, G&A, and profit anticipated to be incurred in the project. That is, the customer and the contractor agree on a price, and that is the price paid to the contractor, no matter the cost. The customer does not care whether

---

[1] Project Management Institute Standard Committee, *A Guide to the Project Management Body of Knowledge* (Upper Darby, PA: Project Management Institute, 1996), p. 127.
[2] *Ibid*.

the contractor or developer makes a profit on the job; the customer simply wants a finished product or service at the end of a specified time at the agreed-upon price. In years gone by, the government sometimes offered a *"cost-plus"* contract. Under such a contract, the contractor received a profit (typically 10%) based on the total project expenditures. The contractor had no incentive to reduce costs and frequently would load the project with unneeded personnel. It was a wonderful way to train new employees in the organization's procedures. After six months to a year, the employees gained the experience to contribute meaningfully to the organization's activities. Some of them would likely be transferred to a different job—perhaps under a fixed-price contract—and replaced by another crop of new hires. The government would pay for all of this not-too-efficient, but permissible, "featherbedding." In defense of cost-plus contracts, some contractors refused to bid on a new and potentially difficult development project that required the use of unproven technologies for fear of underestimating the costs and, consequently, losing money. The government offered the cost-plus contract to entice companies to pursue difficult new and risky developments.

Sometimes, circumstances demand that a project be completed by a given date, and the customer willingly agrees to pay a premium for that outcome. The customer then develops a contract that is intended to motivate the developer by offering a fixed price plus an incentive fee. That is, the customer pays the agreed-upon price to the contractor if the contractor completes the project on the scheduled date. However, if the contractor delivers early, then the customer pays the contractor the agreed-upon price plus an additional percentage of the price (the incentive fee). The downside of this arrangement involves a penalty if the contractor delivers late. The penalty represents risk, and the project manager must carefully monitor the execution of the plans to avoid having to return money to the customer.

Technical Risk

Small-business information technology, electronic, mechanical, and electro-mechanical system and software developers frequently face a variety of technical risks in a new project. A substantial risk exists if an organization has not previously delivered a similar system or software package. The utilization of software, hardware, or manufacturing tools not previously used by an organization also entails risk. Introducing changes into the development or fabrication process results in risk. Frequently, the consequences of these risks surround the schedule, which may incur additional labor hours to complete the various tasks. It may take longer than anticipated for the staff to learn to use a new tool or to gain comfort with a new process. *Murphy's laws* never take a vacation: (1) If anything can go wrong, it will. (2) Nothing is as easy as it looks. (3) Everything takes longer than you think it will.

A new technology brings with it all manner of risk. By its very nature, a research project contains significant risk, because the staff does not know whether it will succeed. The maturity of the technology used on a project has a major bearing on the overall system risk.

TABLE 10–1				

Technology Risk

Technology	Elapsed Time in Years Since Introduction	Employee Training	Availability of Training	Reliability of Software or Electronic Hardware
Leading edge	< 1	Maximum	Few courses available	Poor
State of the art	1–3	Moderate	Courses become available	Good
Mature	3–5	Minimal	Plentiful courses	Excellent
Sunset	5–8	Moderate	Fewer courses available	Excellent
Legacy	> 8	Seek specialists	No courses	Excellent

Table 10–1 indicates that the use of a *leading-edge* technology will raise the eyebrows of most project managers. Whether software or hardware, unproven or recently introduced technology will have *bugs*—unknown problems that limit the use of the application software, product, or service. Sometimes, engineers on technology's front cusp insist on using *beta software*. The term "beta" characterizes software that is in an advanced state of development, but is still being tested and is not yet officially released for production. Beta software is acknowledged to have problems, but manufacturers release it to knowledgeable customers to help "wring out" the bugs just before production. The customer willingly accepts the risk entailed in using unproven software in order to take advantage of unique features that the customer desires. When using leading-edge technology, functional managers and project managers anticipate setting aside time and money for staff training. If the new technology or software is complex it may take considerable time for the staff to achieve proficiency in its use. Project managers understand that new technology has inadequate documentation. Organizations frequently deliver documentation such as application notes, operational user manuals, maintenance manuals, and training manuals sometime after the product's initial release.

Invariably, most of the organization's computers will need to be upgraded to operate leading-edge software. New developers tend to use the latest available computer features. For cutting-edge software, they will expect a cutting-

Availability of Electronic Hardware Product	Computer Platform to Operate Software	Second-Source Availability of Electronic Hardware	Availability of Documentation	Price of Product
Limited	New or upgraded older system	None	Generally unavailable and error prone. Few application engineers available to assist with problems.	High
Good to excellent	New or upgraded older system	Likely	Improving	Moderate
Excellent	Standard platform	Yes	Complete with all updates	Low
Moderate	Standard platform	Yes, but decreasing	Complete with all updates	Moderate
Limited availability	Limited availability	Limited availability	Complete with all updates	High

edge platform that includes a large hard drive, much memory, intensive graphics, and other features. The project manager must make certain to budget for additional computer hardware to operate the new software.

The project manager should expect reliability issues associated with the purchase and use of new electromechanical and electronic products. Assuming that there are no engineering design issues, large production runs usually require some time to work out the manufacturing kinks. Great demand, together with limited initial production, translates into a high price for the product during the first months following its introduction.

Initially, a new electronic product often has only a single supplier. Some time elapses before other manufacturers decide to offer the product. Usually, the price of the product remains high during the time only a *single source* is supplying it. Another downside to using a sole-source item is that whichever organization purchases it will have major redesign issues if the supplier decides to change or discontinue the component. If the supplier experiences production problems or gains success in the marketplace, then any organization that is not a preferred customer of the supplier may have difficulty acquiring the product. Of course, certain situations demand the use of a sole-source supplier. For example, another company may not offer a product that meets the organization's requirements. If this is the case, then the organization must develop a close rapport with the supplier and stay abreast of any anticipated changes in the product's specification, technology, or price.

For these reasons, many project managers do not use leading-edge technology, preferring instead to employ *state-of-the-art* or *mature technologies* to reduce their risk. It does take some convincing, though, because most engineers and technicians want to use "the latest and greatest" product. They feel that they become obsolete if they do not use the most recent technological innovation.

As a technology progresses from leading edge to state of the art, it becomes reliable and available, and the price stabilizes. Training becomes readily obtainable and second sources emerge.

The project manager's favorite, the mature technology, has everything going for it: availability, price, reliability, multiple sources, and documentation. The product will likely continue to be available for several years to come, which will satisfy system maintenance requirements. By this time, technologists have received training, and the project will not incur any delays in the schedule or surprises in the budget due to lack of training. The software will work on all computers, because computer hardware will have caught up to the features required by the software. Little, if any, risk is involved, and the software is a great choice.

Risk begins to increase if the project personnel intend to use *sunset* or *aged technology*. Technical personnel become harder to recruit and voice their reluctance about working on older technology. Even while working on the project, they may seek other opportunities within and external to the organization so that they can work on projects with newer technologies. Changing jobs may result in schedule delays while a new person assumes a transferee's responsibilities. Multiple sources of the product disappear as the demand for the product decreases and manufacturers no longer enjoy the profits they would like.

Only companies specializing in sales of obsolete products will help obtain materials and supplies for *legacy* systems—and even then only at a high cost. Few personnel in an organization have familiarity with obsolete products, and even fewer want to work on them. Recent graduates will have no background at all in this technology. In a Pentium 4 world, who wants to work on a computer with an 80386 or 80486 processor?

Technical and Operational Performance

Some customers request that the contractor demonstrate compliance with every requirement listed in the specification. An operational performance test of that magnitude requires significant preparation, as well as time to actually perform the test. If required, it is customarily performed during the factory or site acceptance test. The project manager should anticipate that things will not go smoothly, which will cost schedule and labor hours.

At times, customers require that a hardware product achieve a minimum reliability or a maximum repair time. The *mean time between failures (MTBF)* is a measure of a hardware system's reliability, signifying the approximate theoretical time the hardware system will operate between failures.

Reliability engineers can calculate the MTBF with the use of standard failure rate tables. Because no such data exist for newer technologies, the MTBF for such technologies may not be able to be calculated accurately. As a result, the customer may request a "live" MTBF test, also known as a reliability demonstration, before accepting the product. If the specification for this test includes a provision to set the elapsed test time to zero following every failure, the schedule and budget could be severely affected. Such a provision should be stricken from the customer's list of test requirements during the proposal phase.

A new packaging approach may bring with it difficulty in meeting a customer's desired *mean time to repair (MTTR)*. If the customer requires that the product be repaired quickly, it may include a provision in the contract designating a specific MTTR goal—perhaps 30 minutes. Proving that the goal has been met in a particular instance may also require an extensive array of testing, the cost of which the project manager should estimate and for which the customer should pay.

The risk involved in both the MTBF and MTTR tests is associated with the possibility of failure. Correcting the product will inevitably cost a great deal of money. Upon the failure of this type of test, many organizations would rather extend the warranty on the product or offer the customer a number of replacement units in lieu of correcting the system and repeating the reliability or time-to-repair test.

Damages

Some projects critical to an organization's operation may cause great harm to the business if they result in products that are inoperative or that do not meet contract specifications after installation. To forestall this eventuality, the organization may include a statement in its terms and conditions requiring the project developer to pay for lost business or may demand some other compensation during the time the developer makes corrections. The contract may not even be worth the risk of this type of damage or the ensuing court fight. The project manager should delete this clause from the customer's terms and conditions during the proposal phase.

Labor Rates and Forward Pricing Projections

Some projects require several years to complete. A multiyear procurement brings with it a highly valued outcome: work for an extended time. However, risks abound, not the least of which is the need to reflect the increased labor costs in the estimate. Typically, the staff receives 3–4% annual salary increases. Material costs rarely go down. Accordingly, the multiyear price to the customer must reflect increases in salaries and the cost of materials. In addition, some project managers word the price statements to take inflation into account. The contractor states that all prices are given in a particular year's dollars—say, 2003 dollars. Then, if rampant inflation takes over the economy in 2004, the customer pays the additional inflationary costs.

Business Risk Issues

From time to time, a contractor decides to move into a new business area and offers a very low price affording the contractor little, if any, profit. The practice is intended to influence the customer to place the order with the said contractor. Under these circumstances, the project manager scrutinizes labor and material expenditures continually during the course of the project, in order not to overrun the budget. The contractor willingly undertakes the risk of exceeding the budget in the hope of establishing itself as a potent player in the new business area.

Sometimes a customer structures a project in phases, with each successive phase contingent upon the successful completion of the previous one. A contractor may decide to bid a low price on the first phase, believing that the customer will be reluctant to switch contractors if the terms of the first phase are fulfilled. The contractor anticipates recovering the profit during subsequent phases. This strategy, known as *cost amortization*, has worked successfully many times. As long as the contractor does not become too greedy, the customer will tend to remain with it. The organizations develop a rapport and understand each other's method of operating. It is easier for the customer to continue the relationship than to seek a new developer, especially if the contractor met the technical requirement and delivered the product on time.

Outsourcing, the process of subcontracting work to outside organizations, has always been a way of doing business, but it places a burden on the project manager, who must make sure that subcontractors are monitored to verify that they will deliver a technically acceptable product or service on schedule and at the agreed-upon price. Organizations outsource for a variety of reasons, including the following:

- The selected contractor may not have the critical technical skills to perform some aspect of the job.
- The selected contractor may have the technical skills and knowledge to perform some aspect of the job, but may not have the resources to complete the set of tasks within the required schedule.
- The customer may direct the selected contractor to use a particular subcontractor.
- The contractor may have entered into an agreement with another organization to subcontract a portion of the job to a team consisting of members of the two organizations.

Organizations commonly enter into a team relationship to make the total package of experience and available resources more attractive than either organization alone could provide. Members from both organizations are selected for the combined team because they complement one another by providing greater technical or managerial depth than a team from either organization alone could provide. Sometimes an organization selects a person for the team because that individual understands the customer and the organization believes that he or she can provide insight into the customer's operations.

Outsourcing brings with it a whole host of issues and risks. Can the organization that receives the outsourcing contract do the job? Does it have a history of success with similar projects? Does it have the technical expertise required for the project? Does it have the facilities, tools, and other needed resources in place? Does it have the financial wherewithal required to accomplish the task? Can it fit the project into its schedule? Can it do the job within budget and still maintain the necessary quality? Does it have the resources required to test the product or service? Can it provide maintenance and repair services and training, if required, after the product or service is delivered? Finally, has the outsourcing organization allocated sufficient labor to monitor the contract awardee's progress?

Terms and Conditions

The project manager should review the customer's terms and conditions contained in the RFP or RFQ during the proposal phase. Potential risk factors must be called to the attention of executive management for discussion and resolution. Among these factors may be an unusual warranty—for example, an extended warranty or a warranty that includes the installation of new versions of the software during the first year after its delivery and installation. Software compatibility may be an issue. For instance, if the system the organization intends to be delivered includes third-party software, new, untested versions of the software may not operate satisfactorily in the customer's environment. In general, an organization that intends to update software should do so only if it receives payment for the task, usually on a time and material basis.

The project manager must make certain that a satisfactory payment schedule exists on longer development contracts. Customers prefer to pay for a job at its conclusion, but an organization must use its own money until it receives payment. Accordingly, provision should be made for payment following the completion of each significant milestone or deliverable.

Companies collect patents for protection purposes. If company A appears to infringe on one of company B's patents, company B slaps company A with a lawsuit. Often, after receiving notice of the lawsuit, company A will examine company B's patents in an effort to countersue for patent infringement. In all likelihood, the parties will settle out of court. Frequently, customers include in the terms and conditions of the contract the right to own all patents that emanate from a development contract. Organizations try to keep patent rights for inventions that they develop even if the customer pays for them. The project manager settles these stipulations before the parties sign the final contract.

Other Costs

Capital expenditures involve the purchase of equipment, facilities, or other non-labor resources above a preset financial minimum that will serve several different projects. Capital expenditures do not usually include equipment that serves a single project. Instead, each project requires the purchase of its own unique tools and equipment. In an effort to reduce costs, project managers review required equipment and tools and try to include them as capital expenditures.

Mitigating Risk at the Proposal Stage

After examining the different types of risk discovered during the proposal phase, the project manager quantifies the risk in accordance with Table 10–2. Together with the functional managers, the project manager calculates the cost of a WBS item and breaks it down into two parts. The first part corresponds to the likely cost of labor and materials for the WBS task. The second part corresponds to the additional cost resulting from a worst-case risk scenario. The project manager assigns a risk probability of 25%, 50%, or 75% to this scenario. The weighted risk is the product of the probability of risk and the risk cost estimate. The WBS item cost corresponds to the sum of the likely WBS item cost and the weighted risk cost. The result of this calculation transfers to the proposal cost spreadsheet shown in Table 7–7, with the project's financial risk included in the cost.

Senior managers generally review the risks associated with a project before submitting the price to the customer. Depending on their desire to win the contract or even on their "gut feeling," they will take all or a portion of the identified risk and add it to the baseline project cost to arrive at a total project cost, which the organization then submits to the customer.

Risk Management during the Project

During the proposal phase, the project team completes a risk management analysis that includes risk identification, risk assessment, and risk abatement. As part of the latter task, the team develops plans that define the actions to be taken should the unwanted events occur. This proactive planning function identifies and ranks elements of risk that could compromise a successful project outcome. Finally, the team sets aside contingency funds to minimize the financial impact of any untoward events.

During the project's execution phase, a host of situations can arise that could cause delays, cost overruns, or performance problems stemming from a failure to achieve technical or operational requirements. Perhaps the most common reason for delays involves changing requirements. As they learn about the capabilities of the product or service they contracted for, customers have a tendency to "fine-tune" their needs. To ensure a profit and deliver the project on schedule, the project manager must control the scope of the job. This translates into controlling the customer and implementing a change control process. Toward those ends, the project manager must insist that the customer submit a formal change order request that describes in detail the nature of the change. This enables the contractor to respond with a price and schedule impact statement. Only after the customer approves the change and agrees to a price increase does the work proceed. The project manager never agrees to a verbal approval. Instead, an authorized customer representative must sign and date the change order. In this manner, the project manager gains assurance that the customer

TABLE 10–2

Quantifying Risk

WBS Item	Task Description	Item Cost ($)	Risk Cost ($)	Probability of Risk	Weighted Risk ($)	Total Item Cost ($)
Total						

understands and agrees to the cost and schedule ramifications of the change. Generally, changes made early in the schedule cost the least to implement.

Modern systems use many complex interconnected components containing multiple hardware and software interfaces. Frequently, the interfaces contain unknown quirks and represent a source of integration problems. Once a software or hardware module operates well consistently, engineers should be urged to use it on similar interfaces rather than redesigning it just for the technical challenge.

Technologists dislike preparing documentation; they love to design. They will accede to testing a system, but they generally dislike writing. Because of that aversion, they will postpone writing as long as possible. The risk in procrastinating is not only that documentation may never get written, but also that the technologist may forget important details that should be contained in the material. Incomplete documentation may cause support (e.g., maintenance and training) problems down the road. During status reviews, the project manager gently reminds all associates of unfinished tasks.

Frequently, the customer has the contractual right to review and approve acceptance tests and other written material. Here again, the project manager prompts the customer to expedite documentation review and approval. Failure to do so can slow the project's progress, because the project manager may halt some activities for fear that, without approval of documentation, some work would require modification, thereby costing additional time and labor.

Rarely is staff turnover planned for. The project manager should anticipate that a small percentage of the staff will depart during the project effort for a variety of reasons, such as illness, disability, family leave, sabbaticals, or simply transferral to a different job. Nowadays, people with skills that are in demand often hop from job to job in an effort to broaden their technical experience base as well as increase their salary. Leaving a position in midstream causes a significant disruption to the work flow. The recruitment of new workers requires time to advertise, interview prospective applicants, and select an appropriate match. The newly hired person needs time to adjust to the company's processes and procedures. Sometimes, the new employee must undergo a period of training. Meanwhile, tasks go undone and the project falls behind schedule. If too many people leave, the organization should investigate the reasons. It may face a broad salary, benefit, or working condition problem that requires attention by the human resource department and upper management.

A special staffing problem involves the use of consultants. At times, a team decides to use consultants to "kick-start" a project. That is, the team brings in experts to get the project off to a fast start. In some situations, temporary workers supplement the existing employee base. In these cases, the project manager must ensure that adequate provisions for a transfer of knowledge from consultant to contractor takes place.

Preparing for recovery from a disaster represents a sound business strategy. The project manager should plan for fire, flood, earthquake, and terrorist attack. Perhaps one cannot prepare for the kind of terrorist attack that struck the World Trade Center in New York City and the Pentagon on September 11, 2001, but the project and the organization should be protected as best as possible. Installing a backup power source to supply power to a system or facility is a good idea. A sticky problem arises in connection with a computer failure. Some people think that having a copy of the computer hard drive on a zip drive or CD-ROM will protect against loss of data. But if the zip drive or CD-ROM is housed in the same facility as the computer, a fire or flood could destroy both the computer hard drive and the backup devices. Accordingly, backup data should be placed in an off-site storage location away from the project manager's office and the manufacturing facility, and similarly for engineering drawings, schematics, software source code, and documentation. Some organizations use a bank vault or safe deposit box or a commercial repository for this purpose and transfer material to that location weekly. Computers should be backed up daily or weekly. Some installations permit setting an automatic daily hard-drive back-up that simplifies the process.

Among the other risk areas that confront the project are the following:

- technical errors or misjudgments
- omissions of tasks
- unspecified design changes
- unavailability of components or equipment
- management commitment to project
- changes in senior management forcing extensive and frequent status reporting
- estimating and scheduling errors
- actions taken by the collective-bargaining unit
- late delivery of products
- changes in priority that result in loss of resources
- delayed approvals and acceptances
- weather and other random events
- incorrect estimation of the learning curve
- unavailable or unreliable tools and methods
- experience, skills, background, and dedication of the project team

MITIGATING RISK

The project team attempts to produce a desired outcome while minimizing the risk of failure, which may take any of the following forms:

- late delivery
- unacceptable installation of a product or service at the customer's site
- running over budget
- technical inadequacies in a product or service
- unacceptable technical performance

- unreliability of a product or service
- inadequate maintainability of a product or service
- inadequate documentation
- inadequate customer training
- inadequate support for a product or service after delivery
- safety issues relating to a product or service
- unacceptable attitude toward a customer
- slow help-desk response

Risk management involves identifying the risk areas before the project begins—that is, during the proposal phase. Once the project manager and the team identify the risks, they are tracked as the project unfolds. Invariably, new risks emerge. Staying on top of the project enables the team to take action before problems that delay activities occur. The project manager works closely with team members to modify developments and reallocate resources in order to control and minimize risk. In that way, the team can move along the best path to meet the project's objectives.

REVIEW QUESTIONS

1. With what does risk management deal?
2. Identify four processes and actions aimed at managing risk.
3. Describe the difference between a cost-plus contract and a "firm, fixed-price award." Which would you prefer and why?
4. Suppose senior management dictates the use of a new project scheduling and project tracking software tool. Describe the issues associated with the use of this new tool. What steps can the project manager who must use the tool take to minimize risks?
5. The engineering staff has decided to use a new composite material to construct an enclosure for a system that is under contract. The engineering department believes that the new product has superior properties (e.g., it is inexpensive, lightweight, strong, and malleable) compared with the properties of traditional materials used for this application. What problems do you think may arise from using the new material? Describe steps you can take to minimize these problems.
6. Discuss the advantages and disadvantages associated with using new technology.
7. Suppose the engineering department recommends the purchase of a newly introduced attachment to a personal computer that would be ideal for use on a project that you are managing. The device will reduce the size, weight, and manufacturing time of the new system under design. The engineering department estimates that the new device will yield a 10% reduction in the cost of the material used on the project. Sentrex

Technologies, a multibillion-dollar, long-established company, is the only firm that manufactures the unit.

   a) Does the use of the device represent a risk?

   b) If a risk exists, describe it. What can the project manager and the engineering organization do to mitigate the risk?

8. Describe the advantages and disadvantages of using newer versus older technology in systems.

9. Discuss the difference between MTBF and MTTR.

10. Describe the circumstances under which an organization might offer a product or service with little or no profit. Under these circumstances, what must a project manager do?

11. Describe the circumstances under which a company might team with another organization to deliver a product or service. What risks does such a partnership entail? What can a project manager do to mitigate the risks?

12. What does "outsourcing" mean? Identify the risks associated with outsourcing? What can a project manager do to mitigate the risks?

13. Describe the process of preparing for risks during the proposal phase.

14. What is the purpose of contingency funds?

15. How can an organization plan for staff turnover?

16. What does "controlling the customer" mean? How does a project manager do that?

17. What steps can people take to protect against natural or human-induced disasters?

CHAPTER 11

PROJECT TRACKING, REPORTING, AND PROCUREMENT

> *There is nothing in this world constant, but inconstancy.*
> Jonathan Swift, "Critical Essay upon the Faculties of the Mind" (1707)
>
> *Change alone is unchanging.*
> Heraclitus (circa 535–475 B.C.E),
> Herakleitos and Diogenes, pt. 1, fragment 23

OBJECTIVES

After studying this chapter, you should be able to

- Understand the importance of project tracking
- Recognize the constituencies from whom a project manager requests information
- Understand the contents of reports
- Understand the frequency of reporting
- Understand the information required to begin to track a project
- Analyze project tracking data
- Recognize when a project is in financial or technical trouble
- Identify the stakeholders responsible for financial or technical problems
- Understand the steps used to end a project
- Prepare yourself to lead a lessons-learned session

INTRODUCTION

Following the proposal and awarding of the contract, the moment arrives at which the satisfaction of all the organization's promises must be begun. Once the project is underway, *project tracking* and *reporting* become uppermost on the list of the project manager's activities. During this stage, the project manager acts primarily as an observer from a functional department. The project manager monitors the status of the project and keeps the customer happy—and far away from the technical organization. The project manager tracks the project's progress against the implementation plan, all the time watching for signs of risk emerging. Many project managers obtain information through the practice of "*management by wandering around.*" Just talking with people uncovers a variety of concerns and issues that no one ever puts on paper. Most project managers try to cultivate relationships with team members, users of products or services, suppliers, customers, and senior managers. Then they visit these individuals in order to assess the progress of the project. Talking informally with all of them frequently uncovers issues that might otherwise take time to surface. Few managers, however, discuss employee attitudes and morale, job iniquities, etc., during status reviews. Generally, any manager who does raise these issues during reviews has reached a crisis level. Wandering around can enable the project manager to evaluate the status of a project from a qualitative as well as a quantitative perspective.

Typical monitoring activities include attending functional department meetings, performing customer reviews and project status reviews, and briefing executive management. The project manager's attendance at functional department briefings is usually inversely proportional to his or her workload. However, attendance is mandatory if the team has identified the emergence of some risk considered during the proposal phase. For high-risk project activities, daily monitoring includes reviewing information on the status of the project, meeting with key project leaders to understand the progress of activities, and making changes to priorities when necessary. For lower risk project activities, the project manager might limit monitoring to reviewing monthly status reports, attending regularly scheduled briefings by project staff, and conducting random visits to the project site to assess the project's progress.

Project tracking serves the need for senior management, functional managers, and customers to understand the issues associated with the job. Before commencing tracking, the project manager should gain familiarity with the history, management, and development methodology of the project. After completing these preliminary steps, the project manager will attain the necessary background to proceed with project tracking, which involves

- monitoring and reviewing the project's accomplishments and results against estimates of the project's scope, resources, schedule, and cost
- verifying that the organization receives material procurements on time
- maintaining contact with subcontractors and receiving information about the status of their assigned work
- developing work-around plans to correct technical, schedule, cost, and subcontracting plans that go awry
- verifying that resources become available when required

- acting on feedback from the user or some other customer

Project tracking and reporting compares the planned versus the actual status of

- the project's schedule and milestones (including changes to dates scheduled for key deliverables or milestones and the planned completion date of the project)
- the project's budget (including the cash flow and funding sources)
- the project's scope, objectives, or requirements (if any changes occur to them)

The project manager remains aware of changes to the project's sponsorship or management and of other relevant organizational adjustments that may affect the work. Most status briefings and reports begin with a summary of accomplishments attained since the last reporting period. Reports frequently conclude with a summary of past, current, and future issues, including steps to mitigate actual or potential problems and an updated risk analysis.

Project tracking methods and requirements vary based on the project's size, budget, complexity, and impact on the affected organizations. Management of a project includes processes for tracking and communicating the status of the project and for performing risk assessments. The project manager has the responsibility for tailoring the frequency of reporting to meet the specific needs of the project. All projects terminate with a report that summarizes the final costs, issues, and lessons learned.

Table 11–1 presents some guidelines for the frequency of monitoring project activities. Most project managers examine the progress of the schedule and actual versus planned spending on a weekly basis. The project manager contacts functional departments and suppliers at least weekly to stay abreast of developing technical, resource, and procurement issues. As discussed in previous chapters, both under- and overspending represent areas of concern. Does a project's progress correspond to its level of spending, or does overspending indicate a technical problem? Does underspending indicate that people are not working on the job? Weekly stakeholder meetings can root out the answers to these questions. The project manager uses common sense in deciding the amount of information gained from these meetings that is to be shared with the customer. Too much negative information will give the customer cause for concern, which is undesirable. However, only fictional projects contain no problems; an experienced customer or project manager becomes suspicious if activities proceed without any problems arising. Senior management does not want to know about every "hiccup" in the development process. Usually, a monthly project overview satisfies upper management's need to remain aware of the project's status. The project manager maintains weekly contact with the purchasing department in order to keep abreast of significant purchases of, or subcontracts involving, components, equipment, or service.

Project Tracking Example

Perhaps project tracking and reporting can be best understood by an example that illustrates the data examined by the project manager when monitoring and controlling the project. The example discussed next describes a plan to provide

TABLE 11–1

Frequency of Project Management Reviews and Interactions

	Customer	Functional Departments	Suppliers	Senior Management	Quality Assurance	Purchasing
Progress of activities compared with schedule	Weekly	Weekly	Weekly	Monthly, unless problems exist	Monthly	Weekly
Actual spending compared with planned spending	Weekly	Weekly	Weekly	Monthly, unless problems exist	Monthly	Weekly
Purchases of components, equipment, and services	As required	Weekly	As required	As required	As required	Weekly
Technical issues	ASAP	ASAP	ASAP	As required	As required	ASAP
Financial issues	As required	ASAP	ASAP	As required	As required	ASAP
Technical interchange meetings	As required	As required	As required	As required	As required	As required
Preliminary design review(s)	Once or twice per project	Once or twice per project	Once or twice per project	As required	Once or twice per project	Once or twice per project
Critical design review	Once per project	Once per project	Once per project	Once per project	Once per project	Once per project
Testing issues (e.g., factory, site, thermal, reliability, maintainability, ruggedness, etc.)	As required	Weekly	As required	As required	As required	As required
Documentation	Once per document	As required	As required	As required	As required	As required

Note: ASAP = as soon as possible after identifying a problem.

FIGURE 11–1

Proposed plan for factory employee access project

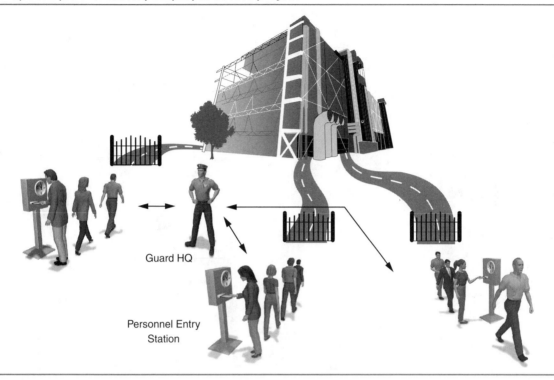

Guard HQ

Personnel Entry
Station

a customer with a custom-built employee security entry system, shown conceptually in Figure 11–1. The customer operates an industrial facility surrounded by a fence with three entrances. The customer is concerned about the security of the plant and wishes to control access to it by requiring each employee to carry and use a magnetic identification card. Before entering the facility, each employee swipes the identification card through a magnetic card reader and places his or her thumb on a scanner. The ID card contains personal and biometric information about the employee. The card reader verifies that the person swiping the card is an employee of the plant by matching the person's fingerprint with data stored on the card. Simultaneously, the system accesses a central database to confirm that the person works at the facility, has the appropriate security clearance for the site, and has completed all training (e.g., in hazardous materials) required for the job. After performing these checks in five seconds or less, the control computer sends a signal to the gate at the entrance to permit or reject the person's request for entry. The customer requires the contractor to install three identical access control systems that will monitor the entry locations and to link each system to a central guard headquarters.

The contractor that received the award decided to use as much commercial off-the-shelf components and equipment as possible in an effort to reduce costs and development time. The proposed schedule, shown in Figure 11–2a, was to last

FIGURE 11–2

Factory employee access project design, fabrication, and installation schedule

(a) Planned schedule

ID	WBS	❶	Task Name	Duration
1	1		System definition	1 wk
2	**2**		**Design**	**39 days**
3	**2.1**		**Hardware**	**34 days**
4	2.1.1		Define hardware–software interfaces	4 days
5	2.1.2		Electrical and electronic design	5 wks
6	2.1.3		Mechanical	6 wks
7	2.2		Software	6 wks
8	2.3		Networking	4 wks
9	2.4		Design review	1 wk
10	3		Purchase materials	3 wks
11	4		Fabricate system	1 wk
12	5		System integration and factory test	1 wk
13	6		Crate and ship components	1 wk
14	7		Site installation and testing	1 wk
15	8		Documentation	1 wk
16	**9**		**Training**	**40 days**
17	9.1		Preparation for training	3 wks
18	9.2		Conduct training class	5 days

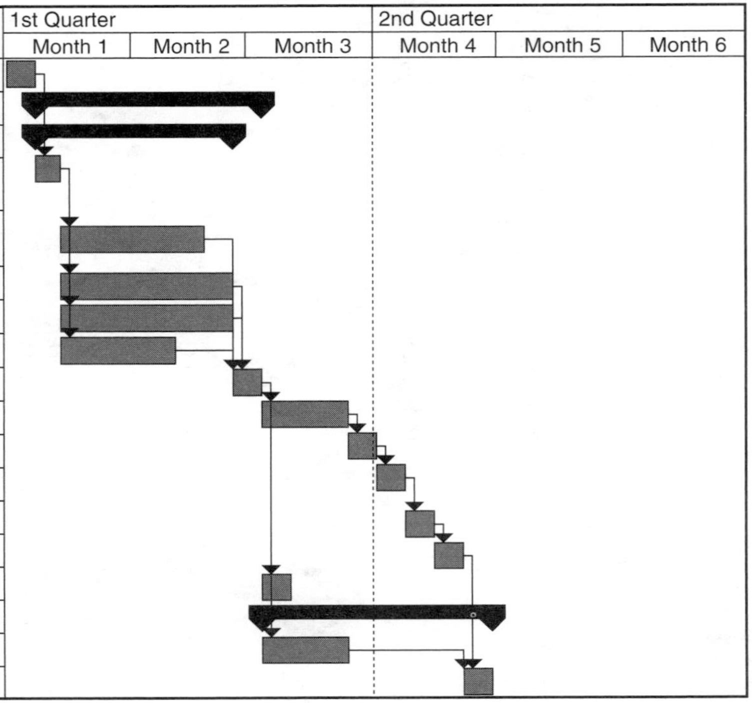

(b) Actual work status four weeks into the project

ID	WBS	ⓘ	Task Name	Duration	Remaining Duration	1st Quarter			2nd Quarter
						Month 1	Month 2	Month 3	Month 4
1	1	✓	System definition	1 wk	0 wks				
2	**2**		**Design**	**39 days**	**24.72 days**				
3	**2.1**		**Hardware**	**34 days**	**20.03 days**				
4	2.1.1		Define hardware–software interfaces	4 days	1 day				
5	2.1.2		Electrical and electronic design	5 wks	3.75 wks				
6	2.1.3		Mechanical	6 wks	3 wks				
7	2.2		Software	6 wks	4.5 wks				
8	2.3		Networking	4 wks	2 wks				
9	2.4		Design review	1 wk	1 wk				
10	3		Purchase materials	3 wks	3 wks				
11	4		Fabricate system	1 wk	1 wk				
12	5		System integration and factory testing	1 wk	1 wk				
13	6		Crate and ship components	1 wk	1 wk				
14	7		Site installation and testing	1 wk	1 wk				
15	8		Documentation	1 wk	1 wk				
16	**9**		**Training**	**40 days**	**40 days**				
17	9.1		Preparation for training	3 wks	3 wks				
18	9.2		Conduct training class	5 days	5 days				

243

16 weeks from the awarding of the contract to installation of the product and training of personnel. The contractor required the following departments and personnel to participate in the effort to complete the work on the project: electrical engineering, mechanical engineering, software engineering, networking engineering, factory technicians, field service technicians, project management, publications, quality assurance, training, shipping, and purchasing. These functional departments contributed to the labor hour estimate for each element of the simplified WBS shown in Table 11–2. Table 11–3 illustrates the plan for the time dis-

---

TABLE 11–2

Factory Employee Access Control Project Labor Hours Plan

| Project Task | ENGINEERING | | | | Factory Technicians | Field Service Technicians |
	Electrical	Mechanical	Software	Networking		
1. System definition	40	40	40	20		
2. Design						
2.1. Hardware						
2.1.1. Define hardware–software interfaces	10	10	10	10		
2.1.2. Electrical and electronic design	60					
2.1.3. Mechanical		120				
2.2. Software			160			
2.3. Networking				40		
2.4. Design review	15	25	25	10		
3. Purchase materials	4	4	4	4		
4. Fabricate system	4	4		2	120	20
5. System integration and factory testing	50	50	50	30	30	40
6. Crate and ship components						4
7. Site installation and testing	8	8	8	8		80
8. Documentation	16	16	16	8		
9. Training						
Total	207	277	313	132	150	144

tribution of the labor. The data shown in the tables represent a joint planning effort between the project manager and all contributors to the project.

The labor hour spending plan shown in Figure 11–3 does not follow the "traditional" inverted-U characteristic described in Chapter 3, because of the project's small size and short duration. Limited funding on the project prohibited the staff from spending all of their time on this job. The nature of small, short-term jobs requires people to complete their assigned tasks quickly and move onto another project. Even the project manager does not charge all of his

Project Management	Publications	Training	Quality Assurance	Shipping	Purchasing	Total Labor
10			10			160
4						44
6						66
10						130
16						176
4						44
25						
1					40	57
12						162
20			20			290
4				8		16
16			10			138
5	40		10			111
6		80				86
139	40	80	50	8	40	1580

TABLE 11-3

Factory Employee Access Control Project Labor Hours Spending Plan

(a) Distribution of Planned Labor Hours, by Week

Department	1	2	3	4	5	6	7	8	9	10	11	12	13	14	15	16	Total
Electrical engineering	20	30	40	20		15	8	2	2	2	2	40	10	8	8		207
Mechanical engineering	20	30	40	40	40	25	8	2	2	2	2	40	10	8	8		277
Software engineering	20	30	40	88	40	25	8	2	2			40	10		8		313
Networking engineering	10	20	20	10		10	8	2	2	2		30	10		8		132
Factory technicians										60	60	20	10				150
Field service technicians											20	20	20	4	80		144
Project management	8	8	8	8	8	20	8	8	8	8	8	8	8	4	10	9	139
Publications															40		40
Quality assurance	10												20	10	10		50
Training	8												6	6	20	40	80
Shipping														8			8
Purchasing					24		10	3	3								40
Total labor	96	118	148	166	88	119	50	19	19	74	92	198	104	48	192	49	1580

(b) Cumulative Planned Labor Hours, by Week

Department	1	2	3	4	5	6	7	8	9	10	11	12	13	14	15	16
Electrical engineering	20	50	90	110	110	125	133	135	137	139	141	181	191	199	207	207
Mechanical engineering	20	50	90	130	170	195	203	205	207	209	211	251	261	269	277	277
Software engineering	20	50	90	178	218	243	251	253	255	255	255	295	305	305	313	313
Networking engineering	10	30	50	60	60	70	78	80	82	84	84	114	124	124	132	132
Factory technicians	0	0	0	0	0	0	0	0	0	60	120	140	150	150	150	150
Field service technicians	0	0	0	0	0	0	0	0	0	0	20	40	60	64	144	144
Project management	8	16	24	32	40	60	68	76	84	92	100	108	116	120	130	139
Publications	0	0	0	0	0	0	0	0	0	0	0	0	0	0	40	40
Quality assurance	10	10	10	10	10	10	10	10	10	10	10	10	30	40	50	50
Training	8	8	8	8	8	8	8	8	8	8	8	8	14	20	40	80
Shipping	0	0	0	0	0	0	0	0	0	0	0	0	0	8	8	8
Purchasing	0	0	0	0	24	24	34	37	40	40	40	40	40	40	40	40
Total labor	96	214	362	528	616	735	785	804	823	897	989	1187	1291	1339	1531	1580

FIGURE 11–3

Planned project labor hours distribution for the factory employee access project

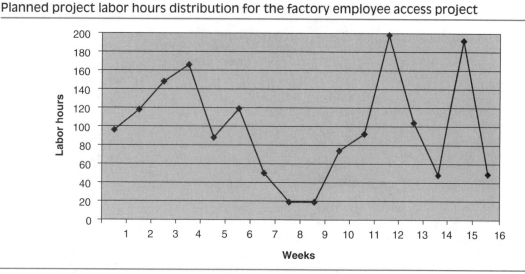

or her time to this job. Project managers can manage four to five projects of such a size and spread their weekly work hours over all of the jobs. With a spending plan distribution such as that presented, the project manager scrutinizes actual costs carefully to ensure that employees do their work and stop charging time to the job after the completion of their tasks.

The project manager begins to gain control of the project by reviewing and understanding its planned budget and schedule. Once the project begins, the project manager has the responsibility to deliver the product or service within budget, on time, and in a technically satisfactory manner. Workers charging time to the job enter the hours they work on each task in the WBS into a database that collects this information. At the end of each week, a financial administrative assistant prepares a variety of reports for the project manager and the functional managers to examine. These reports enable those managers to compare actual with planned expenditures of labor and materials in a variety of ways. At the same time, the project manager examines the work accomplished by the functional departments to verify that they have adhered to the planned schedule. Significant differences between expected and actual spending demand further investigation.

The example being discussed focuses on the labor hours expended by the workers at the end of the project's fourth week. The example does not examine purchases of materials. Table 11–2 describes the functional department's budget for each task composing the WBS. Table 11–3 presents the expected spending for each functional department over the length of the job. Each week, the project's administrative assistant prepares data similar to those shown in Tables 11–4 through 11–6. The data reflect the status of the job at the end of the fourth week. Tables 11–4a and b identify actual spending on the project by each functional department during the first four weeks of the

TABLE 11–4

Actual Factory Employee Access Control Project Labor Hours

a) Actual Labor Hours, by Week and Functional Department

										Week Number							
Department	**1**	**2**	**3**	**4**	**5**	**6**	**7**	**8**	**9**	**10**	**11**	**12**	**13**	**14**	**15**	**16**	
Electrical engineering	5	22	60	30													
Mechanical engineering	20	32	40	65													
Software engineering	4	16	40	58													
Networking engineering	2	8	27	10													
Factory technicians																	
Field Service technicians																	
Project management	10	8	8	8													
Publications																	
Quality assurance	8			4													
Training	8																
Shipping																	
Purchasing																	
Total labor	57	86	175	175													

c) Actual Functional Department Labor Hours Charged to Each Project Task

Labor Hours Spent at the End of the Fourth Week

	ENGINEERING					
Project Task	**Electrical**	**Mechanical**	**Soft-ware**	**Net-working**	**Factory Technicians**	**Field Service Technicians**
1. System definition	27	40	20	12		
2. Design						
2.1. Hardware						
2.1.1. Define hardware–software interfaces	22	12	20	10		
2.1.2. Electrical and electronic design	64					
2.1.3. Mechanical		102				
2.2. Software			78			
2.3. Networking				25		
2.4. Design review						
3. Purchase materials	4	3				
4. Fabricate system						
5. System integration and factory testing						
6. Crate and ship components						
7. Site installation and testing						
8. Documentation						
9. Training						
Total	117	157	118	47	0	0

b) Cumulative Actual Labor Hours, by Week and Functional Department

Department	Week Number															
	1	2	3	4	5	6	7	8	9	10	11	12	13	14	15	16
Electrical engineering	5	27	87	117												
Mechanical engineering	20	52	92	157												
Software engineering	4	20	60	118												
Networking engineering	2	10	37	47												
Factory technicians	0	0	0	0												
Field Service technicians	0	0	0	0												
Project management	10	18	26	34												
Publications	0	0	0	0												
Quality assurance	8	8	8	12												
Training	8	8	8	8												
Shipping	0	0	0	0												
Purchasing	0	0	0	0												
Total labor	57	143	318	493												

Project Management	Publications	Training	Quality Assurance	Shipping	Purchasing	Total Labor
12		6	8			125
						0
						0
6		2	4			76
4						68
4						106
6						84
						25
						0
2						9
						0
						0
						0
						0
						0
						0
34	0	8	12	0	0	493

TABLE 11–5

Comparison of Cumulative Planned Spending Versus Actual Project Labor Charges at the End of the Fourth Week

Department	Cumulative Planned Hours, Week 4	Cumulative Actual Hours, Week 4	±10% Over- or Underspent
Electrical engineering	110	117	
Mechanical engineering	130	157	Over
Software engineering	178	118	Under
Networking engineering	60	47	Under
Factory technicians	0	0	
Field service technicians	0	0	
Project management	32	34	
Publications	0	0	
Quality assurance	10	12	Over
Training	8	8	
Shipping	0	0	
Purchasing	0	0	

project; Table 11–4c summarizes the total labor charged to each WBS task during that time. Figure 11–4 graphically illustrates the interim actual costs with the planned labor costs.

Many project managers begin their weekly status analysis by comparing the total hours actually charged to the project by each functional department with the expected spending plan. The project manager or the project financial administrator compares the expected data from Table 11–3 with the actual labor hours

FIGURE 11–4

Planned versus actual costs four weeks into the factory employee access project

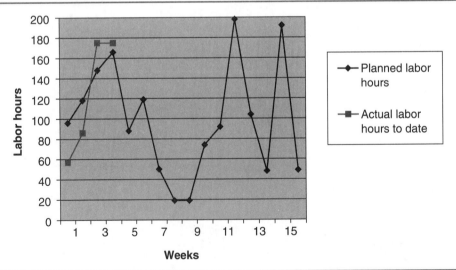

charged from Table 11–4 and notes any discrepancies between the anticipated rate of spending and the hours actually worked on the project. During the first two weeks, for example, although the team expected to spend 214 (96 and 118) hours on the job, it actually spent 143 (57 and 86) hours. During the third and fourth weeks, the team attempted to catch up by working 175 hours each week.

Functional managers may rationalize not placing the required number of people on the job. From their perspective, they have a limited number of people in the department, and they usually feel a responsibility to supply labor for long-term, complex jobs. Functional department managers tend to use short-term projects for "fill-in" work during a lull in the long-term job. Consequently, they may not assign staff to the short-term effort until they can fit it into their timetable. Many functional managers incorrectly perceive the short-term project as less important than the longer effort—a perception that, unfortunately, can result in work falling behind schedule.

At the four-week point of the project under discussion, it became evident that several groups did not put the required number of people on the job. Arbitrarily, it was established that time charged to within ±10% of the spending plan would be satisfactory. The project manager or the project financial administrator creates the comparison in Table 11–5 from the expected data in Table 11–3 and the actual time charged in Table 11–4 to determine which departments put the correct number of people on the project. Examining Table 11–5 leads to the conclusion that the electrical engineering department, factory technicians, field service technicians, project management, and the publications, training, shipping, and purchasing departments spent the number of hours planned for in the labor budget. Whether these departments completed the requisite work corresponding to the expenditures is unknown; all that is known is that their personnel worked the requisite time on the job. The mechanical engineering and quality assurance departments overspent the ±10% guideline. The quality assurance department's 20% overrun of two hours may be ignored, because the figure is too small compared with the overall budget. However, the 20% overrun by the mechanical engineering department does raise questions. Did the department complete the work it set out to accomplish? Did it move ahead of schedule? By contrast, both the software engineering and networking engineering departments underspent their allotted labor funding. Those departments appear not to have put the required amount of labor into the job. Why did they do that? Did they overestimate the complexity of the job, or do they lack the personnel? Did they complete their assigned tasks? Comparing actual time charges with the planned labor expenditures simply does not provide sufficient information to determine the project's status. Further investigation is required.

The planned schedule shown in Figure 11–2a indicates that at the end of the fourth week, WBS activities 1 and 2.1.1 should have been completed. WBS activities 2.1.2, 2.2.3, 2.2, and 2.3 should have had approximately 50% of the work done. As they do at the end of every week, the functional managers provided the project manager with information on the status of the fourth week's schedule. For the project manager to receive a meaningful estimate, each task must have a well-defined output so that both the functional managers and the project manager can objectively confirm the percentage of the task completed.

TABLE 11–6

Ratio of Actual Labor Hours Spent to Planned Labor Hour Estimate at the Fourth Week into the Project

| Project Task | ENGINEERING | | | | Factory Technicians | Field Service Technicians |
	Electrical	Mechanical	Soft-ware	Net-working		
1. System definition	68%	100%	50%	60%		
2. Design						
2.1. Hardware						
2.1.1. Define hardware–software interface	220%	120%	200%	100%		
2.1.2. Electrical and electronic design	107%					
2.1.3. Mechanical		85%				
2.2. Software			49%			
2.3. Networking				63%		
2.4. Design review	0%	0%	0%	0%		
3. Purchase materials	100%	75%	0%	0%		
4. Fabricate system	0%	0%		0%	0%	0%
5. System integration and factory testing	0%	0%	0%	0%	0%	0%
6. Crate and ship components						0%
7. Site installation and testing	0%	0%	0%	0%		0%
8. Documentation	0%	0%	0%	0%		
9. Training						
Total	57%	57%	38%	36%	0%	0%

The project manager or his or her designee places the data received into the column in Table 11–6 entitled "Estimate of Work Completed." The project financial administrator creates the remainder of Table 11–6 by forming the ratio of the actual labor hours charged (Table 11–4c) to the planned labor hour estimate (Table 11–2), shown as a percentage.

Each WBS item is shown in detail in Table 11–6. The data on WBS 1 state that the departments collectively consider the work on the task completed.

Project Manage-ment	Publications	Training	Quality Assurance	Shipping	Purchasing	Total Labor	Estimate of Work Completed
120%		—	80%			78%	100%
150%		—	—			173%	75%
67%						103%	75%
40%						82%	50%
38%						48%	75%
0%						57%	50%
0%							
200%					0%	16%	
0%						0%	
0%			0%			0%	
0%				0%		0%	
0%			0%			0%	
0%	0%		0%			0%	
0%		0%				0%	
24%	0%	10%	24%	0%	0%	31%	

The electrical department charged 68% of the estimated hours to WBS 1, whereas project management charged 120% of its plan. That is, the project management group overspent its budget by 20% on this task. Earlier, it was noted that the software department did not place all the planned labor on the job, but nonetheless completed the task. So this issue is satisfactorily resolved. The training department charged time to WBS 1, but did not include any such charges in its original estimate. Quality assurance underspent. Overall, then,

WBS item 1 worked out well. The team completed it with only 78% of its planned expenditures actually spent. The work was completed on time and under budget—music to a project manager's ears!

WBS task 2.1.1 turns out to be quite a different story, however. The planned schedule indicates that the task should have been done, but the departments reported that it was only 75% complete. Every department overspent its labor budget on the task. The training and quality assurance departments charged unplanned time to the task. What happened? The project manager must visit each department as soon as possible. Has a difficult technical problem arisen? Has the customer requested the engineers to use a different software application or a different piece of equipment than that agreed upon in the proposal? Has a supplier changed the specification for a piece of equipment, thereby creating havoc among the design engineers? Do the users have incomplete or inaccurate data associated with the use of equipment or software? Did the team simply underestimate the complexity of the job? The project manager must quickly discover and resolve the problem(s). Table 11–7 identifies typical issues that may arise during a project's early phases. More often than not, a problem that arises during an early phase is due to a misunderstanding of the requirements, a failure to place people on the job at the required times, an underestimate of the complexity of the job, or a subcontractor failing to perform as expected. With regard to the latter issue, many organizations prefer to place work with reliable subcontractors with whom they have developed trusted relationships, even if the task costs a bit more. This, of course, is in accordance with one of Deming's 14 points:

> End the practice of awarding business on the basis of price tag. Instead, minimize total cost. Move toward a single supplier for any one item, on a long-term relationship of loyalty and trust.

Receiving reliable hardware or software on time so that it does not delay other work is crucial to the success of the job.

TABLE 11–7

Typical Issues Arising During a Project's Early Stages

Issue	Project Manager's Action
Stakeholders uncover an undefined parameter associated with a task or requirement	• Request affected stakeholders to define the parameter in question, using appropriate standards and guidelines. • Inform affected stakeholders (but not the customer) of the change. • Following stakeholders' agreement to the change, inform the customer of the plan in writing.
Unclear requirement in the specification	• Review the unclear requirement with the relevant functional organization(s). Agree on an interpretation that affects the project only minimally. • Inform stakeholders (but not the customer) of the change.

TABLE 11–7

	• Following stakeholder's agreement to the change, inform the customer, in writing, of the contractor's interpretation of the specification requirement. • Seek clarification from the customer only if absolutely necessary.
Customer has not provided technical data required to perform a task	• Request that the customer submit data to the contractor by a specific date. • If the customer fails to deliver the data, meet with the customer to discuss the issues. • As a last resort, inform the customer that the organization will stop work on the job if technical personnel do not receive the required information.
Customer has second thoughts about a requirement in the original agreement and has not provided technical personnel required data	• Request that the customer submit data to the contractor by a specific date. • If the customer fails to deliver the data, meet with the customer to discuss the issues. • Consider trading requirements to offset the impact of the change on the cost and schedule. • As a last resort, inform the customer that the organization will stop work on the job if technical personnel do not receive the required information.
Customer has introduced changes by bypassing the project manager and talking directly to the engineers on the project	• The project manager must prevent the customer from directly contacting the organization's personnel in the future without permission. • The project manager must firmly, but gently, inform the customer of the organization's protocols for requesting changes. • Indicate that the contractor will proceed with the original agreement.
Unavailability of selected components, equipment, or software	• Seek an alternative source for the material desired. • Select different components, equipment, or software. • Inform stakeholders if changes to components, equipment, or software are made.
Unanticipated technical issue	• Resolve issue by obtaining internal or external (consultant) expertise. • Understand the impact of the alternative solutions on the project's cost and schedule. • Agree on a solution to the problem with the affected internal stakeholders. • If the issue is visible to the customer, meet with the customer to discuss alternatives and a solution.
Unavailability of manufacturer's data	• Contact manufacturer or manufacturer's representative, and arrange for a technical discussion between organization's and manufacturer's technical personnel.
Labor not placed on job	• Meet with functional departments to resolve issue.

If the delay associated with WBS task 2.1.1 results from the likelihood of not meeting a customer requirement, then a highly significant issue has surfaced. The functional departments and the project manager must develop several alternative plans and then notify senior management. After bringing senior management on board, the customer should be notified. Often, a good project manager can trade a difficult implementation requirement for another feature that the customer values.

Note that in this example the project manager examined both functional department spending and the status of WBS activities. Formal techniques for performing this analysis exist. In particular, project managers sometimes use earned-value analyses to quantify a project's status. These analyses rely on the original project estimates and actual progress to determine the project's status. Table 11–8 identifies the earned-value definitions. Figure 11–5 illustrates the relationships among several of the variables in the table for data reviewed during the first week of October. On the basis of this information, the project manager concludes that the project is behind schedule and over budget. The graph denotes the estimate at the completion of the project, based on the formula provided in Table 11–8.

Project managers monitor the schedule and cost performance indices on a weekly basis to gain a quick understanding of developing problems. Indices greater than unity signify that all is going well; indices less than unity signify possible problems. When confronted with a long list of tasks, the project manager can easily scan the list to identify those tasks with a CPI or SPI less than unity. The farther below unity, the more is the concern. In this way, the method automatically ranks the tasks calling for the project manager's attention. The earned-value method affords a continual estimate of the project's cost

FIGURE 11–5

Earned-value relationships

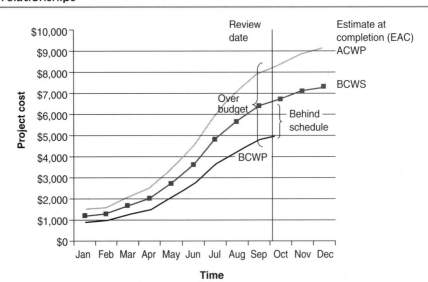

TABLE 11-8

Earned-Value Definitions

Term	Abbreviation	Formula	Derived from	Description
Budgeted cost of work scheduled	BCWS		Budget estimate	Time-phased budget for each task in the entire project
Budgeted cost of work performed	BCWP		Budget estimate	Amount of money the project manager expected to spend for the work on each task completed by a specific date
Budget at completion	BAC		Budget estimate	Approved budget to complete all the work on the project
Estimate to complete	ETC		Actual funds spent	Funding required to complete the remaining work on the project. Estimate calculated at designated points during the project
Estimate at completion	EAC	= ACWP + ETC	Actual funds spent	Estimate of the total funding that will be spent on the project. Estimate calculated at designated points during the project
Actual cost of work performed	ACWP		Actual funds spent	Actual costs for each project task
Cost variance	CV	= BCWP − ACWP	Budgeted and actual funds	A positive value signifies that less money than anticipated has been spent on the task. A negative value signifies that more money than anticipated has been spent on the task
Schedule variance	SV	= BCWP − BCWS	Budgeted and actual funds	A positive value signifies that the task is ahead of schedule. A negative value signifies that the task is behind schedule
Cost performance index	CPI	= BCWP/ACWP	Budgeted and actual funds	CPI greater than 1 signifies that all is going well on the task. CPI less than 1 signifies that problems are associated with the task and the team has spent too much
Schedule performance index	SPI	= BCWP/BCWS	Budgeted and actual funds	SPI greater than 1 indicates that the work is ahead of schedule. SPI less than 1 signifies that the work is behind schedule
Cost at completion	CAC	= TOTAL BUDGET × (ACWP/BCWP)	Budgeted and actual funds	Estimated total project cost based on progress to date
Cost to complete		= Cost at completion − ACWP	Budgeted and actual funds	

at completion, thereby enabling the project manager to respond to one of management's first questions: How much will it cost to solve the problem?

Whatever method of analysis is used, it should be performed in a regular and consistent manner, preferably each week. The project manager examines the project's labor, financial, and schedule data for all WBS tasks in a manner similar to that shown in this example. Meetings then take place with functional department managers to discuss actions required to resolve problems. Stakeholders find it crucial to keep their communication channels active and inform one another of changes. The project manager always informs the customer of changes in writing.

SUMMARY OF MONITORING AND TRACKING ACTIVITIES

The project team can begin to resolve problems only if it knows that a deviation from the plan has occurred. If so, the team assesses the impact of the variance on the overall delivery of the promised product. After identifying the problem, the team formulates a plan to take corrective actions that offset the unwelcome news. Project monitoring detects processes or outputs that deviate from the plan(s) and task costs that deviate from the budget. Project managers pay particular attention to items on the critical path and to the risk areas identified earlier in the process. Resolving problems in accordance with basic control principles will improve the chances of project success. Achieving success requires a disciplined approach in order to track the project's status, anticipate potential problems, and resolve problems quickly.

SUBCONTRACTING

From time to time, an organization decides to subcontract one or more of a project's tasks to external organizations. Following are some of the reasons for subcontracting:

- The organization lacks expertise in a relevant area.
- The labor available to complete the task is insufficient.
- The contract stipulates that one or more tasks be subcontracted.
- The schedule requires some tasks to be subcontracted in order for them to be completed on time.
- Another organization can complete the task for a lower price.

The project manager has the responsibility for coordinating the activities required to contract out the work, as well as the responsibility for monitoring the progress of those activities. Of course, the buyer expects the vendor to provide a quality product or service that meets the specified requirements on schedule and at the negotiated price.

At times, a project manager is not sure whether to permit an internal organization to perform a task or subcontract it to an external organization. Perhaps the internal organization's price appears high, the organization has raised significant technical concerns, or the functional groups have raised labor or scheduling issues. Under these circumstances, the project manager may choose to conduct a *make-or-buy analysis*, which compares the advantages and disadvantages of performing the task in-house versus selecting an external vendor to carry out the effort. If the schedule allows, the project manager may prepare an RFQ or an RFP for distribution to industry, although it could be two or more months before all the responses are received and the contract is awarded.

Seeking to subcontract work sometimes represents a "fishing" expedition. The project manager and the functional department managers want information—perhaps to corroborate the fact that they have pursued a good technical approach. They carefully evaluate the bids received to get a handle on their price and technical content. An ethical question arises if an organization performs this exercise solely for the purpose of gathering information about competitors. Vendors recognize that every time they respond to an RFP, they give the prospective buyer valuable information about their organization and its technical abilities. Unfortunately, this is a cost and risk of doing business. After receiving the bids, the project manager analyzes the information they provide and then decides whether it is in the best interests of the organization to perform the task on its own or subcontract the work out.

Selecting Qualified Vendors

The organization demands that the vendor chosen for a job provide a competitively priced product or service that meets the contract's needs. Purchases made with funds stemming from a contract with a federal government agency require vendors to adhere to certain terms and conditions—for example, equal employment opportunity and civil rights requirements, fair-wage standards, and anti-kickback regulations. Organizations evaluate potential suppliers for compliance with governmental regulations, as well as with quality assurance plans and other terms. Because the process takes a considerable amount of time, many organizations develop lists of preferred vendors to hasten the selection process.

If an organization has never selected a vendor for the required product or service, it might begin the task by doing any or all of the following:

- consulting colleagues in other departments or organizations who have purchased a similar product or service
- checking the Internet
- using library references, such as the *Thomas Register* of *American Manufacturers*
- consulting the Yellow Pages for a listing of local suppliers
- examining trade publications, directories, vendor catalogues, and professional journals
- placing advertisements in general circulation publications such as newspapers or in specialty publications like professional journals

After a buyer creates a list of potential vendors, it evaluates each of their capabilities. The purchasing department obtains a Dun & Bradstreet (D&B) financial report on each proposed vendor. In addition to information on the vendor's creditworthiness and financial stability, some D&Bs include brief profiles of key management personnel and historical information on the company. The purchasing department may also check the supplier's reliability with local Better Business Bureaus. If the prospective subcontract is important to the project's success, the project manager may visit the vendor's facilities to verify that it has the equipment and labor pool required to complete the project. The project manager also may evaluate the vendor's quality assurance process and determine whether it uses state-of-the art technology. The purchasing department usually requests and checks the vendor's references. Following these steps should narrow the field to a manageable set of vendors that will be asked to bid on the needed product or service.

Preparing and Evaluating a Bid

A buyer requires from two to four weeks to prepare an RFP or RFQ. Vendors need from four to six weeks to prepare a proposal response or quote, and the buyer requires about two weeks to evaluate the documents and make a decision on the proposal or quote. The process gives an organization a standard for comparing price, quality, and service, thereby allowing the organization to make an informed and objective choice among potential suppliers.

The buying organization prepares a bid package as described in Chapter 5. Recall that the RFP and RFQ include a clear statement of the item sought, a specification, and a statement of work (SOW) containing a work-breakdown structure (WBS), a schedule, and a blank specification compliance matrix that the vendor completes to signify its compliance with each requirement. This process helps to identify the vendor that can meet the buyer's requirements for the best price.

If members of functional departments believe that the subcontract represents a substantial challenge requiring a highly competent technical labor pool, they request the vendor to include in its response a description of the qualifications of those individuals who may be involved in implementing the goals and objectives of the RFP. Sometimes the writers of the RFP seek input from the vendors because they are unsure whether the product or service that they have requested will satisfactorily implement the solution to their problem. If so, they include a statement in the bid package requesting bidders to describe how they would meet a specific objective, what unique contributions they would make toward the project, and what alternative proposals they would offer. The vendors might also be asked to solve specific problems concerning time constraints, new technology, or on-the-job training for end users. Of course, these requests, in effect, are asking the vendors to provide free consulting services, so they may not respond unless a substantial contract is involved.

At times, the buyer holds a prebidding conference during which the organization distributes and clarifies the solicitation for all preferred vendors. The conference ensures that all vendors have a clear, mutual understanding of the procurement (technical requirements, contract requirements, etc.). Conducting an open meeting prevents any vendor from having an unfair advantage due to information it alone has obtained.

The buyer distributes identical copies of the solicitation and any subsequent changes in the bid specification to all prospective suppliers. One of the first pages in the solicitation should clearly state the deadline for submittal and the person in the organization to whom the vendors should address their response. The buyer records the date and time upon receipt of the bid response packages from the vendors.

Most proposals contain a set of objective *evaluation criteria*, which the buyer uses to rate the proposals. Including these criteria in the solicitation not only assists vendors in the preparation of their work, but also crystallizes those items the buyer deems most important. The following items may be among the evaluation criteria:

- *Technical approach.* Does the proposal demonstrate that the vendor understands and meets the project's requirements?
- *Life-cycle cost.* Is the life-cycle cost of the product low enough? The initial purchase price may not be the only cost factor. Some buyers express interest in a low operating cost as well. If so, the seller must describe all the costs in detail and illustrate how the product affords a low cost of ownership.
- *Technical capability.* Does the seller present a convincing argument that it has the technical skills and knowledge needed to complete the subcontract?
- *Management approach.* Does the seller have management processes and procedures in place (including quality assurance) to ensure a successful project?
- *Financial capacity.* Does the seller demonstrate that it has the financial wherewithal to complete the project?
- *Past performance history.* Has the vendor delivered similar systems or services in the past?
- *After-sale support and services.* Can the seller provide services such as training, help-desk support, and maintenance of the product?

Often, in quantifying the data for evaluation purposes, the buyer assigns a weighting system to minimize the effect of personal prejudice on selecting a source. Most weighting systems assign a numerical weight to each of the evaluation criteria, rate the prospective sellers according to each criterion, multiply the weight by the rating, and total the resultant products to compute an overall score. Some buyers use a screening system that establishes minimum requirements for one or more of the evaluation criteria. That is, failure to meet the minimum requirement automatically disqualifies a bid. The buyer states these "go–no go" criteria clearly in the solicitation.

The buyer carefully examines all of the bids that have been received. Frequently, three or more people read the responses and meet to discuss them. These reviewers narrow the field by determining which vendors are "responsive"—that is, provide all the information asked for and address all the issues in the RFQ or RFP. The specification compliance matrix affords evaluators a quick summary of sellers' responsiveness. Unless a seller has a compelling reason for failing to comply with a requirement, that seller should be eliminated from the competition.

Technical personnel generally review the technical proposal without knowledge of the vendor's price. Members of the purchasing department review the proposed prices. When the two groups meet, their members compare prices and technical content and reach a conclusion as to whom to award the subcontract.

Most purchasing managers and project managers are wary of a vendor who under-bids the competition substantially. Such a vendor may have submitted a "low-ball" price to win the bid, but may not have the resources to deliver a quality product or deliver the product on schedule. A significantly lower price may also indicate that the vendor has misunderstood or misinterpreted the requirements.

Administering a Contract

Following the award, the project manager must ensure that the vendor delivers as promised. *Contract administration* is the process of ensuring that the seller performs as expected. On larger projects with multiple product and service providers, coordinating the interfaces among the various providers becomes a major task. The project manager, assuming responsibility for contract admin-istration, applies the tracking and monitoring processes described earlier in the chapter and seeks to integrate the subcontractor's outputs into the overall proj-ect. Project management activities include the following:

- Monitoring and tracking the subcontractor's cost, schedule, and techni-cal performance
- Employing quality assurance techniques to verify the adequacy of the subcontractor's product
- Using change control practices to ensure the proper approval of changes
- Communicating information to all stakeholders
- Observing the factory and site acceptance tests to verify that the prod-uct conforms with the requirements of the contract

Finally, the project manager approves payments to the subcontractor that are linked to well-defined milestones of the project.

PROJECT COMPLETION

As the end of the project approaches, the subcontractors deliver the required prod-ucts and services. Factory technicians have integrated the software and hardware. Field service technicians have installed the products and services at the cus-tomer's site. Engineers and technicians have completed the acceptance tests. The technologists and technical writers have completed the required documentation. Training personnel have prepared the training material and will soon deliver the courses to the customer's designated personnel. The process of closing out a con-tract involves confirming that the organization correctly and satisfactory com-pleted and delivered all work required by the contract. The project manager requests the appropriate departments to review open invoices and payment records to settle the project's financial statements. The project manager also par-ticipates in the process of updating records to reflect the final costs and techni-cal results of the project and then archiving this information for future use.

Postproject Review: Lessons Learned

Most organizations agree that a postproject evaluation should be performed. However, hardly anybody ever does it. "Right now we're too busy, but we'll get to it later," they say. Well, they usually don't, and they go out and make the same mistakes on the next job. But a *lessons-learned* session—a project "post-mortem"—helps the team do a better job on future projects. During this brief activity, the organization assesses the technical-, cost-, and schedule-related project outcomes, examining the project's planning, organizing, directing, controlling, executing, and budgeting phases. Did the organization achieve the desired results? What went right and what went wrong? Why? What should and should not be done in the future? Which organizational method or process was difficult or frustrating to use? Did the selected suppliers deliver technically satisfactory products and services on schedule and within budget? Did the stakeholders participate effectively and understand their role in the project? If not, what steps should be taken to improve their participation and understanding? The project manager communicates the results of a lessons-learned session to other members of the organization, so that all can benefit from improvements in the management of future projects.

The project financial administrators collect the total project-related expenditures through the cost-tracking system. By analyzing actual expenditures versus budgeted expenditures, the project team can refine its cost-estimating techniques and improve future estimates. In the event of a cost overrun, the team should attempt to explain the variances with the idea of learning from mistakes and should not assign blame. This exercise requires tact and diplomacy, for it can turn into a finger-pointing session during which no one learns very much.

Other appropriate topics discussed during a lessons-learned session include the following:

- the project management process
- the product or service development process
- the subcontracting method used on the project
- the training received or provided
- the data migration task (used in database projects)
- the technology used
- the software used
- the selection of the project team
- suggested changes in organizational policies and procedures

Management can use the results of outcome measures to track the effect that various decisions, policies, and practices have on operations. Perhaps most important of all, the team should identify, describe, and promote successful practices for use in the next project.

REVIEW QUESTIONS

1. Describe the activities that the project manager engages in after the project begins.
2. Why does the project manager not want technical personnel to engage in discussions with the customer without a project manager present?
3. Describe the project tracking activities in which the project manager participates.

4. Which of the following does project tracking involve?
   a) monitoring and reviewing the accomplishments and results of the project and comparing them with estimates of the project's scope, resources, schedule, and cost
   b) informing less enthusiastic team members that they "better shape up, or we'll see to it that they work third shift for the rest of the project"
   c) accompanying project team members on their activities
   d) verifying that the organization receives material procurements on time
   e) maintaining contact with subcontractors and receiving information on the status of their assigned work
   f) visiting subcontractors
   g) performing time and motion studies on project team members
   h) disciplining project team members for not completing work on time
   i) developing work-around plans to correct technical, schedule, cost, and subcontracting plans that go awry
   j) verifying that resources become available when required
   k) informing customers that they "better shape up, or we'll cancel the contract"
   l) acting on feedback from the user or customer.
5. Add a, b, c, and d to make a statement. Is the new statement true or false? Project tracking and reporting compares the planned versus actual status of a project in order to monitor...
   a) changes to a project's sponsorship, management, or organization
   b) a project's schedule and milestones
   c) a project's budget
   d) a project's scope, objectives, or requirements
6. Describe the contents of typical project status briefings.
7. Use the last three columns to check or fill in the frequency of the status meetings listed in the first column.

	Weekly	Monthly	Other (Describe)
Functional department activity progress, planned versus actual	_____	_____	_____
Subcontractor/supplier activity progress, planned versus actual	_____	_____	_____
Functional department spending, planned versus actual	_____	_____	_____
Preliminary design review	_____	_____	_____
Critical design review	_____	_____	_____
Site acceptance test	_____	_____	_____
Technical issues identified by functional department	_____	_____	_____
Technical interchange meetings between functional groups and suppliers	_____	_____	_____
Status meetings with purchasing department	_____	_____	_____

8. Describe the implications associated with the following:
    a) a functional department using fewer labor hours than expected
    b) a functional department using more labor hours than expected
9. Describe the steps to take to verify what you have stated in questions 8a and b.
10. Describe the advantages and disadvantages of always informing your customer of the results of weekly status meetings held with your functional departments.
11. Discuss the following statement: Project managers must use Tables 11–2 through 11–6 regularly to verify the status of a project.
12. The text states that some project managers manage several projects simultaneously. Discuss the characteristics of a person who engages in this kind of activity. Do you think it is more difficult to manage several small projects than one very large project? Explain.
13. Examine WBS elements 2.1.2 and 2.1.3 in Figure 11–2 in the project tracking example described in the text. Analyze the data to determine the status of the electrical/electronic design and mechanical design groups. Are the groups on schedule and within budget? Determine the variance, if any, from the plan.
14. Describe five problems that may arise during a project's early stages, and identify actions the project manager can take to resolve the problems.
15. Why would a prime contractor subcontract a portion of a job?
16. Do you believe that it is ethical for a company to submit an RFP to several companies solely for the purpose of gathering information on what the competition is doing? Initially, the prospective "buyer" has no intent of purchasing the product or service. Explain your answer.
17. A product-testing laboratory has decided to replace an old analog electronic environmental control system with a new digital system. This unit controls the temperature and humidity in three environmental chambers to within ±1%. The system consists of a digital environmental control electronics unit (DECEU) and three environmental units (EUs), each placed in a chamber consisting of temperature and humidity sensors and heater and humidifier/dehumidifier units, as shown in the following diagram:

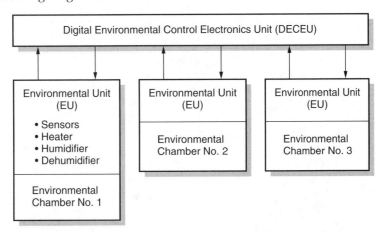

The operator enters the required temperature and humidity for each environmental chamber on a console associated with the DECEU. The DECEU monitors and controls the temperature and humidity in each environmental chamber. The accompanying tables (charts a through c) show the planned schedule, planned labor hours, planned spending, actual labor hours, and percentage of the task completed at the end of two months.

a) Plot the project's planned labor hour estimate versus time. On the same graph, draw the actual hours worked by the departments. What conclusion(s) can you draw?

b) What problem do you see with the functional department labor hours assigned to WBS task numbers 4.1.1, 4.1.2, and 8.2? What should the project manager do about this problem during the planning stage?

c) Prepare a two-month status table comparing the cumulative planned project spending versus the cumulative actual project labor charges for each department.

    i. Have all of the departments assigned the required amount of labor to the project?

    ii. For the first two months, which departments under- or overspent their allotted labor funding budget? By how much?

d) Compare actual time charged with planned labor expenditures for each department. To accomplish this, create a chart similar to Table 11–6 that contains the ratio of the actual labor hours charged to the planned labor hour estimate, shown as a percentage.

    i. Do these data provide sufficient information to determine the project's status? Explain.

    ii. Now add a column containing the functional department's estimate of the work completed for each WBS task. Do these data provide sufficient information to determine the project's status? Explain.

    iii. To which departments does the project manager need to pay attention? Explain.

(a) Digital environmental control system, schedule plan

ID	WBS	❶	Task Name	Duration	Start	Finish	Predeces	Dec	Jan	Feb	Mar	Apr	May	Jun
									1st Quarter			2nd Quarter		
1	1		Award contract	0 days	Jan 2	Jan 2								
2	2		Review system definition	2 days	Jan 2	Jan 3	1							
3	3		Define hardware–software interfaces	3 days	Jan 6	Jan 8	2							
4	4		**Design**	**30 days**	**Jan 9**	**Feb 19**								
5	4.1		**Hardware**	**20 days**	**Jan 9**	**Feb 5**								
6	4.1.1		EU, electrical and mechanical	3 wks	Jan 9	Jan 29	3							
7	4.1.2		DECEU, electrical and mechanical	4 wks	Jan 9	Feb 5	3							
8	4.2		Software	6 wks	Jan 9	Feb 19	3							
9	5		Design review	2 days	Feb 20	Feb 21	5,8							
10	6		**Prototype system**	**40 days**	**Feb 24**	**Apr 18**								
11	6.1		Purchase material	4 wks	Feb 24	Mar 21	9							
12	6.2		Fabricate system	1.5 wks	Feb 24	Mar 5	9							
13	6.3		Integrate and test system	3 wks	Mar 24	Apr 11	12,11							
14	6.4		Update system drawings	1 wk	Apr 14	Apr 18	13							
15	7		Final production build review	2 days	Apr 14	Apr 15	13							
16	8		**Three-system production build**	**27 days**	**Apr 16**	**May 22**								
17	8.1		Purchase material	3 wks	Apr 16	May 6	15							
18	8.2		Fabricate systems	1.5 wks	Apr 16	Apr 25	15							
19	8.3		Integrate systems	2 wks	May 7	May 20	17,18							
20	8.4		Perform factory acceptance test	2 days	May 21	May 22	19							
21	9		Crate and ship materials	5 days	May 23	May 29	20							
22	10		Site installation	1 wk	May 30	Jun 5	21							
23	11		Site acceptance test	2 days	Jun 6	Jun 9	22							
24	12		Documentation	4 wks	May 23	Jun 19	15,20							
25	13		**Training**	**7 days**	**Jun 20**	**Jun 30**								
26	13.1		Preparation for training	1 wk	Jun 20	Jun 26	24							
27	13.2		Conduct training class	2 days	Jun 27	Jun 30	26,23							

(b) Digital Environmental Control System, Project Labor Hours Plan

		ENGINEERING			Factory Technicians	Field Service Technicians
	Project Task	Electrical	Mechanical	Software		
1.	Award contract					
2.	Review system definition	40	40	40		
3.	Define hardware–software interfaces	40	20	80		
4.	Design					
4.1.	Hardware					
4.1.1.	EU, Electrical and mechanical	200	400			
4.1.2.	DECEU, Electrical and mechanical	320	200			
4.2.	Software			450		
5.	Design review	40	40	40		
6.	Prototype system					
6.1.	Purchase material	20	20			
6.2.	Fabricate system				120	
6.3.	Integrate and test system	100	100	120	50	
6.4.	Update system drawings	20	20		40	
7.	Final production build review	40	40	40		
8.	Three-system production build					
8.1.	Purchase material	10	10			
8.2.	Fabricate systems	10	10		300	
8.3.	Integrate systems	50	50	100	20	40
8.4.	Perform factory acceptance test	20	20	20		20
9.	Crate and ship materials					
10.	Site installation	10	10	10		60
11.	Site acceptance test	20	20	20		30
12.	Documentation	50	50	80		
13.	Training					
13.1.	Preparation for training					
13.2.	Conduct training class					
Total		990	1050	1000	530	150

(c) Digital Environmental Control System Project Spending Plan, Monthly Distribution of Planned Labor Hours

Monthly Budgeted Hours

Department or Area	1	2	3	4	5	6	Total
Electrical engineering	250	250	200	125	100	65	990
Mechanical engineering	250	300	210	125	100	65	1050
Software engineering	200	300	220	80	100	100	1000
Factory technicians		80	200	200	50		530
Field service technicians					50	100	150
Project management	80	80	80	60	70	80	450
Publications						50	50
Quality assurance	25	10	10	30	30	40	145
Training						56	56
Shipping					40		40
Purchasing		50	50	50	40		190
Total labor	805	1070	970	670	580	556	4651

Project Management	Publications	Training	Quality Assurance	Shipping	Purchasing	Total Labor
10			10			140
10						150
60						660
45						565
50						500
30			25			175
15					100	155
10						130
40						410
10						90
30			25		10	185
10					80	110
20						340
25			20			305
20			20			120
				40		40
10			10			110
20			20			130
10	50		15			255
10		40				50
15		16				31
450	50	56	145	40	190	4651

(d) Digital environmental control system, actual project spending

Monthly Distribution of Actual Labor Hours in First Two Months

Department or Area	1	2	3	4	5	6	Total
Electrical engineering	150	300					450
Mechanical engineering	225	200					425
Software engineering	150	400					550
Factory technicians		20					20
Field service technicians							0
Project management	100	90					190
Publications							0
Quality assurance	40						40
Training							0
Shipping							0
Purchasing		20					20
Total labor	665	1030					1695

(e) Digital Environmental Control System, Percentage of Task Completed at End of Two Months

WBS No.	Project Task	Percent Task Complete
1.	Award contract	100%
2.	Review system definition	90%
3.	Define hardware–software interfaces	75%
4.	Design	
4.1.	Hardware	
4.1.1.	EU, electrical and mechanical	20%
4.1.2.	DECEU, electrical and mechanical	20%
4.2.	Software	25%
5.	Design review	
6.	Prototype system	
6.1.	Purchase material	20%
6.2.	Fabricate system	10%
6.3.	Integrate and test system	
6.4.	Update system drawings	
7.	Final production build review	
8.	Three-system production build	
8.1.	Purchase material	
8.2.	Fabricate systems	
8.3.	Integrate systems	
8.4.	Perform factory acceptance test	
9.	Crate and ship materials	
10.	Site installation	
11.	Site acceptance test	
12.	Documentation	
13.	Training	
13.1.	Preparation for training	
13.2.	Conduct training class	

18. Why would a buyer hold a prebidding conference?
19. What is the purpose of proposal evaluation criteria?
20. List five items that might serve as the basis for evaluating proposals.
21. Explain the difference between the price of a product and the life-cycle price. Describe the circumstances that would favor the selection of a vendor offering a low price rather than a vendor that offers a low life-cycle price.
22. What activities are involved in administering a contract or subcontract?
23. Following the completion of a project, what is the purpose of a lessons-learned evaluation session?

CHAPTER 12

EPILOGUE

THE BLIND MEN AND THE ELEPHANT

It was six men of Indostan
To learning much inclined,
Who went to see the Elephant
(Though all of them were blind),
That each by observation
Might satisfy his mind.

The *First* approached the Elephant,
And happening to fall
Against his broad and sturdy side,
At once began to bawl:
"God bless me! but the Elephant
Is very like a wall!"

The *Second*, feeling of the tusk,
Cried, "Ho! what have we here
So very round and smooth and sharp?
To me 'tis mighty clear
This wonder of an Elephant
Is very like a spear!"

The *Third* approached the animal,
And happening to take
The squirming trunk within his hands,
Thus boldly up and spake:
"I see," quoth he, "the Elephant
Is very like a snake."

The *Fourth* reached out his eager hand,
And felt about the knee.
"What most this wondrous beast is like
Is mighty plain," quoth he;
"'Tis clear enough the Elephant
Is very like a tree!"

The *Fifth* who chanced to touch the ear,
Said: "E'en the blindest man
Can tell what this resembles most:
Deny the fact who can,
This marvel of an Elephant
Is very like a fan!"

The *Sixth* no sooner had begun
About the beast to grope,
Than, seizing on the swinging tail
That fell within his scope,
"I see," quoth he, "the Elephant
Is very like a rope!"

And so these men of Indostan
Disputed loud and long,
Each in his own opinion
Exceeding stiff and strong,
Though each was partly in the right,
And all were in the wrong!

So, oft in theologic wars,
The disputants, I ween,
Rail on in utter ignorance
Of what each other mean,
And prate about an Elephant
Not one of them has seen!

"The Blind Men and the Elephant," translated
by John Godfrey Saxe (1816–1887),
is a Hindu fable that occurs in the Udana,
a Canonical Hindu scripture.

INTRODUCTION

While managers view separation into departments or divisions as an efficient way of structuring organizations, modern corporations often have barriers between divisions, which limit their ability to interact. The result is much like the fable of the blind men and the elephant. In that tale, each person's perception is colored by where he stands. And so it is within the organization: Each department focuses on its own specific area of the business, while losing the vision of the big picture. Each operational business island may employ different operating procedures, different tools, different software applications, and different databases and may not integrate well with other parts of the organization. Using common tools and procedures, the project manager attempts to meld these disparate teams into a cohesive unit.

The project manager focuses on the project and spreads the "big picture" vision to the entire organizational team. Every day, newspapers print stories about the lack of communication, coordination, and integration associated with major projects undertaken by various organizations. For example, *The New York Times* reported that projects associated with the New York City Board of Education were incurring costs that were more than 10 times the Board of Education's estimates and were two years behind schedule.[1] Apparently, the project manager at the New York City Board of Education had failed to perform up to expectations: Stakeholders did not see the "big picture." The project manager's work certainly does not stop with plans: His or her success depends on *implementing* the plans and *monitoring* and *controlling* the project.

> According to one government agency's report about its own projects, they take much longer and cost about 50% more than comparable projects by other federal agencies or projects in the private sector. Moreover, [they] commonly overrun their budgets and schedules [and] have resulted in facilities that do not function as intended, projects that are abandoned before they are completed, or facilities that have been so long delayed that, upon completion, they no longer serve any purpose. In short, the DOE's . . . record calls into question the credibility of [the agency's] procedures for developing designs and cost estimates and managing projects.[2]

The report concluded that the agency had to "undertake a broad program of reform for the entire project management process."[3] The committee's findings and recommendations read like a project management text's table of contents. Some of them are as follows:

- Establish adequate policies, procedures, documentation, and reporting.
- Define requirements. Prepare a statement of work.

---

[1] Wyatt, E., "School cost overruns no secrect, official says," *The New York Times* (July 20, 2001): DI.
[2] Committee to Assess the Policies and Practices of the Department of Energy to Design, Manage, and Procure Environmental Restoration, Waste Management, and Other Construction Projects, *Improving Project Management in the Department of Energy* (Washington, DC: National Academy Press, 2000); on the Internet at *http://www.nap.edu/openbook/0809066263/RI.html*.
[3] *Ibid*.

- Identify and control risks.
- Use performance measures and incentives.
- Control project changes. Implement a system for managing change.
- Define project organizational lines of authority and the responsibilities of all parties.
- Implement an ISO 9000 certification process.
- Mandate a reporting system that tracks and communicates the cost, schedule, and scope of a project.
- Develop contingency plans and set aside contingency funds.
- Train managers in project management skills.
- Formalize procedures for conducting independent project reviews.
- Provide fiscal rewards for contractors who meet or exceed schedule, cost, and scope of performance targets.
- Structure the organization so as to provide focused and consistent management attention to projects. Establish an office of project management operating at a high organizational level.

According to the committee's report, project management failed at the Department of Energy (DOE). The DOE's unique demands make it imperative that project management concepts be implemented into the agency's operation. Although the DOE's complex projects frequently rely on technologies that have not been proven in the field, the report concluded that the agency's problems are more institutional than technical. The DOE would have to change its culture and focus on the problems of cost and schedule overruns, which involved DOE policies and procedures for identifying, planning, procuring, and managing projects. The report stated clearly that improving the project management methods would go a long way to reigning in technical, cost, and scheduling problems that the agency experienced.

PROJECT MANAGEMENT CAREER

Project management is a widely recognized and accepted career track. Project managers become involved at the birth of a project (the proposal stage) and remain to the final site acceptance test. Budgets range from as low as $100,000 for a small job to many hundreds of millions of dollars for a job that will extend over several years. Projects may involve new development, limited production, or maintenance. Most project managers are assigned to a single job, although some manage multiple projects simultaneously, usually requiring a similar set of skills.

Project managers use a wide assortment of tools to plan, estimate, and track various aspects of jobs. The project manager's core competencies involve both social and technical skills. Social skills influence stakeholders' behavior and attitudes. Communication and negotiation build relationships among all stakeholders. Social skills represent the grease for the skids to influence people to make things happen. Technical skills involve planning, scheduling, and controlling. The project manager uses technical skills to identify the project's technical goals and procedures and to ascertain the progress of the project.

Project Management Social and Technical Skills

Organizations measure the project manager's output on his or her ability to get thing's done on time, within budget, and in accordance with the customer's specifications. Accomplishing this demands a broad range of skills. Invariably, technology students enter a technical program with the goal of learning as many technical subjects as they can cram into their schedule. Then, six months to a year after the students start work at their first job, employers voice a common and consistent complaint: "The new employees just out of school have outstanding technical skills, but they lack social skills. They lack organizational and people skills. They lack customer sensitivity." The social and people skills these employers are referring to include communication, leadership, management, adapting to change, ability to listen, and willingness to go the extra mile—in essence, the skills embodied in the TACT acronym discussed in Chapter 1. This split in thinking limits the new employees' professional growth and advancement within the organization until they develop those skills. Many technology students choose to ignore social skills during their college years, realizing their importance only after they have discovered their limited upward movement within the organization.

Social and People Skills.   The new project manager should focus on developing social skills and abilities in the following areas:

- *Leadership*. The project manager sets a vision, communicates the vision, aligns the team with the vision, and identifies the steps required to achieve the vision. If change, which is inevitable, will improve a product or service, then the project manager assists the team in changing its technology, processes, procedures, suppliers, and, if necessary, personnel.

- *Management*. The project manager plans, organizes, controls, delegates, and communicates. In this regard, it is often wise to use McGregor's theory Y approach: coercive power will not work over the long run. Employ collaborative team concepts to get the project done. If a conflict exists between the project and the organization's business goals, the project manager requests clarification from senior management.

- *Flexibility*. More often than not, several viable options for solving problems present themselves. To increase the likelihood that all these options will be considered, the team members participate in the solution process. The project manager remains open to alternative solutions, juggling resources and adapting to and dealing with situations during periods of change. If the resolution of a problem endangers the schedule, the project manager offers employees support, in the form of resources or a word of encouragement.

- *Promises*. The project manager keeps his or her commitments and, reciprocally, expects others to keep their commitments.

- *Communication.* The project manager makes his or her expectations known in clear, precise, and unequivocal language. "Walking around" is one technique of managing that enables the project manager to remain accessible, no matter how busy he or she is. Negotiation is indispensable, and win–win situations are the key: Following an embarrassing negotiation loss, a humiliated stakeholder may become unmotivated and not perform up to expectations. If stakeholders are permitted a graceful exit, the entire team will benefit.

- *Feedback.* The project manager provides feedback to team members, either by acknowledging a job well done or offering constructive criticism. The latter should be to the point and brief.

- *Toleration of ambiguity.* Mathematical and engineering analyses generally result in a single answer. Some technologists have difficulty working in an environment in which there may be several reasonable answers to a problem. Solutions in business and human relations rarely involve clear-cut answers. More often than not, there will be a variety of ways of "skinning the cat," and it will be difficult to discern which is optimal. Team members should select the approach with which they feel most comfortable, unless the customer mandates the solution or the team's approach demands excessive funding.

- *Conflict resolution.* Issues arise during the course of the project. Sometimes the stakeholders voice strong opinions about an issue. The good project manager learns to resolve conflicts among stakeholders, assuage their sensitivities, and calm things down. Again, win–win solutions are vital in this regard.

- *Coping mechanisms for anxiety and stress reduction.* Technologists are often uncomfortable dealing with people, who are not always logical and who can voice their illogical opinions with passion and strong conviction. The project manager has to convince technicians to redirect themselves. Senior managers, customers, suppliers, and functional designers often have conflicting views. Projects frequently have tight schedules, which leads to anxiety. Coping with these issues requires a huge amount of energy and frequently leads to stress. The project manager should learn coping mechanisms to minimize the impact of stress on one's health and family life.

Technical skills. Beyond possessing the social and people skills discussed, project managers must have a command of the processes and tools required to get the job done. The project management processes discussed in this volume include planning, estimating, scheduling, tracking, controlling, and measuring. Following are some of the areas in which skills that are critical to achieving successful project management are found:

- *Project definition.* Every project demands a plan based on a set of requirements defined by the customer and deemed realistic by the contractor. Project managers must be able to define the project's business objectives and goals, deliverable products, assumptions and constraints, communication plan (how status and information will be shared with all stakeholders), and top-level implementation plan.

- *Tools.* Spreadsheets, word-processing programs, schedule preparation software such as Microsoft Schedule, and tracking tools like Primavera are all part of the project manager's arsenal of instruments used to carry out his or her job. The responsibility assignment matrix and specification compliance matrix may be used in conjunction with these instruments. Checklists verify whether tasks have been completed. Enterprise resource-planning systems that promote easy employee access and broad status checking enable the project manager to stay on top of expenditures, monitor purchases, and understand the labor charges on the job.

- *Estimating.* The project manager compiles estimates during the proposal phase, developing a lessons-learned list from past projects to provide a "sanity check" on functional managers' estimates. Although the project manager should never change functional managers' estimates without their knowledge and approval, the project manager should anticipate a job's cost. A major disparity between any of the functional managers' estimates and the project manager's rough order-of-magnitude appraisal is cause for a discussion.

- *Monitoring and control of status and processes.* Monitoring all fundamental data, the project manager compares labor and material expenditures on every project task against the plan. The project manager examines the technical progress of the project, identifies supplier issues as they arise, talks with the constituent organizations if things appear to be out of kilter, and asks questions to get to the root of problems. This replanning goes on continually as the organization obtains more information.

- *Control of the customer.* The project manager keeps the customer informed of the status of the project, requesting that the customer sign and date approvals to indicate its agreement with progress to date. The customer's signature also is obtained for design reviews and factory and site acceptance tests. Involving the customer reduces the likelihood that it will demand changes due to a lack of knowledge or understanding. One of the most difficult tasks requires the project manager to say no to a customer that requests changes that are beyond the scope of the project. But it has to be done: The project manager must balance the need to delight the customer with the organization's demand for a profit.

- *Consensus building.* The project manager develops team-building skills in him- or herself and in all members of the team.

- *Continuing education.* Technical skills can be improved by pursuing a certification such as the CompTIA Project + or the Project Management Institute's Project Management Professional program. Attending conferences and local seminars and reading project management journals will enable the interested project manager to keep abreast of new developments and revisit old methods to keep them fresh in one's mind.

APPENDIX 1

Typical Employee Performance Appraisal Forms

Four lessons of self-knowledge
One: You are your own best teacher.
Two: Accept responsibility. Blame no one.
Three: You can learn anything you want to learn.
Four: True understanding comes from reflecting on your experience.
—Warren Bennis, *On Becoming a Leader*

PERFORMANCE APPRAISAL

EMPLOYEE NAME:	EMPLOYEE ID NO.:
POSITION TITLE:	LABOR GRADE:
REVIEWER:	REVIEW DATE:

PERFORMANCE ASSESSMENT

Objectives for This Period	Assessment

PERFORMANCE FACTORS

Circle the factor associated with each performance factor that best describes the individual's job performance during this review period.

OUTSTANDING: Employee consistently exceeds expectations or requirements in this area.
MEETS REQUIREMENTS: Employee meets expectations or requirements.
NEEDS IMPROVEMENT: Employee meets some requirements, but needs improvement in this area.
UNSATISFACTORY: Employee does not meet requirements.

QUALITY: Continuously achieves the highest quality possible. Strives to get the job done right the first time. Supports the organization's quality policies. Customer-focused with both external and internal customers.

   Unsatisfactory   Needs Improvement   Meets Requirements   Outstanding

Comments:

COMMITMENT & INITIATIVE: Initiates actions that show continuous improvement; creatively solves problems. Can temporarily assume unaccustomed or additional duties. Dependable and prompt.

   Unsatisfactory   Needs Improvement   Meets Requirements   Outstanding

Comments:

ATTITUDE: Gets along well with others. Team player. Positive and cooperative.

| Unsatisfactory | Needs Improvement | Meets Requirements | Outstanding |

Comments:

JUDGMENT/DECISION MAKING: Makes sound judgments and decisions.

| Unsatisfactory | Needs Improvement | Meets Requirements | Outstanding |

Comments:

PLANNING AND ORGANIZATION: Analyzes priorities. Organizes and executes short- and long-term effective plans.

| Unsatisfactory | Needs Improvement | Meets Requirements | Outstanding |

Comments:

COMMUNICATION: Effectively communicates with coworkers and customers, both verbally and in writing, in a timely manner.

| Unsatisfactory | Needs Improvement | Meets Requirements | Outstanding |

Comments:

JOB KNOWLEDGE: Knowledgeable in methods and skills required for the position/field.

| Unsatisfactory | Needs Improvement | Meets Requirements | Outstanding |

Comments:

PRODUCTIVITY: Achieves expected outcomes within budget and on schedule without sacrificing quality.

| Unsatisfactory | Needs Improvement | Meets Requirements | Outstanding |

Comments:

MANAGING CHANGE: Effectively initiates and/or adapts to changes in operations.

| Unsatisfactory | Needs Improvement | Meets Requirements | Outstanding |

Comments:

SAFETY: Complies with and supports safety policies and procedures.

| Unsatisfactory | Needs Improvement | Meets Requirements | Outstanding |

Comments:

COACHING: Empowers and involves employees in making decisions and solving problems. Encourages teamwork. Acts as coach and mentor.

| Unsatisfactory | Needs Improvement | Meets Requirements | Outstanding |

Comments:

Describe the employee's major accomplishments during the performance period:

_____
_____
_____
_____
_____
_____
_____
_____

OVERALL RATING: Based upon the expectations for the position, circle the overall rating of the employee's performance during the past review period.

Unsatisfactory   Needs Improvement   Meets Requirements   Outstanding

OBJECTIVES FOR NEXT REVIEW PERIOD

TASK	DUE DATE

DEVELOPMENT GUIDANCE

Development guidance for the employee's current position as well as possible future positions.

_____
_____
_____
_____

EMPLOYEE COMMENTS

_____
_____
_____
_____

APPROVAL SIGNATURES

Reviewer:	Date:
Approval:	Date:

Employee Signature:	Date:

EMPLOYEE PERFORMANCE APPRAISAL

Employee Name: _____ Title: _____

Salary Labor Grade: _____ Employee ID No.: _____ Dept. No.: _____

Evaluation Period Dates: _____

Check the level that most closely identifies the quality of performance for the following factors:

Performance Factor	Outstanding	Good	Competent	Needs Improvement	Unacceptable
A. Technical Effectiveness					
B. Defines, Analyzes, and Solves Problems					
C. Planning and Organization					
D. Personal Time Management: Prioritizes and Uses Time Effectively (Meets Deadlines, Is Punctual and has Good Attendance)					
E. Self Motivation: Exhibits Initiative					
F. Oral Communication: Expresses Ideas to Ensure Understanding					
G. Written Communication: Expresses Ideas to Ensure Understanding					
H. Teamwork: Cooperates with Peers, Supervisors, and Customers					
I. Leadership: Organizes and Motivates Others					
J. Supports Diversity					
K. Supervisory Effectiveness: Delegates Assignments, Recognizes Potential in Others					

ESSAY

Comment on the employee's overall performance during the evaluation period. Detail specific accomplishments. Comment on

- Team performance
- Diversity initiatives
- Environmental, health, and safety contributions
- Meeting objectives/goals
- Outstanding contributions/achievements
- Career development activities

PERFORMANCE SUMMARY

Considering the previous performance factors, the essay, and employee's overall evaluation of productivity against expectations, check the box that best describes the SUMMARY level of performance.

Outstanding ☐   Competent ☐   Needs Development ☐   Unacceptable ☐

SIGNATURES

_____   _____
Reviewer   Date

_____   _____
Approved   Date

EMPLOYEE COMMENTS:

_____   _____
Employee Signature   Date

EMPLOYEE EVALUATION

Name: _____   Employee Number: _____

Department: _____

Job Title: _____

Supervisor: _____

Rate employee's performance on a scale of 1 (needs improvement) to 4 (excellent) in each area:

	Needs Improvement	Fair	Good	Excellent
1. Work attitude:	1	2	3	4

Comments: _____

2. Ability to work with others:	1	2	3	4

Comments: _____

3. Independent decision making:	1	2	3	4

Comments: _____

4. Quality of work:	1	2	3	4

Comments: _____

5. Initiative:	1	2	3	4

Comments: _____

7. Organizational skills:	1	2	3	4

Comments: _____

8. Attendance/Punctuality:	1	2	3	4

Comments: _____

9. Technical ability:	1	2	3	4

Comments: _____

10. Verbal ability:	1	2	3	4

Comments: _____

11. Writing ability:	1	2	3	4

Comments: _____

EMPLOYEE EVALUATION (continued)

	Needs Improvement	Fair	Good	Excellent
12. Dependability:	1	2	3	4

Comments: _____

13. Appearance:	1	2	3	4

Comments: _____

14. Overall performance:	1	2	3	4

Comments: _____

15. Recommendations for professional growth:

_____

_____

_____

_____

_____

This report has been discussed with the employee on _____
                                                        Date

_____
Employee name (please print)

_____   _____
Employee Signature   Date

_____   _____
Supervisor name (please print)   Title

_____   _____
Supervisor Signature   Date

APPENDIX 2

Ethical Codes of Selected Professional Organizations

We are all faced with a series of great opportunities
brilliantly disguised as unsolvable problems.
—John W. Gardner

AMERICAN CHEMICAL SOCIETY

The Chemist's Code of Conduct

The American Chemical Society expects its members to adhere to the highest ethical standards. Indeed, the federal Charter of the Society (1937) explicitly lists among its objectives "**the improvement of the qualifications and usefulness of chemists through high standards of professional ethics, education, and attainments . . . .**" Chemists have professional obligations to the public, to colleagues, and to science. One expression of these obligations is embodied in "The Chemist's Creed," approved by the ACS Council in 1965. The principles of conduct enumerated below are intended to replace "The Chemist's Creed." They were prepared by the Council Committee on Professional Relations, approved by the Council (March 16, 1994), and adopted by the Board of Directors (June 3, 1994) for the guidance of society members in various professional dealings, especially those involving conflicts of interest.

Chemists Acknowledge Responsibilities to

- **The Public**   Chemists have a professional responsibly to serve the public interest and welfare and to further knowledge of science. Chemists should actively be concerned with the health and welfare of coworkers, the consumer, and the community. Public comments on scientific matters should be made with care and precision, without unsubstantiated, exaggerated, or premature statements.
- **The Science of Chemistry**   Chemists should seek to advance chemical science, understand the limitations of their knowledge, and respect the

285

truth. Chemists should ensure that their scientific contributions, and those of the collaborators, are thorough, accurate, and unbiased in design, implementation, and presentation.

- **The Profession** Chemists should remain current with developments in their field, share ideas and information, keep accurate and complete laboratory records, maintain integrity in all conduct and publications, and give due credit to the contributions of others. Conflicts of interest and scientific misconduct, such as fabrication, falsification, and plagiarism, are incompatible with this Code.
- **The Employer** Chemists should promote and protect the legitimate interests of their employers, perform work honestly and competently, fulfill obligations, and safeguard proprietary information.
- **Employees** Chemists, as employers, should treat subordinates with respect for their professionalism and concern for their well-being, and provide them with a safe, congenial working environment, fair compensation, and proper acknowledgment of their scientific contributions.
- **Students** Chemists should regard the tutelage of students as a trust conferred by society for the promotion of the student's learning and professional development. Each student should be treated respectfully and without exploitation.
- **Associates** Chemists should treat associates with respect, regardless of the level of their formal education, encourage them, learn with them, share ideas honestly, and give credit for their contributions.
- **Clients** Chemists should serve clients faithfully and incorruptibly, respect confidentiality, advise honestly, and charge fairly.
- **The Environment** Chemists should understand and anticipate the environmental consequences of their work. Chemists have a responsibility to avoid pollution and to protect the environment.

http://www.acs.org

AMERICAN SOCIETY OF MECHANICAL ENGINEERS (ASME)

Code of Ethics of Engineers

The Fundamental Principles: Engineers uphold and advance the integrity, honor, and dignity of the engineering profession by

I. Using their knowledge and skill for the enhancement of human welfare;

II. Being honest and impartial, and serving with fidelity the public, their employers and clients; and

III. Striving to increase the competence and prestige of the engineering profession.

The Fundamental Canons

1. Engineers shall hold paramount the safety, health, and welfare of the public in the performance of their professional duties.
2. Engineers shall perform services only in the areas of their competence.
3. Engineers shall continue their professional development throughout their careers and shall provide opportunities for the professional and ethical development of those engineers under their supervision.
4. Engineers shall act in professional matters for each employer or client as faithful agents or trustees, and shall avoid conflicts of interest or the appearance of conflicts of interest.
5. Engineers shall build their professional reputation on the merit of their services and shall not compete unfairly with others.
6. Engineers shall associate only with reputable persons or organizations.
7. Engineers shall issue public statements only in an objective and truthful manner.
8. Engineers shall consider environmental impact in the performance of their professional duties.

http://www.asme.org/asme/policies/p15-7.html

Reprinted with permission from the ASME.

THE INSTITUTE OF ELECTRICAL AND ELECTRONICS ENGINEERS (IEEE)

Code of Ethics

We, the members of the IEEE, in recognition of the importance of our technologies affecting the quality of life throughout the world, and in accepting a personal obligation to our profession, its members, and the communities we serve, do hereby commit ourselves to the highest ethical and professional conduct and agree

1. to accept responsibility in making engineering decisions consistent with the safety, health, and welfare of the public, and to disclose promptly factors that might endanger the public or the environment;
2. to avoid real or perceived conflicts of interest whenever possible, and to disclose them to affected parties when they do exist;
3. to be honest and realistic in stating claims or estimates based on available data;
4. to reject bribery in all its forms;
5. to improve the understanding of technology, its appropriate application, and potential consequences;
6. to maintain and improve our technical competence and to undertake technological tasks for others only if qualified by training or experience, or after full disclosure of pertinent limitations;
7. to seek, accept, and offer honest criticism of technical work, to acknowledge and correct errors, and to credit properly the contributions of others;

8. to treat fairly all persons regardless of such factors as race, religion, gender, disability, age, or national origin;

9. to avoid injuring others, their property, reputation, or employment by false or malicious action;

10. to assist colleagues and coworkers in their professional development and to support them in following this code of ethics.

Approved by the IEEE Board of Directors, August 1990
http://www.ieeeusa.org/documents/CAREER/CAREER_LIBRARY/ethics.html

Reprinted with permission from the IEEE.

PROJECT MANAGEMENT INSTITUTE (PMI)

Member Code of Ethics

The Project Management Institute (PMI) is a professional organization dedicated to the development and promotion of the field of project management. The purpose of the PMI *Member Code of Ethics* is to define and clarify the ethical responsibilities for present and future PMI members.

Preamble: In the pursuit of the project management profession, it is vital that PMI members conduct their work in an ethical manner in order to earn and maintain the confidence of team members, colleagues, employees, employers, customers/clients, the public, and the global community.

Member Code of Ethics: As a professional in the field of project management, PMI members pledge to uphold and abide by the following:

- I will maintain high standards of integrity and professional conduct
- I will accept responsibility for my actions
- I will continually seek to enhance my professional capabilities
- I will practice with fairness and honesty
- I will encourage others in the profession to act in an ethical and professional manner.

PMI Member Standards of Conduct

Member Standards of Conduct: The following PMI *Member Standards of Conduct* describes the obligations and expectations associated with membership in the Project Management Institute. All PMI Members must conduct their activities consistent with the *Member Standards of Conduct*.

    I. **Professional Obligations**.

        A. Professional Behavior.

            1. PMI Members will fully and accurately disclose any professional or business-related conflicts or potential conflicts of interest in a timely manner.

2. PMI Members will refrain from offering or accepting payments, or other forms of compensation or tangible benefits, which: (a) do not conform with applicable laws; and (b) may provide unfair advantage for themselves, their business or others they may represent.

3. PMI Members who conduct research or similar professional activities will do so in a manner that is fair, honest, accurate, unbiased, and otherwise appropriate, and will maintain appropriate, accurate, and complete records with respect to such research and professional activities.

4. PMI Members will respect and protect the intellectual property rights of others, and will properly disclose and recognize the professional, intellectual, and research contributions of others.

5. PMI Members will strive to enhance their professional capabilities, skills and knowledge; and will accurately and truthfully represent and advertise their professional services and qualifications.

B. Relationship with Customers, Clients, and Employers.

1. PMI Members will provide customers, clients, and employers with fair, honest, complete and accurate information concerning: (a) their qualifications; (b) their professional services; and (c) the preparation of estimates concerning costs, services, and expected results.

2. PMI Members will honor and maintain the confidentiality and privacy of customer, client, employer, and similar work information, including the confidentiality of customer or client identities, assignments undertaken, and other information obtained throughout the course of a professional relationship, unless: (a) granted permission by the customer, client, or employer; or (b) the maintenance of the confidentiality is otherwise unethical or unlawful.

3. PMI Members will not take personal, business, or financial advantage of confidential or private information acquired during the course of their professional relationships, nor will they provide such information to others.

C. Relationship with the Public and the Global Community.

1. PMI Members will honor and meet all applicable legal and ethical obligations, including the laws, rules, and customs of the community and nation in which they function, work, or conduct professional activities.

2. PMI Members will perform their work consistent and in conformance with professional standards to ensure that the public is protected from harm.

II. **Obligations to PMI.**

A. Responsibilities of PMI Membership.

1. PMI Members will abide by the bylaws, policies, rules, requirements, and procedures of the Project Management Institute, and will not knowingly engage or assist in any activities intended to

compromise the integrity, reputation, property, and/or legal rights of the Institute.

2. PMI Members will abide by the laws, regulations, and other requirements of their respective communities and nations, and will not knowingly engage in, or assist in, any activities intended to have negative implications, including criminal conduct, professional misconduct, or malfeasance.

3. PMI Members will cooperate with the Institute concerning the review of possible ethics violations, and other PMI matters, completely, consistent with applicable policies and requirements.

4. PMI Members will accurately, completely, and truthfully represent information to PMI.

PMI Member Ethical Standards

Member Ethics Case Procedures: The following ethics case procedures are the only rules for processing possible violations of these ethical standards. These procedures are applicable to members of the Project Management Institute (hereinafter referred to as PMI or the Institute), and those who are seeking Institute membership. PMI members and individuals seeking PMI membership understand and agree that these procedures are a fair process for resolving all ethics matters duly adopted by PMI; and they will be bound by decisions made, and requirements issued, pursuant to these procedures.

A. **General Provisions**

1. *Nature of the Process.* PMI has the only authority to resolve and end any ethics matter, regardless of circumstances. By applying for membership in the Institute, PMI members and applicants agree that they will accept the authority of the Institute to apply the *Member Code of Ethics*, *Member Standards of Conduct*, and the *Member Ethics Case Procedures*, and other relevant policies to resolve ethics matters.

   These ethics procedures are not a formal legal process; therefore, many legal rules and practices are not observed, and the procedures are designed to operate without the assistance of attorneys. Any party, of course, may be represented by an attorney with respect to an ethics matter. If a party has retained an attorney, that attorney may be directed to communicate with the Institute through the PMI Legal Counsel. The parties are encouraged to communicate directly with the Institute. The Institute may use the services of PMI Legal Counsel without limitation.

2. *Participants.* Ethics cases may be decided by the PMI Ethics Review Committee, the Ethics Appeals Committee, and/or any authorized designee. A PMI member or applicant who is the subject of an ethics complaint or investigation will be identified as the Respondent. The person(s) initiating an ethics complaint will be identified as the Complainant(s).

3. *Time Requirements.* The Institute will make every reasonable effort to follow the time requirements noted in these procedures. However, the Institute's failure to meet a time requirement will not prohibit the final resolution of any ethics matter, or otherwise prevent PMI from acting under these procedures. Complainants and Respondents are required to comply with all time requirements specified in these procedures. Time extensions or postponements may be granted by the Institute if a timely written request explains a reasonable cause.

4. *Relaxation of Requirements/Global Accommodations.* In light of the global nature of the international project management community, including differences related to the language, custom, geographic location, and other characteristics of PMI members and applicants, the Institute recognizes that PMI members and applicants may have difficulty meeting certain time or other requirements in these procedures. Accordingly, a PMI member or applicant may submit to the Executive Director a written request for an extension of one or more of the time requirements; or, a reasonable accommodation related to matters of language, custom, geographic location, or the like. The Executive Director will forward such requests to the Chair of the Ethics Review Committee or the Chair of the Ethics Appeal Committee, as applicable. Generally, requests for such time extensions that seek to increase a deadline and other reasonable accommodations will be granted.

5. *Litigation/Other Proceedings.* The Institute may accept and resolve ethics complaints when civil or criminal litigation, or other proceedings related to the complaint, are also before a court, regulatory agency or professional body. The Institute may also continue or delay the resolution of any ethics complaints in such cases.

6. *Improper Disclosure.* The Institute may issue any appropriate directive(s) and requirement(s) where a PMI member or applicant provides a misleading disclosure, or fails to disclose requested information related to: PMI membership; an ethics complaint; an ethics case; or similar matter. Where a discipline, order, directive, or other requirement is issued by the Institute under this Section, the member or applicant involved may seek review and appeal pursuant to these procedures.

7. *Confidentiality.* In order to protect the privacy of the parties involved in an ethics case, all material prepared by, or submitted to, the Institute will be confidential, unless otherwise authorized by these procedures. Among other information, the Institute will not consider the following materials to be confidential: materials which are disclosed as the result of a legal requirement; materials which are disclosed upon the written request of the member or applicant who is the subject of an ethics complaint or investigation, any information relating to the member or applicant which he/she would like released to other

professional organizations or third parties, and which is not otherwise confidential; and, all final published rulings, decisions, requirements, orders, and/or reports of the Ethics Review Committee or the Ethics Appeals Committee.

8. *Failure to Cooperate.* If any party refuses to fully cooperate with the Institute concerning matters arising under these procedures without good cause, the Institute may: terminate the ethics complaint of an uncooperative Complainant; or, impose any sanction or requirement included within these rules if a Respondent is uncooperative. Where a discipline, order, requirement, or other directive is issued by the Institute under this Section, the member or applicant involved may seek review and appeal pursuant to these procedures.

9. *Resignation from the Institute.* Should a Respondent attempt to relinquish PMI membership or withdraw an application during the course of any ethics case, the Institute reserves the right to continue the matter to a final and binding resolution according to these procedures.

B. **Submission of Ethics Complaints/Acceptance or Rejection.**

1. *Executive Director.* Any person, group, organization, or, in appropriate cases, the Institute (Complainant) may initiate an ethics complaint. Each Complainant must submit to the Executive Director a detailed written description of the factual allegations supporting the ethics complaint, including the specific provisions of the *Member Code of Ethics* or *Member Standards of Conduct* relevant to the allegations set forth in the complaint. The Executive Director will forward the complaint to the Ethics Review Committee Chair for review, consideration, and assignment.

2. *Ethics Review Committee.* The Ethics Review Committee will be responsible for the investigation and resolution of each ethics complaint. Upon receipt of a complaint, the Review Committee will determine whether sufficient detail is presented to constitute a formal ethics complaint, based upon the specific *Member Code of Ethics* or *Member Standards of Conduct* provisions identified by the complaint, and to permit the Review Committee to conduct an appropriate review.

3. *Complaint Acceptance/Rejection Criteria.* In order to determine if an ethics complaint is accepted or rejected, the Ethics Review Committee will consider whether: a proven complaint would constitute a violation of the specific *Member Code of Ethics* or *Member Standards of Conduct* provisions identified by the Complainant in the original submission; the passage of time since the alleged violation requires that the complaint be rejected; relevant, reliable information or proof concerning the charge is available; the Complainant is willing to provide testimony or other evidence concerning the complaint; and, there is reasonable cause to believe that the charge appears to be justified, considering the proof available.

3.a. *Complaint Acceptance.* Upon a determination that an ethics complaint is appropriate, the Ethics Review Committee will issue a formal Ethics Complaint Notice identifying each *Member Code of Ethics* and *Member Standards of Conduct* violation alleged, and the supporting factual basis for each complaint. This Notice will be delivered to the Respondent, and will be marked *Confidential.* The Review Committee may request additional information to supplement or explain an allegation.

3.b. *Complaint Rejection.* If the Ethics Review Committee determines that an allegation or complaint change should not be a formal ethics complaint, the Review Committee will return all information submitted and notify the Complainant of the rejection and its basis by correspondence.

 3.b.1. *Appeal of Complaint Rejection Determination.* Within forty-five (45) days of the mailing date of complaint rejection correspondence, the Complainant may appeal to the Ethics Appeals Committee by stating in writing the procedural errors he/she believes were made by the Ethics Review Committee with respect to the charge rejection, if any; the specific provisions of the *Member Code of Ethics* and *Member Standards of Conduct* believed violated; and, the specific information he/she believes supports the acceptance of a complaint. The Ethics Appeals Committee will review the Complainant's appeal and issue a decision based upon the record. The Appeals Committee may accept the Review Committee decision and reject the complaint, or any part thereof; or, reverse the Review Committee decision and direct that a complaint be issued and the case resolved under these procedures.

4. *Ethics Complaint Response.* Within forty-five (45) days of the mailing date of an Ethics Complaint Notice, the Respondent must submit a response to the Ethics Review Committee. The Ethics Complaint Response must include a full response to each complaint, and a copy of each document relevant to the resolution of the ethics complaint. The Review Committee may request additional information to supplement a response.

5. *Complaint Referral.* If the Ethics Review Committee determines that the factual allegations presented by a Complainant, or the information revealed by an investigation, may constitute a violation of *Member Code of Ethics* or *Member Standards of Conduct* provisions not directly related to those presented by the Complainant, the Review Committee may take any of the following actions: notify the Respondent of possible, unrelated Code or Standards violations, and any recommended corrective actions; refer the matter to the Complainant for review and possible resubmission of a revised or new complaint; refer the matter to other Institute, government, or professional bodies for review; or, other appropriate actions/referrals.

C. **Preliminary Actions and Orders.**

Preliminary and Temporary Orders. The Ethics Review Committee, or the Ethics Appeals Committee, may require the Respondent to do, or to refrain from doing, certain acts by Preliminary and Temporary Order reasonably related to the complaint under consideration pending the final resolution of the case or investigation. Such orders may include, but are not limited to, a requirement that the Respondent voluntarily and immediately cease from representing himself or herself as a PMI member or applicant, or as otherwise associated with the Institute until further notice; or, a restriction that the Respondent may not pursue a PMI position or office pending the final resolution of the ethics matter under review. The Ethics Review Committee or the Ethics Appeals Committee may discipline a Respondent who fails to comply with a Temporary or Preliminary Order. Preliminary and Temporary Orders are not subject to appeal, but may be reconsidered by the Committees upon written request of the Respondent presenting substantial reasons that the order is no longer necessary.

D. **Ethics Review Committee Hearings.**

1. *Ethics Review Committee.* The PMI Board of Directors will appoint at least seven (7) PMI members to serve as the Ethics Review Committee to investigate and resolve ethics complaint matters. The PMI Chair, with Board of Directors approval, will appoint a Committee Chair from the seven members, who will supervise the work of the Committee. The Chair may appoint one or more Vice-Chairs to assist him/her, and to also preside over each Ethics Hearing. As directed by the Committee Chair, three (3) disinterested members of the Ethics Review Committee will be assigned to each case, and will conduct an informal Ethics Hearing designed to collect and weigh all of the available information and proof, and will have full authority to convene, preside over, continue, decide, and conclude an Ethics Hearing.

2. *Hearing Schedule, Notice, and Attendance.* The hearing date, time, and location for each ethics case will be scheduled by the Ethics Review Committee in consultation with the parties, and both parties will be notified in writing. Each party may attend the hearing in person or via telephone conference, where all participants will be able to communicate with each other.

3. *Participation of Legal Representatives/Conduct of the Hearing.* Upon request by the Ethics Review Committee, the PMI Chair, or the PMI Board of Directors, the PMI Legal Counsel shall be available to assist the Committee at an Ethics Hearing, with privilege of the floor, and may conduct the hearing in consultation with the Ethics Review Committee. Legal or other representatives of the parties do not have such privilege and are bound by the determinations and rulings of the Ethics Review Committee and PMI Legal Counsel. No formal legal rules of evidence, cross-examination, oath, and other procedures will apply to hearings. The PMI member or applicant, or a legal representative, will

be permitted to ask questions of witnesses at the discretion of the Ethics Review Committee. Objections relating to relevance of information and other procedural issues will be decided by the Ethics Review Committee and these decisions are not subject to appeal.

4. *Hearing Record.* A taped, written, or other record of the Ethics Hearing will be made by the Ethics Review Committee, another PMI representative, or a stenographer/recorder, as determined by the Review Committee.

5. *Hearing Expenses.* Parties will be responsible for their expenses associated with an ethics investigation or case, including the costs associated with any witnesses or legal counsel. The Institute will bear other general costs of conducting the Ethics Hearing, including costs associated with the activities of PMI representatives.

6. *Closing of the Hearing Record.* Any Ethics Hearing may proceed to a conclusion and decision, whether or not the parties are present, based on the appropriate written record, as determined by the Ethics Review Committee. The Review Committee will review the hearing record, as well as any submissions presented by the parties and other relevant information, and thereafter, will determine the outcome of the ethics case by majority vote in a closed session. The hearing record will be closed following the conclusion of the hearing, unless otherwise directed by the Ethics Review Committee Chair or a Vice-Chair.

7. *Ethics Review Committee Decision and Order.* A Decision and Order will be prepared by the Ethics Review Committee after the closing of the record, which will include a summary of the case, including the positions of the parties; a summary of relevant factual findings based on the record of the hearing; a final ruling on the *Member Code of Ethics* and *Member Standards of Conduct* violations charged; and, a statement of any corrective or disciplinary action(s), and other directives issued by the Review Committee. Copies of the Ethics Review Committee Decision and Order shall be sent to the parties. The parties will also be notified that the final decision may be published consistent with the requirements of these procedures.

8. *Disciplinary Actions Available.* When a Respondent is found to have violated one or more provisions of the *Member Code of Ethics* or *Member Standards of Conduct*, the Institute may issue and order one or more of the following disciplinary or remedial actions:

8.a. The denial and rejection of any PMI membership application;

8.b. Private reprimand and censure, including any appropriate conditions or directives;

8.c. Public reprimand and censure, including any appropriate conditions or directives;

8.d. Membership probation for any period up to three (3) years, including any appropriate restrictions or conditions concerning membership rights and any other conditions or directives;

8.e.   Suspension of membership status for a period of no less than six (6) months and no more than three (3) years, including any appropriate conditions or directives;

8.f.   Termination of membership and expulsion from the Institute.

E. **Ethics Appeals Committee/Appeals.**

1. *Time Period for Submitting Appeal.* Within forty-five (45) days of the mailing date of an adverse Ethics Review Committee Decision and Order, the Respondent or the Complainant may submit to the PMI Executive Director a written appeal of all or a portion of the Decision and Order consistent with the requirements of these procedures. The Executive Director will forward the appeal to the Ethics Appeals Committee Chair for review, consideration, and assignment.

2. *Grounds for Appeal.* An adverse Ethics Review Committee Decision and Order may be reversed or otherwise modified by the Ethics Appeals Committee. However, the grounds for appeal of an adverse decision are strictly limited to the following:

    2.a.   *Procedural Error.* The Ethics Review Committee misapplied a procedure contained in these rules, and the misapplication prejudiced the appealing party.

    2.b.   *New or Previously Undiscovered Information.* Following the closing of the Hearing Record, the appealing party has located relevant proof that was not previously in his/her possession; was not reasonably available prior to closure of the record; and, could have affected the Ethics Review Committee decision.

    2.c.   *Misapplication of the Code of Ethics or Standards of Conduct.* The Ethics Review Committee misapplied the provisions of the *Member Code of Ethics* or *Member Standards of Conduct*, and the misapplication prejudiced the appealing party.

    2.d.   *Contrary to the Information Presented.* The Ethics Review Committee decision is contrary to the most substantial information provided in the record.

    2.e.   With respect to Subsections 2.a. and 2.c. above, the Ethics Appeals Committee will consider only arguments that were presented to the Ethics Review Committee prior to the closing of the Hearing Record.

3. *Contents of Appeal Letter.* The appealing party must submit to the PMI Executive Director a letter or other written document directed to the Ethics Appeals Committee and to the other party, which contains the following information and material: the ethics case name; the docket number and date of the Ethics Review Committee Decision; a statement and complete explanation of the reasons for the appeal under Section E.2, including an explanation and basis for any request concerning a reduction in the discipline issued by the Ethics Review Committee; and, copies of any material supporting the appeal.

F. **Ethics Appeals Committee/Appeal Hearings.**

1. *Ethics Appeals Committee.* The PMI Board of Directors will appoint at least seven (7) PMI members to serve as the Ethics Appeals Committee to resolve ethics appeals. The PMI Chair, with Board of Directors approval, will appoint a Committee Chair from the seven members, who will supervise the work of the Appeals Committee. The Chair may appoint one or more Vice-Chairs to assist him/her, and to also preside over each Appeal Hearing. As directed by the Committee Chair, three (3) disinterested members of the Appeals Committee will be assigned to each case, and will have full authority to convene, preside over, continue, decide, and conclude an ethics appeal.

2. *Appeal Hearings.* Following receipt of a complete and proper written appeal, the Ethics Appeals Committee will schedule a date on which to conduct an Appeal Hearing, and the parties will be notified in writing at least forty-five (45) days in advance of the scheduled date. The Appeals Committee will review the hearing record, as well as any appeal submissions presented by the parties and other relevant information, and thereafter will determine and resolve the appeal by majority vote in a closed session.

3. *Request to Appear Before Ethics Appeals Committee.* Either party may request the opportunity to appear before the Ethics Appeals Committee in writing at least forty-five (45) days prior to the date scheduled for the Appeal Hearing. In the event that a request to appear before the Ethics Appeals Committee is approved, the Appeals Committee may limit the appearance in any manner. Denials of requests to appear before the Appeals Committee are not subject to appeal.

4. *Ethics Appeals Committee Decision and Order.* Following the conclusion of an Appeal Hearing, the Ethics Appeals Committee will issue an Appeal Decision and Order stating: the outcome and resolution of the appeal, including a summary of relevant portions of the Ethics Review Committee Decision and Order; a summary of any relevant procedural or factual findings made by the Appeals Committee; the Ethics Appeals Committee's ruling(s) and decision(s) with respect to the matters under appeal; and, the Appeals Committee's final Decision and Order accepting, affirming, reversing, amending, or otherwise modifying any portion of the Ethics Review Committee Decision and Order, including any final disciplinary action or sanction issued by the Appeals Committee. Copies of the Ethics Appeals Committee Decision and Order shall be sent to the parties. The parties will also be notified that the final decision may be published, consistent with the requirements of these procedures.

G. **Finalizing Ethics Cases.**

1. *Events Which Will Cause Closure of an Ethics Case.* An ethics case will be closed when any of the following occur: the ethics complaint has been rejected pursuant to these procedures; a final decision has

been issued by the Ethics Review Committee without appeal pursuant to these procedures; a final decision has been issued by the Ethics Appeals Committee pursuant to these procedures; or, an ethics complaint has been terminated or withdrawn by the Complainant(s).

2. *Events Which Will Cause an Ethics Case Decision and Order to Become Final.* The Ethics Case Decision and Order issued by the Ethics Review Committee that is not appealed within the prescribed time requirements will be considered final. The Ethics Case Decision and Order issued by the Ethics Appeals Committee will be considered final.

3. *Referral and Notification Actions.* PMI may notify appropriate governmental, professional, or similar bodies of any actions taken concerning a Respondent by sending a copy of the final Ethics Case Decision and Order issued by the Ethics Review Committee and/or the Ethics Appeals Committee, or by sending another appropriate notice. This notification may be done at any point after the time period for the Respondent to appeal an adverse decision has elapsed. During the appeal period, the Institute may respond to inquiries regarding the existence of ethics cases and indicate the existence of such proceedings.

4. *Publication of Final Disciplinary Action.* PMI may publish a notification of a final Ethics Case Decision and Order following the issuance of an Ethics Review Committee or Ethics Appeals Committee decision or ruling. This notification may be published following the conclusion of any appeals available to the Respondent. Any party may request publication of any final decision.

H. **Probation and Suspension Orders/Reinstatement Procedures.**

1. *Probation Orders/Reinstatement or Referral.* Following the expiration of a final decision/order which includes a probation requirement under these procedures, the Ethics Review Committee will determine whether the Respondent has satisfied the terms of the probation order, and will do the following: if the Respondent has satisfied the terms of probation in full, the Review Committee will immediately verify that the probation has been completed and reinstate the individual to full membership status following the acceptance of a complete membership application and full payment of all membership dues; or, if the Respondent has not satisfied the terms of probation in full, the Review Committee will issue any appropriate action consistent with these procedures, including, but not limited to, the imposition of an additional probation term(s).

2. *Suspension Orders/Reinstatement Requests.* After the expiration of a final decision/order which includes a suspension requirement issued under these procedures, a Respondent may submit to the Ethics Review Committee a request for membership reinstatement, which will consist of a written statement including: the relevant ethics case name, docket number, and the date that the final Ethics Decision and

Order was issued; a statement of the reasons that support or justify the acceptance of the reinstatement request; and, copies of any relevant documentary or other material supporting the request.

3. *Ethics Review Committee Reinstatement Request Decisions.* Following the submission of a complete membership reinstatement request, the Ethics Review Committee will schedule and conduct a hearing to review and rule on the request. During these deliberations, the Review Committee will review the information presented by the Respondent and any other relevant information, and prepare and issue a final Decision and Order stating whether: the request is granted, denied, or continued to a later date; and, if appropriate, any conditions of membership. Copies of the Review Committee Decision and Order will be sent to the parties. While no appeal of the Decision and Order is permitted, the Respondent may submit a new request pursuant to this Section, one (1) year or more after the issuance of the Review Committee Decision and Order rejecting the request.

http://www.pmi.org

APPENDIX 3

Wilderness Survival Answer and Rationale Sheet

Keep away from people who try to belittle your ambitions.
Small people always do that, but the really great make you feel that you, too, can
become great.
—Mark Twain

Managing a project starts with a team. The project manager must assemble technical and non-technical personnel who have unique skills, knowledge and experience to ensure the success of the project's objectives. Managers attempt to create a collaborative environment that promotes a consensus.

This exercise attempts to build the student's confidence in the judgment of the team by asking questions about a topic with which most people are unfamiliar. The expectation is that the number of questions that the team answers correctly will be higher than the number of questions that the individual answers correctly. By discussing the question and examining it from different viewpoints, the team will likely reach a better decision than the individual.

This appendix identifies the recommended courses of action for each of the situations listed on the Wilderness Survival Work Sheet found in the questions associated with Chapter 1. These answers come from the comprehensive course on woodland survival taught by the Interpretive Service, Monroe County (New York) Parks Department. The responses are considered to be the best rules of thumb for most situations; specific situations, however, might require other courses of action.

1. (a) *call "help" loudly, but in a low register.* Low tones carry farther, especially in dense woodland. There is a much better chance of being heard if you call loudly, but in a low key. "Help" is a good word to use, because it alerts your companions to your plight. Yelling or screaming not only would be less effective, but might be passed off as bird calls by your friends far away.

2. (a) *make a lot of noise with your feet.* Snakes do not like people and will usually do everything they can to get out of your way. Unless you

surprise or corner a snake, there is a good chance that you will not even see one, let alone come into contact with it. Some snakes do feed at night, and walking softly may bring you right on top of a snake.

3. (c) *put a bit of the plant on your lower lip for five minutes; if it seems all right, try a little.* The best approach, of course, is to eat only those plants that you recognize as safe. However, when you are in doubt and very hungry, you may use the lip test. If the plant is poisonous, you will get a very unpleasant sensation on your lip. Red berries alone do not tell you much about the plant's edibility (unless, of course, you recognize the plant by the berries), and birds just do not have the same digestive systems we do.

4. (c) *drink as much as you think you need when you need it.* The danger here is dehydration, and once the process starts, your liter of water will not do much to reverse it. Saving or rationing will not help, especially if you are lying unconscious somewhere from sunstroke or dehydration. So, use the water as you need it, and be aware of your need to find a source of water as soon as possible.

5. (c) *dig in the streambed at the outside of a bend.* This is the part of the river or stream that flows the fastest, is less silted, is deepest, and is the last part to go dry.

6. (c) *midway up the slope.* A sudden rainstorm might turn the ravine into a raging torrent. This has happened to many campers and hikers before they had a chance to escape. The ridgeline, on the other hand, increases your exposure to rain, wind, and lightning should a storm break. The best location is on the slope.

7. (b) *put the batteries under your armpits to warm them, and then replace them in the flashlight.* Flashlight batteries lose much of their power, and weak batteries run down faster in the cold. Warming the batteries, especially if they are already weak, will restore them for a while. You would normally avoid night travel, of course, unless you were in open country where you could use the stars for navigation. There are just too many obstacles (logs, branches, uneven ground, and so on) that might injure you—and a broken leg, injured eye, or twisted ankle would not help your plight right now. Once the sun sets, darkness falls quickly in wooded areas; it would usually be best to stay at your campsite.

8. (a) *yellow.* A yellow flame indicates incomplete combustion and a strong possibility of carbon monoxide buildup. Each year, carbon monoxide poisoning kills many campers as they sleep or doze in tents, cabins, or other enclosed spaces.

9. (a) *leave your boots and pack on.* Errors in fording rivers are a major cause of fatal accidents. Sharp rocks or uneven footing demands that you keep your boots on. If your pack is well balanced, wearing it will provide you the most stability in the swift current. A waterproof, zippered backpack will usually float, even when loaded with normal camping gear; if you step off into a hole or deep spot, the pack could become a lifesaver.

10. (b) *across the stream.* Errors in facing the wrong way in fording a stream are the cause of many drownings. Facing upstream is the worst alternative; the current could push you back and your pack would provide the unbalance to pull you over. You have the best stability facing across the stream, keeping your eye on the exit point on the opposite bank.

11. (c) *in stockinged feet.* Here you can pick your route to some degree, and you can feel where you are stepping. Normal hiking boots become slippery, and going barefooted offers your feet no protection at all.

12. (c) *freeze, but be ready to back away slowly.* Sudden movement will probably startle the bear a lot more than your presence. If the bear is seeking some of your food, do not argue with it; let it forage and be on its way. Otherwise, back very slowly toward some refuge (trees, an outcropping of rock, etc.)

Reprinted with permission from the Nature Center at Mendon Ponds Park, Monroe County Parks Department.

APPENDIX 4

ISO 9000 Quality Management Principles

No one can make you feel inferior without your consent.
—Eleanor Roosevelt

This appendix introduces the eight quality management principles defined in ISO 9000:2000, *Quality Management Systems Fundamentals and Vocabulary*, and in ISO 9004:2000, *Quality Management Systems Guidelines for Performance Improvements*. The documents may be found on the ISO Web site (*http://www.iso.ch/iso/en/iso9000-14000/iso9000/qmp.html*). The principles contained therein may be used by management as a framework to guide organizations toward improved performance.

Principle 1 Customer focus. Organizations depend on their customers and therefore should understand current and future customer needs, should meet customer requirements, and should strive to exceed customer expectations.

Key benefits:

- increased revenue and market share obtained through flexible and fast responses to market opportunities
- increased effectiveness in the use of the organization's resources to enhance customer satisfaction
- improved customer loyalty, leading to repeat business

Applying the principle of customer focus typically leads to

- researching and understanding customer needs and expectations
- ensuring that the objectives of the organization are linked to customer needs and expectations
- communicating customer needs and expectations throughout the organization
- measuring customer satisfaction and acting on the results
- systematically managing customer relationships

- ensuring a balanced approach between satisfying customers and other interested parties (such as owners, employees, suppliers, financiers, local communities, and society as a whole)

Principle 2 Leadership. Leaders establish a unity of purpose and direction of the organization. They should create and maintain an internal environment in which people can become fully involved in achieving the organization's objectives.

Key benefits:

- People will understand and be motivated toward the organization's goals and objectives.
- Activities are evaluated, aligned, and implemented in a unified way.
- Miscommunication between levels of an organization will be minimized.

Applying the principle of leadership typically leads to

- considering the needs of all interested parties, including customers, owners, employees, suppliers, financiers, local communities, and society as a whole
- establishing a clear vision of the organization's future
- setting challenging goals and targets
- creating and sustaining shared values, fairness, and ethical role models at all levels of the organization
- establishing trust and eliminating fear
- providing people with the required resources, training, and freedom to act with responsibility and accountability
- inspiring, encouraging, and recognizing people's contributions

Principle 3 Involvement of people. People at all levels are the essence of an organization, and their full involvement enables their abilities to be used for the organization's benefit.

Key benefits:

- motivated, committed, and involved people within the organization
- innovation and creativity in furthering the organization's objectives
- people being accountable for their own performance
- people eager to participate in, and contribute to, continual improvement

Applying the principle of involvement of people typically leads to

- people understanding the importance of their contribution and role in the organization
- people identifying constraints on their performance

- people accepting ownership of problems and their responsibility for solving them
- people evaluating their performance against their personal goals and objectives
- people actively seeking opportunities to enhance their competence, knowledge, and experience
- people freely sharing knowledge and experience
- people openly discussing problems and issues

Principle 4 Process approach. A desired result is achieved more efficiently when activities and related resources are managed as a process.

Key benefits:

- lower costs and shorter cycle times through the effective use of resources
- improved, consistent, and predictable results
- focused and prioritized opportunities for improvement

Applying the principle of process approach typically leads to

- systematically defining the activities necessary to obtain a desired result
- establishing clear responsibility and accountability for managing key activities
- analyzing and measuring the capability of key activities
- identifying the interfaces of key activities within and between the functions of the organization
- focusing on the factors, such as resources, methods, and materials, that will improve key activities of the organization
- evaluating risks, consequences, and impacts of activities on customers, suppliers, and other interested parties

Principle 5 System approach to management. Identifying, understanding, and managing interrelated processes as a system contributes to the organization's effectiveness and efficiency in achieving its objectives.

Key benefits:

- integration and alignment of the processes that will best achieve the desired results
- ability to focus effort on the key processes
- enabling interested parties to have confidence in the consistency, effectiveness, and efficiency of the organization

Applying the principle of system approach to management typically leads to

- structuring a system to achieve the organization's objectives in the most effective and efficient way

- understanding the interdependencies among the processes of the system
- structured approaches that harmonize and integrate processes
- providing a better understanding of the roles and responsibilities necessary for achieving common objectives and thereby reducing cross-functional barriers
- understanding organizational capabilities and establishing resource constraints before acting
- targeting and defining how specific activities within a system should operate
- improving the system continually through measurement and evaluation

Principle 6 Continual improvement. Continual improvement of the organization's overall performance should be a permanent objective of the organization.

Key benefits:

- advantage in performance through improved organizational capabilities
- alignment of improvement activities at all levels with an organization's strategic intent
- flexibility to react quickly to opportunities

Applying the principle of continual improvement typically leads to

- employing a consistent organizationwide approach to continual improvement of the organization's performance
- providing people with training in the methods and tools of continual improvement
- making the continual improvement of products, processes, and systems an objective for every individual in the organization
- establishing goals to guide, and measures to track, continual improvement
- recognizing and acknowledging improvements

Principle 7 Factual approach to decision making. Effective decisions are based on the analysis of data and information.

Key benefits:

- informed decisions
- an increased ability to demonstrate the effectiveness of past decisions through reference to factual records
- increased ability to review, challenge, and change opinions and decisions

Applying the principle of factual approach to decision making typically leads to

- ensuring that data and information are sufficiently accurate and reliable
- making data accessible to those who need it

- analyzing data and information through the use of valid methods
- making decisions and taking actions based on factual analysis, balanced with experience and intuition

Principle 8 Mutually beneficial supplier relationships. An organization and its suppliers are interdependent, and a mutually beneficial relationship enhances the ability of both to create value

Key benefits:

- increased ability to create value for both parties
- flexibility and speed of joint responses to changing market or customer needs and expectations
- optimization of costs and resources

Applying the principles of mutually beneficial supplier relationships typically leads to

- establishing relationships that balance short-term gains with long-term considerations
- pooling of expertise and resources with partners
- identifying and selecting key suppliers
- clear and open communication
- sharing information and future plans
- establishing joint development and improvement activities
- inspiring, encouraging, and recognizing improvements and achievements by suppliers

REFERENCES

Adams, J. R., and N. S. Kirchof, "Project Management Professionalism and Market Survival" (paper presented at a 1983 symposium of the Project Management Institute).

Aguayo, R., *Dr. Deming: The American Who Taught the Japanese about Quality* (New York: Fireside Books, 1991).

Apgar, M., IV, "The Alternative Workplace: Changing Where and How People Work," *Harvard Business Review* (May/June 1998), reprint no. 98301.

Argyris, C., "Empowerment: The Emperor's New Clothes," *Harvard Business Review* (May/June 1998): 98–105.

Argyris, C., *Organization and Innovation.* (Irwin Press, 1965).

Badiru, A. B., *Project Management Tools for Engineering and Management Professionals* (Norcross, GA: Industrial Engineering and Management Press, 1991).

Barnard, C., *The Functions of the Executive* (Cambridge, MA: Harvard University Press, 1938).

Belgard, W. P., K. K. Fisher, and S. R. Rayner, "Vision, Opportunity, and Tenacity: Three Informal Processes That Influence Transformation," in *Corporate Transformation*, ed. R. Kilmann & T. Covin (San Francisco: Jossey-Bass, 1988), p. 135.

Bennis, W., and B. Nanus, (1985). *Leaders.* New York: Harper & Row.

Blanchard, K., and S. Johnson, *The One Minute Manager* (New York: William Morrow and Company, 1982).

Boehm, B. W. *Software Engineering Economics* (Englewood Cliffs, NJ: Prentice-Hall, 1981).

Collins, J. C., and J. I. Porras, *Built to Last* (New York: Harper Business, 1997).

Committee to Assess the Policies and Practices of the Department of Energy to Design, Manage, and Procure Environmental Restoration, Waste Management, and Other Construction Projects, *Improving Project Management in the Department of Energy* (Washington, DC: National Academy Press, 2000); on the Internet at *http://www.nap.edu/openbook/0309066263/R1.html.*

Covey, S. R. *The Seven Habits of Highly Effective People: Powerful Lessons in Personal Change* (London: Simon and Schuster, 1992).

Davenport, T. H. *Process Innovation* (Boston: Harvard Business School Press, 1993).

Davenport, T. H., and J. E. Short, "The New Industrial Engineering: Information Technology and Business Process Redesign," *Sloan Management Review* (Summer 1990): 11–27.

Deal, T. E., and A. A. Kennedy, *Corporate Cultures: The Rites and Rituals of Corporate Life* (London: Penguin, 1988).

Deming, W. E. *Out of the Crisis* (Cambridge, MA: MIT Center for Advanced Engineering, 1986).

Drucker, P. F., *The Frontiers of Management: Where Tomorrow's Decisions are Being Shaped Today* (New York: Truman Talley Books, 1986).

Drucker, P. F., "Managing Oneself", *Harvard Business Review* (March/April, 1999): 65–74.

Fielder, F. E. *A Theory of Leadership Effectiveness* (New York: McGraw-Hill, 1967).

Freiberg, K., and J. Freiberg, *Nuts! Southwestern Airlines' Crazy Recipe for Business and Personal Success* (Austin, TX: Bard Books, 1996).

Geneen, H., and A. Moscow, *Managing* (New York: Avon Books, 1985).

Goldman, T. "Success in Industry" (paper presented at National Conference on Outcomes Assessment, American Society for Engineering Education, Washington, DC., Sept. 19–20, 1997).

Gulick, L., and L. Urwick, *Papers on the Science of Administration* (New York: Columbia University Press, 1937).

Hallows, J., *Information Systems Project Management* (New York: American Management Association, 1998).

Harris, P. R., and D. L. Harris, "High Performance Team Management," *Leadership and Organization Development Journal* 10 (1989): 28–32.

Harris, P. R., and K. G. Harris, "Managing Effectively through Teams," *Team Performance Management* 2, no. 3 (1996): 23–26.

Harrold, D., "Designing for Six Sigma Capability." Control Engineering Online; on the Internet at *http://www.controleng.com/archives/1999/ctl0101.99/01a103.htm.*

Hasek, G., "The World's 100 Best," *Industry Week.com.* (Aug. 21, 2000): 46–68.

Hayes, D. S., "Evaluation and Application of a Project Charter Template to Improve the Project Planning Process," *Project Management Journal* 31, no. 1, (2000): 14–23.

Hesselbein, F., and P. M. Cohen, *Leader to Leader.* (San Francisco: Jossey-Bass, 1999).

Imai, M., *Kaizen: The Key to Japan's Competitive Success* (New York: Random House, 1986).

Jick, T. D., "The Vision Thing," *Harvard Business Review* (Sept. 26, 1989), reprint no. 9-490-019.

Katzenbach, J. R., and D. R. Smith, "The Discipline of Teams," *Harvard Business Review* (March/April 1993): 111–120, reprint no. 93207.

Katzenbach, J. R., and D. R. Smith, "Why Teams Matter," *The McKinsey Quarterly* 25 (1992): 3–27.

Kerzner, H., *Project Management: A systems approach to planning, scheduling, and controlling,* 7th Edition. (Berea, OH: John Wiley, 2000).

Koonce, R., "Becoming Your Own Career Coach," *Training & Development* 49, no. 1 (January, 1995): 18–25.

Kotter, J. P., *A Force for Change: How Leadership Differs from Management* (New York: The Free Press, 1990).

Maslow, A., *Motivation and Personality* (New York: Harper, 1954).

Mayo, E., *The Human Problems of an Industrial Civilization* (Boston: Harvard University, 1933).

McConkey, D. D. "Are You an Administrator, a Manager or a Leader?" *Business Horizons* (September/October 1989): 15–21.

McGregor, D., *The Human Side of Enterprise* (New York: McGraw-Hill, 1960).

Mintzberg, H., *The Nature of Managerial Work* (New York: Harper & Row, 1973).

Mintzberg, H., *The Rise and Fall of Strategic Planning* (New York: Simon and Schuster 1994).

Moss-Kantor, R., *The Change Masters: Innovation and Entrepreneurship in the American Corporation* (New York: Simon and Schuster, 1983).

Mullins, L. *Hospitality Management: A Human Resources Approach* (London: Pitman, 1992).

Mullins, L., and C. Roberts, "Assessment Strategies: Some Comparisons between the UK and the US Systems of Higher Education," *International Journal of Educational Management* 10, no. 4 (1996): 44.

Paulk, M. C., *A Comparison of ISO 9001 and the Capability Maturity Model for Software*. Technical Report CMU/SEI-94-TR-12, ESC-TR-94-12, Software Engineering Institute, Carnegie Mellon University, Pittsburgh, PA, July 1994).

Paulk, M. C., "The Rational Planning of (Software) Projects" (paper presented at the Proceedings of the First World Congress for Software Quality, San Francisco, CA, June 20–22, 1995).

Pearlman, Jeff, "At Full Blast: Shooting outrageously from the lip, Braves closer John Rocker bangs away at his favorite targets: the Mets, their fans, their city and just about everyone in it" *Sports Illustrated* 91, no. 25 (December 27, 1999): 60.

Peters, T., *Thriving on Chaos: Handbook for a Management Revolution* (New York: Perennial Library, 1988).

Peters, T., and R. H. Waterman, *In Search of Excellence* (New York: Harper and Row, 1982).

Pralahad, C. K., and M. H. Krishnan, "The New Meaning of Quality in the Information Age," *Harvard Business Review* 77, no. 5 (September/October 1999): 109–118.

Project Management Institute Standards Committee, *A Guide to the Project Management Body of Knowledge* (Upper Darby, PA: Project Management Institute, 1996).

Reicheld, F. F., and W. E. Sasser, "Zero defections: Quality Comes to Service," *Harvard Business Review* 76, no. 5 (September/October 1990): 2–8.

Sandomir, R., "His Airness Laces Up Some New Shoes," *The New York Times* (January 23, 2000): Section 4, p. 2.

Seglin, J. L., "The Right Thing: Throwing a Beanball in Business," *The New York Times* (January 16, 2000): Section III, p. 4.

Shenhar, A. J., "From Theory to Practice: Toward a Typology of Project-Management Styles," *IEEE Transactions on Engineering Management* 45, no. 1 (February 1998): 33–48.

Smith, J. A., and I. I. Angeli, "The Use of Quality Function Deployment to Help Adopt a Total Quality Strategy," *Total Quality Management* 6, no. 1 (1995): 35–44.

Sotiriou, D., and D. Wittmer, "Influence Methods of Project Managers: Perceptions of Team Members and Project Managers," *Project Management Journal* 32, no. 3 (September, 2001): 12–20.

Stevenson, R. W., "Growth in jobs at end of year beats estimates," *The New York Times* (January 8, 2000): A1.

Taylor, F. W., *The Principles of Scientific Management* (New York: Harper & Row, 1911).

Tryon and Associates. "Project Charter Template"; on the Internet at *http://www.tryonassoc.com/news/projchartertempl.asp.*

Tuckman, B. W., "Developmental Sequence in Small Groups," *Psychological Bulletin* 63 (1965): 384–399.

Twomey, K., and B. H. Kleiner, "Teamwork: The Essence of the Successful Organization," *Team Performance Management* 2, no. 1 (1996): 6–8.

Verespej, M. A., "Human Resources: Flexible Schedules Benefit All," *Industry Week.Com* (August 21, 2000): 25.

Waterman, R. H., Jr., J. A. Waterman, and B. A. Collard, "Toward a career-resilient workforce," *Harvard Business Review* (July/August, 1994): 87–95.

Whyte, W. F., D. J. Greenwood, and P. Lazes, "Participatory Action Research," in *Participatory Action Research*, ed. W. F. Whyte (Newbury Park, CA: Sage, 1991), 19–55.

Wilson, F., "Great Teams Build Themselves," *Team Performance Management* 2, no. 2, (1996): 27–31.

Wright, T. P., "Factors Affecting the Cost of Airplanes," *Journal of Aeronautical Science* 4, no. 3 (1936): 122–128.

Wyatt, E. "School Cost Overruns No Secret, Official Says," *The New York Times* (July 20, 2001): D1.

Yahoo, *http://biz.yahoo.com/rf/00816/168865.html* (August 16, 2000), from Reuters, (August 16, 2000).

INDEX

3Com, 21

Abbot Laboratories, 21
acceptance theory of authority, 66
Accreditation Board for
    Engineering and Technology
    (ABET), 8, 9
activities, 26
Adams, J. R., 7
Adolor Corporation, 21
Aguayo, R., 197
American Society of Mechanical
    Engineers (ASME), 8, 286–287
Apgar, M., IV, 69
Argyris, C., 75

Barnard, Chester, 66
Belgard, W. P., 22
Bennis, Warren, 55, 62, 77
beta software, 224
bid preparation, 260–262
bidding process, 37
Blue Angels, 39
burdened wage, 147, 153–155

Capability Maturity Model (CMM),
    207–209
Collard, B. A., 9
Collins, J. C, 22
communications, 180–189
    E-mail, 183, 186–187
    encoder-decoder, 184
    listening, 187
    meetings, 184–186
    memos, 186–187
    pathways, 182
    protocol, 182–183
    telephone, 188
    verbal, 4
    written, 4
CompTIA, 276

contingency theory, 60
continuous quality improvement,
    202
contract, 36, 73, 87, 88, 93, 94, 96,
    97, 222–223, 229, 238, 262
    cost-plus, 223
    fixed price, 222
contract work breakdown structure
    (CWBS), 108
core identity, 20, 23
core ideology, 21
corporate values, 22
cost management, 169–173
costs
    direct, 144
    general and administrative
        (G&A), 146–147
    indirect, 144
    material, 144
    material handling, 144
    operational, 146
    other direct costs (ODC), 145
    overhead, 146
    sales commission, 145
    travel and living, 145
critical path, 119, 133
Crosby, Philip, 196, 197
customer
    external, 29, 72
    internal, 29

damages, 227
Davenport, T. H., 29
Dell, Michael, 78
Deming, W. Edwards, 67–69, 192,
    193, 195, 201, 216
    14 points, 68–69, 195
    total quality management, 67
Department of Energy (DOE), 273
direct costs, 144
Drucker, Peter F., 9, 66–67

efficiency, 56
employee appraisal forms, 278–284
employee expectations, 5–7
estimating
    analogy, 163
    bottom-up, 147–151, 161
    COCOMO, 162–163
    learning curve, 164–168
    parametric, 161
    Price-H, 162
    Price-S, 162
    rule-of-thumb, 161
    top down, 161
ethics codes, 285–299
external standards, 204
ExxonMobil, 21

Fayol, Henri, 57
FedEx, 6
Feigenbaum, Armand, 196
Fielder, F. E., 60
financial analysis, 170–172
Fisher, K. K., 22
Follett, Mary Parker, 60
forward pricing, 227
French, J. R. P., 71
functional manager, 39, 119, 136

Gantt chart, 119, 120, 125, 127,
    129, 130, 133, 136
Gantt, Henry, 55, 57, 58
Gates, Bill, 78
Geneen, Harold, 76, 214
General Motors, 74
Gilbreth, Frank and Lillian, 57, 59
goals and objectives, 24
    SMART, 25
Great Wall, 53
Gulick, L., 57

Hawthorne effect, 61

Hawthorne plant, 60, 61
Hayes, D. S., 89
Herzberg, 62
Hewlett-Packard, 21, 22, 61
hygiene factors, 62

Imai, M., 192
indirect costs, 144
Institute of Electrical and
    Electronic Engineers (IEEE), 2,
    8, 29, 36, 204, 205–207,
    287–288
Intel Corporation, 38, 308
International Organization for
    Standardization (ISO), 29,
    209–211
Ishikawa, Karou, 197
ISO 9000, 199, 305–309

Jick, T. D., 22
Johnson, D. G., 7
Jordan, Michael, 11
Juran, Joseph, 193, 194, 196, 201,
    217

kaizen, 197–198, 209
Katzenbach, J. R., 73
Kerzner, H., 192
King, Jr., Martin Luther, 78
Kirchof, N. S., 7
Koonce, R., 9
Kotter, John P., 57, 76
Krishnan, M. H., 192

labor rates, 227
leadership, 76–80
    definition, 76–77
leadership versus management,
    78–80
learning curve, 164–168
lessons learned, 262–263
lifecycle, 36, 37, 160

make-or-buy analysis, 259
management, 36, 51–81
management by objective (MBO),
    66–67
management styles, 70–71, 238
    autocratic, 70
    democratic, 70
    laissez-faire, 70
    participative, 70
    wandering around, 238
Mary Kay, 21
Maslow, Abraham, 62, 63–64

Mayo, Elton, 60
McGregor, Douglas, 62, 64–65
mean time between failures
    (MTBF), 226
mean time to repair (MTTR), 227
MedPrac, 101–107
meetings, 184–186, 188–189
Merck, 22
Microsoft, 22
Microsoft Project 2000, 119–135
    critical path, 133
    task dependencies, 130
    task duration, 127, 129
    timescale, 127
    WBS column, 128
    WBS number, 127
    work completed, 134
milestone, 121, 123
Millennium Restaurant, 21
Mintzberg, H., 57
mission, 20
Murphy's laws, 223

Nanus, Burt, 77
National Aeronautics and Space
    Administration (NASA), 22
New Jersey Bell Telephone, 66
New Jersey Transit, 21
New York City Board of Education,
    272

opportunity review board (ORB), 87
organization
    definition, 20
    functional, 43, 47
    line, 46
    matrix, 45, 47
    organization chart, 42–45
    projectized, 44, 47
organization's expectations, 2
outsourcing, 228–229

Packard, David, 20
Panasonic, 21
Pearlman, Jeff, 13
Peters, Tom, 69
Plan-Do-Check-Act, 193, 194, 216
planning, 86
policy, 29, 30
Porras, J. I., 22
Powell, Colin H., 77
power, 71–73
    coercive, 71
    expert, 72
    formal, 71

information, 72
    referent, 71
    reward, 71
Pralahad, C. K., 192
private company, 29
procedure, 29, 30
process, 29, 30
productivity, 56
professionalism, 7–12
    certifications and licensures, 11
    characteristics, 7
    dissemination of information, 8
    ethics, 9
    lifelong learning, 8–9
    service, 8
profit, 2, 3, 20, 21, 22, 30, 31, 32,
    56, 81, 94, 96, 144, 145–146,
    147, 151, 153, 154, 155, 158,
    169, 170, 173, 192, 197, 222,
    223, 226, 228, 230, 276
program, 39
program manager, 39
project
    charter, 88–90
    cost estimating, 144
    life cycle, 36, 37, 160
    plan, 90–93
    plan troika, 94–114
    scope, 86
    spending profile, 158–160
project management definition, 38
Project Management Institute
    (PMI), 7, 38, 72, 86, 89, 118,
    180, 192, 222, 276, 288–299
project manager responsibilities, 41
project monitoring and tracking,
    258, 272–273
project time management, 118
proposal, 137
public company, 29
Pyramid, 53

quality, 192–217
    assurance, 201, 213–214
    control, 194, 201, 214–216
    cycle, 202
    improvement, 194
    planning, 194, 201, 203–213
    policy, 198–199, 200
quality trilogy, 194

Raven, B. H., 71
Rayner, S. R., 22
Reader's Digest, 21

requirements, also see specification
requirements, 28, 36, 38, 41, 42, 48, 49, 74, 86, 88, 90, 92, 93, 94, 95, 97, 99, 100, 102, 104, 105, 108, 109, 110, 111, 148, 150, 163, 177, 180, 192, 196, 199, 200, 203, 204, 205, 206, 207, 208, 209, 210, 222, 225, 226, 227, 230, 239, 254, 255, 258, 259, 260, 261, 262, 272, 278, 290, 291, 292, 295, 296, 297, 305
resources, 26
responsibility assignment matrix (RAM), 118, 130, 133
RFP, 86–88, 91, 92, 93, 150, 217, 229, 259, 260–262
RFQ, 86–88, 91, 150, 163, 217, 229, 259, 260–262
risk, 222–234
Rocker, John, 13
Roethlisberger, Fritz, 60
Roman Aqueduct, 53
rule, 29, 30

Sandomir, R., 11
Saturn Corporation, 74–75
schedule, 118–137
Seglin, Jeffrey L., 13
Shenhar, A. J., 36
Shewhart, Walter A., 193, 216
Short, J. E., 29
situational theory, 60
six sigma, 211–213
Smith, D. R., 73
social skills, 274–275
SoftApps, 101–107
SoftHuge, 101–107
Sony, 21, 22
Sotiriou, D., 65
Southwest Airlines, 21, 76
SOW example
  deliverables, 103
  documentation, 104
  factory acceptance, 104
  installation schedule, 102
  license, 105
  maintenance, 104
  product description, 101
  quality assurance, 105
  relational database, 104

site acceptance, 104
support, 105
terms and conditions, 105–107
training, 105
warranty, 106–107
specification, 26, 27, 36, 37, 41, 86, 87, 88, 89, 91, 93, 94–96, 97, 98, 100, 104, 105, 109, 110, 111, 112, 136, 140, 148, 162, 172, 173, 181, 192, 204–206, 214, 225, 226, 227, 254, 255, 260, 261, 274
specification compliance matrix, 87, 260, 261
stakeholder, 38, 40, 41, 46, 47, 54, 56, 70, 71, 72, 73, 75, 79, 88, 91, 92, 93, 94, 96, 97, 112, 119, 123
standards, 22, 27–29
  ANSI, 29, 204
  ASQ, 204
  IEEE, 29, 204
  ISO, 27, 29, 199, 200, 204, 205, 209–211, 219, 273, 305–309
  Military, 204
  OSHA, 204
  Software Engineering Institute, 29
  Underwriters Laboratory, 29
Staples, 21
statement of work (SOW), 87, 96–114
  key elements, 97
  sample, 101–107
  template, 98–100
Stevenson, R. W., 2
Stodgill, Ralph M., 77
Stonehenge, 53
strengths, weaknesses, opportunities, threats (SWOT)
  corporate, 23–24
  personal, 25–26
subcontract, 94, 98, 258–262

TACT, 2–4
task entry, 125
task relationship
  finish-to-finish, 122
  finish-to-start, 120, 121
  start-to-start, 122
Taylor, Frederick, 57, 59

teams, 74
technical skills, 275–276
technology
  leading edge, 223–226
  legacy, 223–226
  mature, 223–226
  state of the art, 223–226
  sunset, 223–226
technology risk, 223–226
Temple of the Inscriptions, 53
terms and conditions, 112–113, 229
theory X, 64
theory Y, 65
time card, 114
total quality management (TQM), 67, 68, 198, 214
trades and crafts, 12
Tryon and Associates, 89
Tuckman, B. W., 74

Union of Japanese Scientists and Engineers (JUSE), 193
Urwick, L., 57

vendors, 259–260
Verespej, M. A., 61
Villa-Tech, 151–158
  burdened wages, 153–154
  general and administrative, 153
  ground rules, 151
  overhead, 151–152
  risk, 155–156
vision, 22–23

Walt Disney Company, 22
Waterman, J. A., 9
Waterman, R. H., Jr., 9
Weber, Max, 57, 59, 60
Welch, Jack, 78
Western Electric, 60, 193
Whistleblower's act, 10
Whitehead, T. N., 60
wilderness survival
  answer sheet, 301–303
  worksheet, 15–16
Wittmer, D., 65
work breakdown structure (WBS), 87, 108–112
  sample, 109–112, 124–125
working time, 126, 135–136
Wujeck, J. H., 7